White Women, Race Matters

"... Here is whiteness as something assumed and learned and naturalized, even among anti-racists. And here is an author who is conscious of her own struggles to avoid naturalizing 'race' while documenting how the women she spent hours interviewing experience it nonetheless. A book well worth reading."

Virginia Dominguez
University of California, Santa Cruz

Traditional debates concerning racially hierarchical societies have tended to focus on the experience of being black. *White Women, Race Matters* breaks with this tradition by focussing on the particular experiences of white women in a racially hierarchical society. By considering their lives as contexts for the reproduction of racism but also at times for challenges to it, the work offers a rigorous examination of existing methodologies, practices and assumptions concerning racism and gender relations. Supported by extracts from in-depth life history interviews, *White Women, Race Matters* will provide valuable reading for undergraduates, lecturers and researchers in women's studies, anthropology, cultural studies and sociology.

Ruth Frankenberg is Assistant Professor of American Studies at the University of California at Davis.

Gender, Racism, Ethnicity
Series editors: Kum-Kum Bhavnani, University of California at Santa
Barbara; Avtar Brah, University of London; Gail Lewis, The Open
University; Ann Phoenix, Brunel University

Gender, Racism, Ethnicity is a new series whose main concern is to
promote rigorous feminist analysis of the intersections between gender,
racism, ethnicity, class and sexuality within the contexts of
imperialism, colonialism and neo-colonialism. Intended to contribute
new perspectives to current debates and to introduce fresh analysis, it
will provide valuable teaching texts for undergraduates, lecturers and
researchers in anthropology, women's studies, cultural studies and
sociology.

white women, race matters

THE SOCIAL CONSTRUCTION OF WHITENESS

Ruth Frankenberg

Published by the University of Minnesota Press
2037 University Avenue Southeast, Minneapolis, MN 55455-3092
Printed in the United States of America on acid-free paper

Simultaneously published in the UK
by Routledge
11 New Fetter Lane, London EC4P 4EE

British Library Cataloguing in Publication Data

A catalogue record for this book is available from the British Library.

ISBN 0-415-10510-2 (hbk)
 0-415-10511-0 (pbk)

This work is dedicated to those who struggle for a day beyond racism—to a time when this book will be read as history and not as a study of the present.

Contents

Acknowledgments

This book has been in the making for some time. As a result, family members, teachers, colleagues, readers, students, and friends in several parts of the world have been critical to its completion. I would like to thank Alison Frankenberg, Ronald Frankenberg, and Rose-Anna Frankenberg—those who have known me the longest—for their, love, encouragement, and support. By teaching me in their very different ways to believe in human dignity and equality, my parents provide the bedrock of my own commitment to the pursuit of social justice. I also thank my grandmother, Susan Sherratt, whose life provided me with key lessons about endurance, courage, and female self-determination.

I began work on this project in Santa Cruz, California. My deep thanks to Nancy Chodorow, James Clifford, Donna Haraway, and David Wellman. All four provided encouragement, tools for intellectual work, theoretical insight, and careful, engaged, and serious critique of my work. I could not have wished for a better Ph.D. committee. Also at the University of California, Santa Cruz, Vivek Dhareshwar, Mary John, Tejaswini Niranjana, and other members of the Group for the Critical Study of Colonial Discourse were crucial to my intellectual formation, as were Chela Sandoval, the late Rosa Maria Villafañe-Sisolak, and others associated with the Board of Studies in History of Consciousness and the Santa Cruz campus. David Schneider provided me with a research assistantship at a critical moment, as well as reading and commenting on my work. Billie Harris kept me on track, as it were, infrastructurally. Rosamaria Zayas and bell hooks were the two women who, in 1980, challenged me to rethink very seriously my own position within the racial order and thus set this project in motion.

Beyond Santa Cruz, I have been sustained intellectually, politically, and emotionally through this project by friends and colleagues old and new, including Susan Alexander, Scott Anderson,

Terry Berman, Chetan Bhatt, Kum Kum Bhavnani, Reyna Cowan, Ali Ishtiaq, Katie King, Carol Lopes, Meera Mani, Sunita Mani, Eleanor Soto, Ted Swedenburg, Kamala Visweswaran, Yvonne Yarbro-Bejarano, and members of the Culture Studies Group at the University of Washington, Seattle. Toni Morrison, Michael Omi, Beth Schneider, and Sylvia Yanagisako commented in extremely helpful ways on the manuscript. Dana Collins typed the bibliography for the manuscript, thus saving me from the straw that might well have broken this particular camel's back. Janaki Bakhle and Robert Mosimann at the University of Minnesota Press have been generous in their enthusiasm and practical assistance throughout our work on this project. My heartfelt thanks to Robert Zeiger for keeping my yin out of deficit. Finally, Lata Mani has played an especially significant role in my life, personally and intellectually, through and beyond the research and writing of this text. Our intensive engagement with one another's work has generated an exciting and creative context that has nurtured this project and left its mark on this book.

Thirty anonymous women interviewees are the sine qua non of this text. My deepest thanks to those I interviewed for this book. Whether or not you agree with what I have written here, please know that I have striven to treat your words with the care and thoughtfulness that they deserve.

Material support is also, of course, vital. The Humanities Division of the University of California, Santa Cruz, provided grants in support of my research on two occasions. A Research Professorship from the University of Washington, Seattle, helped me to revise the manuscript.

1

Introduction: Points of Origin, Points of Departure

My argument in this book is that race shapes white women's lives. In the same way that both men's and women's lives are shaped by their gender, and that both heterosexual and lesbian women's experiences in the world are marked by their sexuality, white people *and* people of color live racially structured lives. In other words, any system of differentiation shapes those on whom it bestows privilege as well as those it oppresses. White people are "raced," just as men are "gendered." And in a social context where white people have too often viewed themselves as nonracial or racially neutral, it is crucial to look at the "racialness" of white experience. Through life history interviews, the book examines white women's places in the racial structure of the United States at the end of the twentieth century and views white women's lives as sites both for the reproduction of racism and for challenges to it.

If race shapes white women's lives, the cumulative name that I have given to that shape is "whiteness." Whiteness, I will argue in the pages that follow, has a set of linked dimensions. First, whiteness is a location of structural advantage, of race privilege. Second, it is a "standpoint," a place from which white people look at ourselves, at others, and at society.[1] Third, "whiteness" refers to a set of cultural practices that are usually unmarked and unnamed. This book seeks to begin exploring, mapping, and examining the terrain of whiteness.

There are two analytic dimensions to the book. In beginning to research the significance of race in white women's lives, I expected to learn about, and document, the daily experience of racial structuring and the ways race privilege might be crosscut by other axes of difference and inequality: class, culture, ethnicity, gender, and sexuality. From there, I hoped to comprehend how that daily experience shapes white women's perceptions of the significance of race in the social structure as a whole. As my work proceeded,

1

however, a second dimension of analysis became equally significant, for it became clear that, as much as white women are located in—and speak from—physical environments shaped by race, we are also located in, and perceive our environments by means of, a set of discourses on race, culture, and society whose history spans this century and, beyond it, the broader sweep of Western expansion and colonialism.[2]

The material and discursive dimensions of whiteness are always, in practice, interconnected. Discursive repertoires may reinforce, contradict, conceal, explain, or "explain away" the materiality or the history of a given situation. Their interconnection, rather than material life alone, is in fact what generates "experience"; and, given this, the "experience" of living as a white woman in the United States is continually being transformed. Analytically, chapters of the book at times foreground that which is clearly concrete, tangible, and material about white women's experience of race—childhood, interracial relationships, political activism. At other times my focus is on issues of discourse—the meaning and apparent emptiness of "white" as a cultural identity; the political contexts, strengths, and limitations of different ways of "thinking through race"; the persistence of a discourse against interracial relationships.

Points of Origin

This book emerged out of the 1980s, the decade in which white feminist women like myself could no longer fail to notice the critique of white feminist racism by feminist/radical women of color (a critique that had, in fact, marked the entire "second wave" of feminism).[3] More specifically, the research project had as its inception my own passage through that decade, and my own despair over the confused mess that white feminist women's response to charges of racism had collectively become by 1983–84. At worst—and it appeared from where I was standing that "worst" was much of the time—it seemed as though we white feminists had a limited repertoire of responses when we were charged with racism: confusion over accusations of racism; guilt over racism; anger over repeated criticism; dismissal; stasis. Feminist/radical women of color would also, it seemed, go through phases: anger over racism; efforts to communicate with white women about racism, despite it; frustration; and the temptation (acted upon temporarily or permanently) to withdraw from multiracial work.

Sites of productive multiracial feminist dialogue and activity existed, but they were few and far between.[4] Too often, I witnessed situations in which, as predominantly white feminist workplaces, classrooms, or organizations tried to move to more multiracial formats or agendas, the desire to work together rapidly deteriorated into painful, ugly processes in which racial tension and conflict actually seemed to get worse rather than better as the months went by. There were, it appeared, multiple ways in which the racism of the wider culture was simply being replayed in feminist locations.

Increasingly, this generated for me a sense of contradiction, a need to know more. As a white feminist, I knew that I had not previously known I was "being racist" and that I had never set out to "be racist." I also knew that these desires and intentions had had little effect on outcomes. I, as a coauthor, in however modest a way, of feminist agendas and discourse, was at best failing to challenge racism and, at worst, aiding and abetting it. How had feminism, a movement that, to my knowledge, intended to support and benefit all women, turned out not to be doing so?

In the early 1980s, I found myself straddling two sides of a "race line." On the one hand, I spent time sitting with white feminist university friends (roughly my age, roughly my class), at times in discussion groups and at other times more informally, as we struggled to make sense of the "racism question." The issue was anything but trivial to us. For one thing, it was startling in its implication that we were about to lose our newly found grip on the reins of liberation. (My friends and I were mostly socialist feminists. I, for one, liked the idea that, as women—apparently racially undefined—we had a distinctively radical purview of society, premised in part upon our status as structurally oppressed in relation to men—again apparently racially undefined. We were, however, analytically honest enough to realize that analyses such as that proposed by the Combahee River Collective, pointing to the structural subordination of women of color, and the potentially radical standpoint arising out of that position, changed all that!)[5] Because we were basically well-meaning individuals, the idea of being part of the problem of racism (something I had associated with extremists or institutions but not with myself) was genuinely shocking to us. And the issue was also terrifying, in the sense that we constantly felt that at any second we might err again with respect to racism, that we didn't know the rules and therefore didn't know how to prevent that happening. There was, perhaps, a way racism was disembodied in our discussions, sometimes an issue of standpoint, sometimes one of etiquette, and definitely an issue that provoked the intense frustration that came of not being able to "get it," or to "get it right."

Meanwhile, I was also spending a great deal of time with a friendship/support network of working-class women of color and white women, some of whom I had also first met through the university. These women were mainly parents (I was not), as well as older, poorer, and positioned very differently than I in the relations of racism in the United States. As I sat with them and traveled their daily pathways—thanks to an unexpectedly profound connection to one woman in particular—an inventory of meanings of racism, of racist behaviors began, de facto, to accumulate in my consciousness. In part, the inventory felt necessary to my ability to cope in those gatherings without offending anyone, but in part my friend made it her business to educate me. I learned by proximity what it means to navigate through a largely hostile terrain, to deal with institutions that do not operate by one's own logic nor in one's interests, and to need those institutions to function in one's favor if one is to survive, let alone to achieve. I realized for almost the first time in my life the gulf of experience and meaning between individuals differentially positioned in relation to systems of domination, and the profundity of cultural difference. (I say *almost* the first time because the culture shock of moving to the United States from Britain at the age of twenty-one had opened my eyes to the latter.)

Uniting the divergent experiences of being both a part of that network and a graduate student was, and remains, beyond my capability. In any case, doing so, and especially conveying the experiences of women of color, in general or in particular, is not my goal in any direct way.[6] More relevant here is the multifaceted impact of both affiliations, and their disjunction, on my own understanding of racism and on the genesis of this project. When my white sisters and I struggled to comprehend a situation we did not understand and had not meant to create, critical questions for me were: How did this happen? How did we get into this mess? What do "they" mean when they tell us white feminism is racist? Translated into research, the same questions looked something like this:

(How) does racism shape white women's lives?

What are the social processes through which white women are created as social actors primed to reproduce racism within the feminist movement?

(How) can white women's lives become sites of resistance to the reproduction of racism?

Socialist feminism had also given me an analytical commitment to three axioms: first, that in "societies structured in dominance"[7] we, as feminists, must always remember that we act from within the social relations and subject positions we seek to change; second, that experience constructs identity; and, third, that there is a direct relationship between "experience" and "worldview" or "standpoint" such that any system of domination can be seen most clearly from the subject positions of those oppressed by it. As the project developed, applying those axioms to positions of privilege or domination, or to subjects simultaneously privileged and oppressed, required me to complicate the second and third of these axioms. The first remained not only intact but even more challenging than it had appeared at the outset.

From the network predominantly made up of women of color, of which I was in some way a part, I carried into the research three realizations: first, that there is frequently a gulf of experience of racism between white people and people of color; second, that white women might have a range of awareness in relation to racism, with greater awareness based on, among other things, their long-term connectedness to communities of color (I did not, I should perhaps clarify, include myself in the latter category at that time); third, that there *is* a cultural/racial specificity to white people, at times more obvious to people who are not white than to white individuals.

What's in a Name?

When I began work on this book, I described it as one that would examine the relationship between white women and racism. In the years between then and now, I have added another conceptualization of it, one that perhaps overlaps, without displacing, my earlier description. For I now also describe this book as a study of the social construction of whiteness.

Calling the project a study of white women and racism marked out the set of concerns that motivated me to begin it, namely, emphasizing that racism was and is something that shapes white women's lives, rather than something that people of color have to live and deal with in a way that bears no relationship or relevance to the lives of white people. For when white people—and I was especially concerned about white feminists, since the project had its origins in the feminist movement—look at racism, we tend to view it as an issue that people of color face and have to struggle with, but not as an issue that generally involves or implicates us. Viewing racism in this way has serious consequences for how white women look at racism, and for how antiracist work might be framed. With this view, white women can see antiracist work as an act of compassion for an "other," an optional, extra project, but not one intimately and organically linked to our own lives. Racism can, in short, be conceived as something external to us rather than as a system that shapes our daily experiences and sense of self.

The "and" in "white women and racism" implies, but does not really define, a link between the two terms. The need to speak of whiteness further specifies what is at stake in speaking of racism in relation to white people. To speak of "the social construction of whiteness" asserts that there are locations, discourses, and material relations to which the term "whiteness" applies. I argue in this book that whiteness refers to a set of locations that are historically, socially, politically, and culturally produced and, moreover, are intrinsically linked to unfolding relations of domination. Naming "whiteness" displaces it from the unmarked, unnamed status that is itself an effect of its dominance. Among the effects on white people both of race privilege and of the dominance of whiteness are their seeming normativity, their structured invisibility. This normativity is, however, unevenly effective. I will explore and seek to explain the invisibility and modes of visibility of racism, race difference, and whiteness. To look at the social construction of whiteness, then, is to look head-on at a site of dominance. (And it may be more difficult for white people to say "Whiteness has nothing to do with me—I'm not white" than to say "Race has nothing to do with me—I'm not racist.") To speak of whiteness is, I think, to assign *everyone* a place in the relations of racism. It is to emphasize that dealing with racism is not merely an option for white people—that, rather, racism shapes white people's lives and identities in a way that is inseparable from other facets of daily life.

To name whiteness also broadens the focus of my study, first because it makes room for the linkage of white subjects to histories not encompassed by, but connected to, that of racism: histories of colonialism and imperialism, and, secondarily, histories of assimilationism in the United States. Second, it allows me to view certain practices and subject positions as racialized (that is, structured by relations of race, usually alongside other structuring principles) rather than necessarily racist—although whiteness is for the most part racialized in the context of racism. Third, by examining and naming the terrain of whiteness, it may, I think, be possible to generate or work toward antiracist forms of whiteness, or at least toward antiracist strategies for reworking the terrain of whiteness.

Several distinct but, I believe, compatible theoretical and methodologial orientations have been distilled into my approach. First, I share in a feminist commitment to drawing on women's daily lives as a resource for analyzing society. Second, I also share what is, in a sense, the converse of that commitment (and also an approach adopted by feminists): the belief that women's daily life experiences can only be adequately understood by "mapping" them onto broader social processes. Third, then, in order to better comprehend the social processes involved in the construction of whiteness, I have drawn on both theoretical and substantive analyses of race, racism, and colonialism in the United States and beyond.

Feminism: Personal, Political, Theoretical

My decision, in 1984, to begin to explore whiteness through white women's life histories drew on a strong current of feminist thought that has used accounts of women's experience as ground for the construction and critique of theory and strategy. Since the consciousness-raising groups of the late 1960s, feminists have transformed accounts of personal experience into politicized and theorized terrain.[8] Through this process, the private, the daily, and the apparently trivial in women's activities came to be understood as shared rather than individual experiences, and as socially and politically constructed. The personal, in short, became political.

In addition to anchoring theories of gender and of society in general, women's accounts of personal experience have served as leverage points from which to criticize canons, whether of social theory or of political movements' agendas for change. During the "second wave" of feminism, from the late 1960s to the present, this kind of critique has challenged at least two canons that are especially relevant here. First, white feminists and feminist/radical women of color have criticized the lack of attention to gender domination—and effective male-centeredness—of left and anti-racist movements. Second, feminist/radical women of color have challenged feminisms dominated by white-centered accounts of female experience. As women activists of a range of racial identities criticized theory based on male standpoints, it became clear that such standpoints obscured or ignored female subordination. And again, as women of color challenged white feminist accounts of "women's place" in society, the partiality of those accounts became visible.

Theorizing "from experience" rested on several key epistemological claims that, over time, became staples of feminist "common sense." The first of these was a critique of "objectivity" or "distance" as the best stances from which to generate knowledge. For, feminists argued, there is a link between where one stands in society and what one perceives. In addition, this epistemological stance made another, stronger claim: that the oppressed can see with the greatest clarity not only their own position but also that of the oppressor/privileged, and indeed the shape of social systems as a whole.[9]

To theorize "from experience" is thus to propose that there is no firm separation to be drawn between woman as member of society and woman as thinker, theorist, or activist. And therefore, as became clear in the context of a critique of white feminist racism, there are multiple problems in attempting (by default) to use white women's lives as a resource for analyzing gender domination in its entirety. Through the 1980s and into the present, work predominantly by women of color has been transforming feminist analysis, drawing attention to the white-centeredness, and more generally the false universalizing claims, of much feminist discourse.[10] Ethnocentrism based on the racial specificity of white women's lives, it was pointed out, limits feminist analysis and strategy in relation to issues such as the family[11] and reproductive rights.[12] In the realm of theory, women of color were the first to advance frameworks for understanding the intersection in women's lives of gender, sexuality, race, and class[13] as well as visions and concepts of multiracial coalition work.[14]

The issue here was not only that white women's daily experiences *differed* from those of our sisters of color. If that had been
the case, simply adding more accounts by women from a variety
of racial locations would have resolved the problem. Instead, it
became clear that white feminist women accounting for our experience were missing its "racialness" and that we were not seeing
what was going on around us: in other words, we lacked an
awareness of how our positions in society were constructed in relation to those of women—and men—of color.

One of my concerns, as I looked at white women's lives
through a specifically racial lens, was, as a result, trying to comprehend those lacunae in perception. I needed to understand not
only how race is lived, but also how it is seen—or more often, in
my immediate political and social networks, *not* seen. In 1983 (before beginning the interviews for this book) I argued that the extent to which white women were "missing" or "not getting" the
significance of race in either our or anyone else's experience had
everything to do with standpoint: because we were race privileged, I argued, we were not in a structural position to see the
effects of racism on our lives, nor the significance of race in the
shaping of U.S. society.[15]

But by themselves, the material, daily relations of race cannot
adequately explain whether, when, and in what terms white
women perceive race as structuring either their own or anyone
else's experience. The "dailiness" of racial separation and the ines-
capability of whiteness as a position of relative privilege cannot
explain the *content* of white women's descriptions of others and of
themselves—the ways, for example, masculinity and femininity
are divided in racial and cultural terms. Similarly, they cannot explain why some white women learn or contest explicitly racist
attitudes from childhood onward, while for others racial inequality is, in the words of one of the women I interviewed, "a reality
enjoyed, but not acknowledged, a privilege lived in, but unknown."

Through the second half of the 1980s, several ongoing areas of
feminist work were critical as I interviewed white women and
analyzed their narratives. First, feminist scholars, mainly women
of color, engaged in the painstaking work of refracting gender
through the lenses of race and culture: examining, for example,
how constructions of womanhood have always been racially and
culturally marked and, in a racist society, even racially exclusive.[16]
This work of rigorous specification exposes the universalism of

the second wave of feminism as largely false—and calls, I suggest, for the reciprocal specification of *white* womanhood.[17] Second, feminists of all racial groups (but, as noted earlier, in a process initiated by women of color) made richer and more complex our theorizations of subjectivity and of society in general. Thus, for example, theorists described the "simultaneity" of the impact of race, class, and gender in shaping the lives of women of color[18] (and, I would add, white women too) and emphasized that subjectivity is "[displaced] across a multiplicity of discourses"[19] rather than produced out of the single axis of gender domination or the twin poles of capitalism and patriarchy. Third, more complex views of the subject produced correspondingly complex epistemologies, understood as emerging out of multifaceted political locations.[20]

While feminist women of color have worked to specify their histories and the contemporary shape of their lives in gendered and racial terms, however, a corresponding particularism has too often been lacking on the part of white feminist women. Thus, as white feminists participate alongside women of color in developing new theoretical articulations of "difference" and the "multiplicity" of women's experiences, there is, I fear, a danger that while increasingly theorists of color speak from concrete conceptualizations of what that multiplicity means to them, for white women visions of "difference" and "multiplicity" may remain abstract.

There are critical exceptions here. In a productive approach to questions about white women and racism, some white feminists began in the late 1970s and 1980s to examine through autobiography the ways race privilege and racism have shaped their own lives.[21] Thus, as these women and others like them continue to articulate feminist practice, they do so with a more multifaceted understanding of the social forces that made them who they are.

My study, and the exploration of white women's life histories upon which this book is based, share these women's commitment to careful and detailed analysis of how racism enters and shapes white women's lives, and to making more visible how our lives are embedded in a range of histories, political struggles, and social forces. My assumption here is one I've held since I first came to politics in the 1970s: that knowledge about a situation is a critical tool in dismantling it.

Theorizing Race

In analyzing the life narratives of white women, I attempt as thoroughly as possible to situate them in relation both to the material relations of racism at specific times and places in the United States, and to the circulation and shifting salience of a range of discourses on race. In the narratives that serve as the primary resource for this book, it is clear that, indeed, race privilege translated directly into forms of social organization that shaped daily life (for example, the de jure and, later, de facto residential, social, and educational segregation that characterized most of these women's childhoods), and that these in turn shaped the women's perceptions of race.

In order to think about white women and race, then, it is critical to reflect on the meaning and history, in the United States, of the category "race" itself, and similarly that of the idea of "racism." I have found most useful those analyses that view race as a socially constructed rather than inherently meaningful category, one linked to relations of power and processes of struggle, and one whose meaning changes over time.[22] Race, like gender, is "real" in the sense that it has real, though changing, effects in the world and real, tangible, and complex impact on individuals' sense of self, experiences, and life chances. In asserting that race and racial difference are socially constructed, I do not minimize their social and political reality, but rather insist that their reality is, precisely, social and political rather than inherent or static.

Historical research underscores the instability of racial categorization. Michael Omi and Howard Winant point out, for example, that:

> [In the U.S. census] Japanese Americans have moved from categories such as "non-white," "Oriental" or simply "Other," to recent inclusion as a specific ethnic group under the broader category of "Asian and Pacific Islanders." The variation both reflects and in turn shapes racial understanding and dynamics.[23]

Again, Jewish Americans, Italian Americans, and Latinos have, at different times and from varying political standpoints, been viewed as both "white" and "nonwhite." And as the history of "interracial" marriage and sexual relationships also demonstrates, "white" is as much as anything else an economic and political category maintained over time by a changing set of exclusionary practices, both legislative and customary.[24]

The women I interviewed replicated another dimension of racial discourse worth noting at this preliminary stage. Racist discourse, I suggest, frequently accords a hypervisibility to African Americans and a relative *invisiblity* to Asian Americans and Native Americans; Latinos are also relatively less visible than African Americans in discursive terms. Needless to say, neither mode of expression of racism is more desirable, or more unpleasant in its effects, than the other. Two white women explicitly singled out African Americans as "racial others," in contrast to Latinos and Asians, viewed as "culturally" but not "*racially*" different from white people. Elsewhere, the women described Asian Americans and Latinos as somehow less different from whites in racial terms. They also at times had more to say about Black-white relations, and more elaborate constructions of African Americans, than about other communities of color. This pattern was in part an effect of the regions in which individual women had grown up: those raised on the West Coast of the United States, for example, explored questions about race and identity in relation to Chicanas and Chicanos as often as to African American men and women.

In this book, I define race difference in a way that is avowedly historically specific, politically engaged, and provisional. I thus view groups who are currently targets of racism—Native Americans, Latinos, African Americans, and Asian/Pacific Americans, as well as other nonwhite immigrants—as being racially different from white people, and from each other. (The study is also premised on the notion that white people, as much as people of color, are racialized.) Part of my concern is, of course, to explore how white women described race and cultural difference, and how their descriptions reflect different moments in the history of race.

Racial naming is also in part an effect of communities' own collective struggles to claim or rearticulate identity. The shifts in census classification of Japanese Americans, for example, resulted in large part from the demands of Asian/Pacific Americans themselves. And in fact, this book bears the marks of a more recent community-initiated "renaming" process, for in the years 1984 to 1986, when the interviews for this book took place, the name "African American" was not yet current, so it was not used by the women I interviewed to describe men and women of African descent living in the United States.

U.S. history is marked by an unevenly evolving history of discourses on race difference. Central to competing analyses of race have been assertions of, and challenges to, a range of claims about differences between people, including physiological or genetic differences, cultural differences, and differences in access to power. One can, in fact, identify a chronological movement in the history of ideas about race in the United States, if only to qualify and complicate that chronology immediately afterward. In a synthesis that has been crucial to this book, Omi and Winant divide that chronology into three stages.[25] For the greater part of U.S. history, as they point out, arguments for the biological inferiority of people of color represented the dominant discourse (or in their terms, paradigm) for thinking about race.[26] Within this discourse, race was constructed as a biological category, and the assertion of white biological superiority was used to justify economic and political inequities ranging from settler colonialism to slavery.

Beginning in the 1920s, a new clustering of concepts gained currency: race difference came to be named in cultural and social terms instead of, or simultaneously with, biological ones. Here, Omi and Winant argue, the notion of "ethnicity" displaced "race" as a descriptor of difference.[27] Within this new paradigm, belonging to an ethnic group came to be understood more behaviorally than biologically (although, since a cultural group continued to be understood in terms of descent rather than practice, one could add that biology continued to underwrite conceptions of identity). Alongside the ethnicity paradigm came an "assimilationist" analysis of what would and should happen to people of color in the United States: like white immigrants, it was argued, people of color would gradually assimilate into the "mainstream" of U.S. society. Ultimately, ethnicity theorists believed, a meritocracy would be achieved. Vital to this perspective was the belief that racial inequality was incompatible with American society, which, within this view, was understood to be fundamentally adequate as a democracy.

The posing of demands for racial equality in terms of the ideal of democracy in the United States also provided the rhetorical and moral force of the early civil rights movement. However, radical antiracist and cultural nationalist movements of the late 1960s and early 1970s—Black Power, La Raza, and the American Indian Movement—brought about a resurgence, reevaluation, and transformation of notions of the *differentness* of peoples of color from the white dominant culture, along with an analysis and critique of racial inequality as a fundamentally structuring feature of U.S. society. Omi and Winant characterize this third phase as one of class- and nation-based paradigms for understanding race and racism.[28] Here, in fact, we come full circle to the second wave of feminism. For, as Omi and Winant (among others) point out, these class- and nation-based movements were themselves the inspiration and in some ways provided the moment of origin for second-wave feminism or "women's liberation." Not only did they provide models for the women's movement,[29] but many women activists either moved from antiracist movements into the feminist movement or participated simultaneously in both.[30] The obvious question here is why, given these origins, by the mid-1970s the most clearly audible feminist discourses were those that failed to address racism. The answer to that question is lengthy and beyond the scope of this book, although related to it.

One way to describe these three moments, paradigms, or discourses is in terms of shifts from "difference" to "similarity," and then "back" to difference radically redefined. The first shift, then, is from a first moment that I will call "essentialist racism," with its emphasis on race difference understood in hierarchical terms of essential, biological inequality, to a discourse of essential "sameness" popularly referred to as "color-blindness"—which I have chosen to name as a double move toward "color evasiveness" and "power evasiveness."[31] This second moment asserts that we are all the same under the skin; that, culturally, we are converging; that, materially, we have the same chances in U.S. society; and that— the sting in the tail—any failure to achieve is therefore the fault of people of color themselves. The third moment insists once again on difference, but in a form very different from that of the first moment. Where the terms of essentialist racism were set by the white dominant culture, in the third moment they are articulated by people of color. Where difference within the terms of essentialist racism alleges the inferiority of people of color, in the third moment difference signals autonomy of culture, values, aesthetic standards, and so on. And, of course, inequality in this third moment refers not to ascribed characteristics, but to the social structure. I will refer to this discursive repertoire as one of "race cognizance."

Having begun this discussion with a chronological description of the emergence of three distinct modes of thinking through race, I should stress that the transitions from one to the next cannot be viewed as paradigm shifts in any total sense, for elements of all three can be found in today's literature on race and racism in the United States and in the rhetoric of activists both for and against racism.[32] Moreover, while it may be fair to say that at a certain point in U.S. history a color- and power-evasive public language of race displaced essentialist racism as the dominant discourse on race, color- and power-evasive discourse remains dominant today; it has not been displaced in its turn by race cognizance. Although continually challenged by the third mode of thinking through race, the color- and power-evasive paradigm has incorporated elements of race cognizance into itself, rather than being in any significant way displaced by it (see chapter 6).

The claim that evasion of color and power is dominant is, perhaps, at first sight counterintuitive at a time when conservative cultural critics are arguing that the United States is being overrun by the new orthodoxy of "multiculturalism"—ostensibly a product of race cognizance. But the situation is much more complicated than conservative critics would claim. First, efforts to move popular discourse toward multiculturalism have thus far been limited in scope and, while having some impact in education and mass media, are not yet a part of most people's daily thought or practice. Second, despite the conservatives' claims, it has in practice proven to be extremely difficult to establish multiculturalist or pluralist approaches to curricula or media in the context of continued structural and institutional white leadership. Proposals for the development of pluralist or multiculturalist curricula are often "watered down" in their pathways through institutional bureaucracies. The versions of multiculturalism that emerge as educational or representational practice are for the most part rearrangements of the selective engagement that evasion of color represents, and are little less power-evasive than the policies and practices that arise out of classical "color-blindness." One can, in fact, argue that struggles between power evasion and race cognizance are being fought on the terrain of multiculturalism.

As I will explore in the chapters that follow, elements of all

three modes of thinking through race were present in the narratives of the women I interviewed. In analyzing the ways in which
they circulated in the narratives, I have found it helpful to characterize as "discursive repertoires" the clusterings of discursive
elements upon which the women drew. "Repertoire" captures, for
me, something of the way in which strategies for thinking
through race were learned, drawn upon, and enacted, repetitively
but not automatically or by rote, chosen but by no means freely
so.[33] ∴ CAN Bₑ UNLEARNED THRO WHITENESS

The Imperial Legacy and the Construction of Whiteness: A Note on Colonial Discourses

Scholarship in the critical study of colonial discourses—that is,
analytical work on discursive repertoires associated with the process of West European colonial exploration, appropriation and
ruling—provided a third part of the context for this study. Given
the inception of the United States as a colony settled by Europeans, and given continued transnational traffic in modes of knowing associated with racial domination, there continue to be close
ties in the United States between racist and colonial discourses, as
well as between constructions of whiteness and of Westernness.
Such ties were evident in the narratives collected for this study.

Analysts of the era of West European colonial expansion that
began in the sixteenth century have documented the cultural dis-
ruptions that took place alongside economic appropriation, as
well as the centrality of the production of knowledge to the success of colonial rule.[34] The term "knowledge" must be used with
caution here, however, since like the racist repertoires that have
characterized much of the "knowledge" generated in the context
of racial domination in the United States, the discourses on the
colonized that the colonizer produced were, for the most part,
distorted at best, fabricated at worst.[35] The notion of "epistemic
violence" captures the idea that associated with West European
colonial expansion is the production of modes of knowing that
enabled and rationalized colonial domination from the standpoint
of the West, and produced ways of conceiving "Other" societies
and cultures whose legacies endure into the present.[36]

Colonization also occasioned the reformulation of European
selves. Central to colonial discourses is the notion of the colonized
subject as irreducibly Other from the standpoint of a white

"self."[37] Equally significant, while discursively generating and marking a range of cultural and racial Others as different from an apparently stable Western or white self, the Western self is itself produced as *an effect of* the Western discursive production of its Others.[38] This means that the Western self and the non-Western other are coconstructed as discursive products, both of whose "realness" stand in extremely complex relationships to the production of knowledge, and to the material violence to which "epistemic violence" is intimately linked. As Gayatri Chakravorty Spivak puts it:

> Europe . . . consolidated itself as sovereign subject by defining its colonies as "Others," even as it constituted them for purposes of administration and the expansion of markets.[39]

There are implications here for the present project. Elements of colonial discourse were at times present in these white women's descriptions of themselves and others. Thus, for example, their descriptions of cultural difference were often dualistic. Whiteness and Americanness seemed comprehensible to many only by reference to the Others excluded from these categories. As later chapters will show, whiteness and Westernness, racism and colonial discourse were frequently interwoven in the women's words. Moreover, the women drew at times on the language of anti-imperialist as well as antiracist movements as they attempted to think critically about racism in their own lives.

In addition to documenting the traces of colonial discourses in white women's thinking, my study of whiteness responds in part to the legacy of colonialism. As I suggested earlier, one effect of colonial discourse is the production of an unmarked, apparently autonomous white/Western self, in contrast with the marked, Other racial and cultural categories with which the racially and culturally dominant category is coconstructed. In this context, it has also for the most part been Other, marked subjects rather than white/Western, unmarked subjects whose racial and cultural identities have been the focus of study.

Within this framework for thinking about self and other, the white Western self as a racial being has for the most part remained unexamined and unnamed. On the one hand, studies of racial and cultural identities have tended to view the range of potential subjects of research as limited to those who differ from the (unnamed) norm.[40] On the other hand, whiteness has elsewhere been simultaneously ignored and universalized: studies of members of the dominant race or culture, unless focused on racism per se, bracket the issues of race and culture and presume by implication the racial neutrality of the subjects of study. (For example, a study of the workplace involving Chicana workers will probably address race and culture; a study of white women workers probably will not.)[41] Further, such studies at times then go on to falsely generalize from a group of white subjects or to draw conclusions about women in general—a procedure for which white North American and West European feminist scholarship has been heavily criticized.

In short, whiteness and Westernness have not, for the most part, been conceived as "the problem" in the eyes of white/Western people, whether in research or elsewhere.[42] In a direct response to this representational matrix, the present study attempts two kinds of subversion. First, it examines the whiteness of white women's experience, rather than leaving it unexplored. Second, in examining the formation and contestation of white women's race consciousness, the study inquires into the social construction of the white gaze. Further, it is by intention an investigation of self rather than of other(s), since it is a study of whiteness and women undertaken by a woman who is white. Clearly, there are limits to my similarity to the women I interviewed: we met across differences of nationality, and at times also of age, class, ethnicity, sexuality, parental status, and political views. Most significantly for the study, however, the women I interviewed and I participated in a shared universe of discourses on race (the significance of this point will be discussed further in chapter 2).

The Scope of the Study

The implications of this study are both particular and general. This is by no means an exhaustive study of whiteness, nor even of white femaleness. The book is intended to make two kinds of contribution. To begin with, it examines thirty articulations of whiteness, seeking to specify how each is marked by the interlocking effects of geographical origin, generation, ethnicity, political orientation, gender, and present-day geographical location, and how each is inscribed in differing ways into a shared history of race in the United States and beyond. Through a process of documentation and analysis, the study proposes and applies a method and theoretical apparatus by means of which to analyze whiteness. Both method and theoretical tools may be applicable to future analyses of racially dominant subject positions.

Chapter 2 describes in more detail the thirty white women I interviewed and the circumstances in which the interviews took place. But the specificities of this study, and their implications, are worth describing here. While the women I interviewed had come from many parts of the United States, and two from beyond it, they do not represent an even spread in terms of their geographical origins: more had grown up on one of the two coasts than in the southern states, and none had lived in the southwestern United States.

Equally important, all of the interviews took place in California. The ways in which the women constructed their experiences were, I am sure, significantly shaped by the material relations and public language(s) of race current on the West Coast of the United States in the mid-1980s. The narratives might, I suspect, have read differently had they been gathered somewhere else. For one thing, the expressions of race conflict and the racist discourses that circulated in Santa Cruz County and in the San Francisco Bay Area in the mid-1980s were, I believe, in general less explicit, less stark, and less sharply defined than those of, say, major cities on the eastern seaboard. Similarly, the history and persistence of far-right racism are, while equally significant, less well known and less a part of popular memory on the West Coast than in the southern United States.[43]

The effects of regional specificity on this group of white women should not be overstated, however. For one thing, although the women were living on the West Coast at the time of these interviews, their senses of self and other were shaped by their own and their families' lives elsewhere, as well as by national and global relations of racism, past and present. For another thing, class and age frequently overrode region in ways that challenged popular wisdom about the relations of U.S. racism: for example, middle-class women from all over the United States, not just those in the southern states, described residentially segregated lives. Nor did a more muted racism in the public language(s) of race on the West Coast translate into a sense that these women's lives were to any lesser extent shaped by the relations of racism extant in their environments and in their histories.

By conscious design on my part, the interviewee group included more women identified with feminism or the left than would have been the case in a random sample of U.S. women. Similarly, many of these women were living their gender identities in ways that challenged their ascribed places in the racial and sexual orders—as partners in interracial relationships, as women without children, or as lesbians. All of this, as later chapters explore, had the potential to shape their articulations of whiteness in both obvious and subtle ways. As will be clear, however, by no means did all of the women interviewed subscribe to feminism, nor to political progressivism of any kind. There is thus a continuum here, from self-consciously feminist and antiracist women to self-styled far-right or conservative women.

The study is not premised on the notion of a random sample whereby these thirty women are, in a "part-for-whole" fashion, a microcosmic representation of the white women of the United States. Rather, through focused attention to a group of women I have sought to map out and situate in sociocultural terms some patterns in the material contexts in which whiteness is lived in the United States in the late twentieth century. In addition, I have contrasted the discursive repertoires through which white women seek to describe and comprehend their positions in the racial order. As important as differentiating between modes of "thinking through race," however, has been showing the *continuities* across discursive repertoires from (ostensibly) "left" or "progressive" to apparently more conservative: the traces of essentialist racism, colonial discourse, and evasion of color and power in the discursive repertoires of women whose intentions are, in fact, quite different; the sharp cutting edges that reinforce racism, embedded in the discursive repertoires of color- and power-evasive women who might well, at the level of intention, be attempting to challenge essentialist racism.

The specifics of the women's backgrounds and identities enabled me to call into question certain elements of "popular wisdom." These interviews did *not*, for example, suggest that one experience of marginality—Jewishness, lesbianism—led white women automatically toward empathy with other oppressed communities, nor that participation in one kind of liberatory movement—feminism, the "left"—led automatically to antiracism (although, as I argue in chapter 6, liberatory movements *did* give some of the women access to specific tools with which to reach toward particular forms of antiracism).

In the context of analyzing narratives of white experience whose particularities are clearly specifiable, I propose ways of looking further afield: directions and contributions to the development of theory and method for thinking about whiteness. My approach emphasizes, first, the salience or meaningfulness of race in the construction of white experience. Here, I am especially concerned to document the ways in which racism is a "white issue," that is, an issue that shapes white experience as well as that of communities of color. Second, I have sought to move well beyond the study of "racial attitudes," developing an analysis of how white people's positions in the racial order are produced through the interplay of discourses on race with the material relations of racism. Third, I seek to move away from a present-oriented, "snapshot" approach to race, developing instead one that views white women's thinking about race as embedded in a long and global history. Fourth, my approach entails a social constructionist emphasis on the social, political, and historical rather than "essential" or natural character of racial positioning.

Conclusion

In this chapter I have set out some of the personal, political, and intellectual history in the context of which I approach the study of white women, race, and whiteness. As I have indicated, the project had its inception in a particular, "local" concern: accounting for and engaging in critique of the racial structuring of second wave feminist discourse and practice. Given this point of origin, I return frequently to feminism, at times focusing in detail on white feminist women's engagement with whiteness and anti-racism, or setting out the implications of this study for new directions in white feminist antiracist practice. However, white feminists are, of course, participants in histories and social processes larger than those of feminism itself. The study looks well beyond feminism and seeks to begin analyzing something broader: the inscription of a diverse group of white women into a racial order whose elements are both daily and lifelong, and are shaped by local, regional, national, and international histories.

My hope is that, in the chapters that follow, race, racial dominance, and whiteness will emerge as complex, lived experiences, as material rather than abstract categories, and as historically situated rather than timeless in their meanings and effects. Chapter

2 begins to bring into focus the women I interviewed and describes the ways in which interviewing white women about race
required me to begin charting a course through both dominant
and "counterhegemonic" race discourses, ways of speaking about
race and whiteness. Chapter 3 documents and analyzes the "social
geographies of race" that shaped the women's childhoods, making
explicit and tangible some of the ways in which white women's
life experience is racially structured. Chapters 4 and 5 both explore—from slightly different angles—interracial relationships as
sites of long-standing contention in U.S. history. Chapter 4 examines white women's thoughts about interracial relationships as
idea and the racialized constructions of masculinity, femininity,
identity, and community that flow from a dominant discourse
against interracial relationships. Chapter 5 focuses more directly
on the experiences of the women who were or had been involved
in interracial partnerships and parenting. Chapter 6 involves the
mapping and critique of a range of ways of "thinking through
race" that emerged in these interviews, locating each in political
and historical contexts and examining what each conceals or reveals about the materiality of racism. Chapter 7 examines the
meaning of whiteness as a cultural form or set of practices, asking
how, when, and why these women named themselves in terms of
racial, cultural, ethnic, regional, or class belonging. The epilogue
draws together the threads of preceding chapters in order both to
articulate a sense of the meanings of whiteness generated through
the text and to seek out possible directions for transforming
whiteness.

2

White on White: The Interviewees and the Method

Conducting the interviews for this book was, in different ways, terrifying, frustrating, challenging, and joyous (not necessarily in that order, either temporally or quantitatively!). The terror came in large part from the fact that interviewing required of me a confrontation with my own personality and cultural training. For interviewing requires one to go out and ask personal questions of strangers and, even before that, to approach unknown people, either in person or by telephone, and ask them for an enormous favor—to give time, and to share personal history, for the most part taking entirely on trust that their time and, more importantly, their words will be treated with respect. The frustration and the challenge came from the special difficulties involved in interviewing white women on what for many of them was, in ways I will explore later, a "taboo" topic that generated areas of memory lapse, silence, shame, and evasion. The joy came from listening, talking, and reveling in the singularity of the women's stories, accents, turns of phrase. It would be patently untrue to suggest that I "agreed" or identified equally with each woman's perspective on society, or with how each articulated the issues of race, culture, and whiteness with which I was preoccupied. Nonetheless, in the context of the interviews themselves, I worked to comprehend the logic of their lives and the words with which they described them.

Vital Statistics

Between 1984 and 1986, I interviewed thirty white women, diverse in age, class, region of origin, sexuality, family situation, and political orientation, but all living in California at the time of the interviews either in Santa Cruz County or the San Francisco Bay Area. The interviews were lengthy: I spent between three and eight hours with each woman (usually over two sessions, but, in

a few instances, one or three), striving to set race in the context
of her life and priorities rather than separate it from other
concerns.

It is crucial at the outset to begin to give an indication of who
these women were, although of course that will become clearer
throughout the book. It is difficult for several reasons to catego-
rize definitively or in any standardized fashion the class or economic backgrounds of these women as a group. For one thing,
given differences of generation, region, and urban or rural upbringing, the class categories with which the women identified
themselves, and even the women's concrete descriptions of their
own or their parents' means of survival, meant different things in
different contexts. Making matters more complicated were the
degrees to which many families' economic fates seesawed in response either to national trends (the Depression, World War II) or
family crises (chiefly the disability, death, or departure of the male
breadwinner).

The women's descriptions of their economic situations in childhood were, of necessity, subjective, since children for the most
part neither know their parents' income nor can calibrate it in relation to the class structure as a whole. More than a few (Evelyn
Steinman, Ginny Rodd, Dot Humphrey, Louise Glebocki, Clare
Traverso)[1] described themselves as having been "poor" for all or
part of their childhoods. And others, it seemed to me from their
descriptions of parents erratically or underemployed, must also
have been so. But talking of class was complicated, an emotional
and rhetorical as well as an objective process. Thus, for some, the
assertion of middle class status was at times a metaphor for race
privilege. And Ginny Rodd, having described how to maintain an
entire family for months at a time on flour and milk alone, dis-
avowed in a different way the image of her rural smallholding
family as "poor" when she said:

> We were all the same. There were no rich where we lived. Or rather, no
> rich, no poor. You couldn't get poor as long as you enjoyed your life.
> You were rich if you loved your family. No rich, no poor. We all
> worked.

The group was by no means confined to one or even a few class
strata, but rather ranged from working class to upper middle and
owning strata; the children of the middle strata were better represented than the very rich or the very poor. In the women's

childhoods, their parents had been, among other things, under- or irregularly employed manual laborers (Marty Douglass, Louise Glebocki), skilled manual or pink-collar workers (Clare Traverso, Sandy Alvarez, Donna Gonzaga, Cathy Thomas), self-employed craftspeople, storekeepers, and small-business owners (Dot Humphrey, Jeanine Cohen, Joan Van Buren, Frieda Kazen, Marjorie Hoffman), rural smallholders (Ginny Rodd), highly paid, skilled professionals (Beth Ellison, Tamara Green, Eve Schraeger, Chris Patterson, Suzie Roberts), and owners of large, successful businesses (Margaret Phillips, Irene Esterley). This list still falsely simplifies a complex picture in certain ways, however. The "self-employed craftspeople, storekeepers, and small-business owners" include, for example, two dry cleaners—one in Johannesburg, South Africa, and the other in New Jersey—the owners of a mom-and-pop hardware store in Queens, New York, a front-yard mechanic in rural Kansas, and a tailor who plied his trade in the lumber camps of upstate Maine in the early decades of the century. Thumbnail sketches of all the women in the appendix characterize their backgrounds and lives in greater detail. But more than that, the stories and incidents upon which I draw, chapter by chapter, bring some women more than others into the foreground in ways that help make concrete where they were "coming from" and where they were during the interview.

The women ranged in age from twenty to ninety-three.[2] As adults, they were diverse but in some ways not proportionately representative of the white female population as a whole. Thus, for example, only twelve of them had children. Eight were lesbian and twenty heterosexual (the sexual orientation of two of the women was not clear to me). The group was more educated than an "average" group, although not dramatically so: one woman had a postgraduate degree, and, at the other end of the scale, five either had not completed high school or were educated only up to the end of high school. Twelve either had bachelor's degrees or were currently working toward them as returning students. Four others had teaching credentials *and* bachelor's degrees.

The women's status in the work force was extremely varied. Nine were not in the paid work force: of these, five were retired after lifetimes of waged work. Four were at the time of the interviews full-time homemakers under retirement age. Of these, one working-class woman had found that her job did not cover the costs of child care so now stayed at home with the children; two

others, both upper middle class, could easily afford to take a break
from wage earning while their husbands supported them. Another had chosen to stay at home with the children although it
meant the family was stretched financially. Twelve, at the time of
the interviews or before retirement, earned their living by means
of "typically female" jobs: there were two waitresses, one paid
domestic worker, two clerical workers, four teachers, one receptionist, one housekeeper, and one retail worker. Four women ran
their own businesses (one owned a retail store, one a travel
agency, the third was an interior designer and the fourth a free-
lance housepainter). Of the rest, one managed the typesetting for
a small press, two worked in feminist nonprofit agencies, one was
an attorney (but currently working outside her field), one was an
editor with a technical publisher, one was a paid labor union organizer, and one was employed part time raising funds for an en-
vironmental action group. Of the retirees not already mentioned,
one had been a government employee at management level, another had worked in left organizations, and one had been a traveling secretary and companion for a woman academic.[3]

In the interviews, I asked the women to explore the landscapes
of their childhoods, building up fine-grained pictures of house-
holds, friends, schools, neighborhoods, and wider communities.
I wanted to know who, racially and ethnically speaking, each
woman had encountered and in what circumstances, how she
came to conceptualize people of different racial and ethnic groups,
and whether she saw herself as a racially or ethnically identified
being. Beyond their common grounding in childhood (however
differently experienced, everyone had one), the interviews di-
verged in accordance with the differences between the women,
for I had hoped to divide the interviews broadly into three
subgroups: first, women who, I imagined, might be more than
usually conscious of gender as a system of domination; second,
white women whom I knew to be more than usually connected
to communities of color (and thus possibly more conscious of racial domination); and, third, women about whom I had no preconceptions besides their gender and their racial identity.

I adopted a purposive rather than a random strategy for gathering interviews. The diversity of the whole group in terms of
age, class, and region was something I monitored consciously
through the two-year research period, as was the range of women

in the three subgroups. In constructing the group, my choice was to intentionally "overrepresent" some "types" of experience, in particular, women involved in feminism, women involved in antiracism, and women in interracial partnerships or families. Feminists were of particular interest given the origins of the project in feminism and given the ways that, I hope, the book will speak in particular to feminist women. Antiracist and interracial experience were of importance, it seemed to me, because of their difference from dominant modes of living whiteness. Theirs were voices that I felt needed to be heard. Finally, however, it was important to me to try to scan as broad a range as possible of ways of living as a white woman in the United States within my economic constraints of conducting research as a graduate student.

Among the women I interviewed because of their involvement in antiracist or feminist activism was Marjorie Hoffman, in her seventies by the time of the interview, who recalled meeting Black children as a volunteer worker in New York settlement houses during the Depression years and also described her move to the southern United States as one of the few white workers in an innovative race relations program. Louise Glebocki was an active member of a Marxist-Leninist party, strongly committed to the struggles of people of color both within and outside the United States. Debby Rothman was an organizer in a labor union whose members were predominantly women of color. Tamara Green, Jeanine Cohen, and Donna Gonzaga were all socialist, feminist, and lesbian activists who had been involved in a range of racially mixed and internationally focused groups and coalitions. Three other women were or had been teachers in schools that served mainly students of color: Frieda Kazen, for example, described as the formative period in her adult life the years she spent teaching in a Harlem elementary school at the height of Black Power activism and the "second Harlem Renaissance." Others had been students of women's studies or active in feminist organizations. Dot Humphrey, for example, had participated in one of the earliest, New York-based women's liberation groups of the second wave of feminism and cofounded a (now defunct) feminist journal. Eve Schraeger had served for several years on the collective of a West Coast women's bookstore. Chris Patterson had worked to create a lesbian feminist coffeehouse in a small southern town.

Two others, Pat Bowen and Cathy Thomas, had both first encountered feminism as undergraduate college students.

Some women had crossed the "color line" in a different way, as partners in heterosexual or lesbian interracial relationships or as the parents of children of "mixed" heritage. As I will argue in chapter 5, these women in fact experienced changed positions in the relations of racism, albeit temporarily, and often as a result gained new insight into the working of racial oppression and boundary marking. For these women, racism had an impact both in the form of external pressure and from within the relationship. As Jeanine Cohen put it, "Racism was in our bedroom."

Not all the women were feminist, leftist, or self-consciously antiracist, however. On the right wing of the political continuum, Alison Honan described herself as a far-right Republican, closest in spirit to the John Birch Society. Others also declared themselves Republican voters, and antiwelfare conservative Evelyn Steinman sardonically referred to herself as an ex-bleeding heart liberal. Still others described themselves as disinterested in, or confused by, politics and current affairs. Joan Bracknell, for example, had not voted for years, in part out of a sense that voting did not achieve anything, and also out of a concern that appearing on the electoral register would make her eligible for jury duty (she had been reluctant to be called to serve on a jury while she was responsible for the care of her invalid mother, but she had not bothered to register in later years). Marty Douglass and her husband had voted Democratic in the last presidential election, but in general Marty felt that she had no understanding of politics.

I was not, of course, interested only in women with strongly and consciously articulated views of political questions in general, or the meaning of race in particular. The words the women chose in telling stories, their enthusiasm, anger, anxiety, or disinterest at different points in our conversations, and their varying interpretations of my research goals all expressed a great deal about the many ways in which race can be lived and seen.

Given the flexibility of an interview (different, for example, from a questionnaire) there was room for diverse interpretations of the issues at hand. Thus, some women took my interest in "white women, race, and ethnic difference" as an invitation to discuss their history of political involvement in antiracism, their personal struggles with it, and so on. For others, the interview called forth a catalogue of all the people of racial and ethnic identities different from their own that they had met in their lifetimes. Yet others felt that, if they did not know anyone racially or culturally different from themselves, they were not qualified to be interviewed.

In addition to leaving space for, and learning from, this range of possible meanings of the question of "white women and racism," I did not discourage apparent digressions of any kind, in part because of my commitment to place race in the context of white women's other interests and concerns. Descriptions of childhood experience of abuse, of the discomfort of feeling like an eccentric or outsider in a small town, of anti-Semitism all provided me with clues about what might make a difference to white women's race consciousness. They also continued to remind me that all women experience a complex interweaving of privilege and oppression, comfort and pain. Other digressions were less obviously relevant but served to point out that race was not always at the forefront of the women's attention: listening to the tapes for one interview, for example, I realized that the woman had spent more time describing a patent diet mix than on any other single topic!

The Researcher and Power

Two sets of power relations shaped this book and my relationships with the women I interviewed. First, there is in general a power imbalance between a researcher and the subjects of research in the sense that the researcher sets the agenda and edits the material, analyzes it, publishes it, and thereby takes both credit and blame for the overall result.

Needless to say, the women who took part in this project did so voluntarily. They also knew they could refuse to answer particular questions, discontinue the interview altogether, or turn the tape recorder off temporarily. They took up the first and third options on occasion. One woman said that her childhood had been so painful that she would prefer not to discuss it at all and chose to begin her narrative from age eighteen. Others turned the tape recorder off while they named particular individuals or organizations.

These practices are standard in any research project. I also urged the women I interviewed to add questions or topics of their own, to ask me about the purpose of specific questions, or to turn the tables by asking me to respond to my own questions. They did all of these things from time to time, but the interviewer role is a well known one, difficult to rework at will. Thus, at least 80 percent of the questions and answers traveled in the "traditional" direction: I asked and they answered.

The problem of the researcher as an "invisible hand" that guides the analysis and the final written text is addressed, in part, by stating it as an issue and by providing as clear an account as possible of both the interviewing strategy and the theoretical positions that underpin the analysis. Critics of the idea of objectivity have pointed out that there is no disinterested position to be adopted in scholarship. I would agree with such critics: in carrying out the research for this book, I viewed myself, as much as the women I interviewed, as situated within the relations of racism. An advantage of qualitative research in this regard is that it presents greater possibilities for multiple interpretation: I hope that, in the chapters that follow, I have left room for disagreement and alternate readings. However, it should be clear too that the editorial choices were mine—while readers can reinterpret the material I have included, they are at a disadvantage with regard to what has been left out.

The second set of power relations, more specific to this project, are the power relations of racism itself, and specifically the effects of the color- and power-evasive discourse on race that, I have argued, was the dominant public language of race at the time the interviews took place. In designing the study, I attempted to develop strategies to explicitly address and subvert some of the power dynamics of racism, as well as the problems of power inequity in all research.

Central to this task was my development of a "dialogical" approach to the interviews. Rather than maintaining the traditionally distant, apparently objective, and so-called blank-faced research persona, I positioned myself as explicitly involved in the questions, at times sharing with interviewees either information about my own life or elements of my own analysis of racism as it developed through the research process.

This approach served two different functions, for in addition to seeking to facilitate discussion about race and racism in a social

context where privilege and particular discourses on race construct zones of silence, repression, and taboo, it served to democ-
ratize the research process, reducing the extent to which I was
positioned as an invisible presence.

The blank-faced or neutral interviewer should, it is suggested,
dodge questions about her own life and opinions, using evasive
responses such as "I'm more interested in *your* life than mine right
now" and "Gee, I guess I never thought about that issue." Within
the logic of this approach, the researcher is also expected to avoid
sharing with interviewees her research goals and her analysis of
the issues at hand. The argument here is that this standardizes and
makes more scientific one's results, minimizing the chance of
"leading" interviewees to say what they believe the researcher
wants to hear.[4] Feminists have criticized the goal of interviewer
neutrality on several counts. Social psychologist Ann Oakley be-
lieves that the approach is unfair to women who may desperately
need information or advice the interviewer has to offer (in the
instance that inspired her critique, Oakley's research was on
motherhood and childbirth and involved interviewing women
who were pregnant for the first time).[5] Further, Oakley argues,
the adoption of the blank-faced persona requires a narrow definition of the interviewee as "data," and thereby keeps in place an
extreme power differential between interviewer and interviewee.
Feminist oral historian Sherna Gluck suggests that it may be necessary to step outside the neutral persona and tell potential interviewees the philosophy behind the project in order to secure their
interest and help.[6]

I agree with Oakley and Gluck, and it seems to me that there
are still more problems with the blank-faced, neutral interviewer.
For one thing, no presentation of self is really neutral. One's
words and nonverbal signals send messages: I was variously
viewed as younger, older, a feminist, an ally or comrade, a person
of the same or not the same sexual orientation as the woman I
was talking to, a person who did or did not have interracial involvements parallel to her own, a "nice girl," a foreigner, Jewish,
white—and probably other things too. Second, evasive or vague
responses mark one as something specific by interviewees, be it
"closed-mouthed," "scientific," "rude," "mainstream," "moder-
ate," or perhaps "strange"—and many of those are negative characterizations in some or all of the communities in which I was

interviewing. My ability to conduct interviews successfully involved a complex set of adjustments in self-presentation, but
never a presentation of myself as neutral.

Racism and Taboo: Problems of Initiating Interviews

Competing discourses on race shaped my research strategies. Any
research project involves raising an overarching question or opening up an area of discussion and receiving a range of responses to
it. The question I put to myself at the beginning of this study was,
more or less, "What is white women's relationship to racism?"
What I said to potential interviewees was, "I'm doing research on
white women and race . . ." As I combed the San Francisco Bay
Area and Santa Cruz County for potential interviewees, my question was greeted with cooperation and interest in some circles,
suspicion and hostility in others. These divergent responses, it
seemed to me, resulted partly from what I was exploring through
the study—the range of possible meanings of whiteness, race, and
racism in the contemporary United States.

   As I have already noted and will explore in much greater detail
in later chapters, the women I interviewed were variously positioned in relation to competing discursive repertoires on race and
racism. Some (especially Marxists) viewed racism primarily as a
structural issue rather than a personal one. While their feelings
about racism were frequently intense, the issue did not feel as
though it was about their own identities, so discussing the topic
was not personally difficult or challenging. Some of the feminist
women did see racism as an intensely personal issue, but, as I
noted earlier, feminist culture has within it precedents for offering
one's personal life for public scrutiny. Further, criticism of feminism by feminist/radical women of color had introduced many
white feminist women to the idea of racism as a personal issue.
Finally, both feminist and Marxist women had been exposed to
the race-cognizant moment in the naming of race, in which it is
argued that race differences must be made visible in order for political analysis of them to take place. It this context, some women
were very responsive to my call for speech.

   A good part of the silence, suspicion, and hostility that my
project attracted came from women whose thinking about race
drew primarily on the color- and power-evasive repertoire. Many
of the women, in addition to having been schooled in evasion of

color and power as the correct response to questions about race, had memories or direct experience of their own and others' inscription into essentialist racism. Given this, putting the words *white* and *race* together broke several taboos simultaneously. My asking to understand more about "whiteness" was, for many women, only comprehensible as a white supremacist gesture, and my focus on white women could only be comprehended as race discrimination. On another level, my interest in white women's race consciousness was also threatening. For, as I will argue in chapter 6, in a racially hierarchical society, white women have to repress, avoid, and conceal a great deal in order to maintain a stance of "not noticing" color. From this point of view, there are apparently only two options open to white women: either one does not have anything to say about race, or one is apt to be deemed "racist" simply by virtue of having something to say.

Some examples of the grounds on which white women refused to be interviewed will help clarify this point. The chairwoman of an antiabortion organization refused over the telephone my request that I come to a group meeting and then ask for volunteers. Her comment was, "I don't know what makes you think our members would have anything to say. Our organization has nothing to do with race." Other telephone calls, to labor union offices and seniors' centers, ended with distinctly chilly or evasive responses that made me feel that *they* felt that *I* was a racist extremist.

On another occasion, I was screened by a multiracial (Asian, Black, and white) committee of staff and participants in a seniors' day center prior to being given permission to solicit interviewees. Here, in spite of a more extended discussion, I was nonetheless refused entry. My interest in interviewing white women was viewed as discriminatory against women of color (and possibly also against men, although I do not know for sure). I was told (reasonably enough) that it would be impossible to make an announcement in the dining room to ask for white women only. It was emphasized to me, in indignant and even shocked tones, that the day center served all groups equally.

There seemed to be no discursive common ground between us. My explanations that there were important reasons to focus on white people and make racism a "white people's problem," as well as that white researchers now needed to let people of color do research within their communities rather than claiming the right to do it for them rang even in my own ears as weak excuses, rather than as a stand in favor of self-representation by communities of color. And, while it was clear to me that a call for white women only could sound like blatant discrimination, I am sure another way could have been found. But this underlines what is distinctive about race as an axis of difference: a call in the dining room for "over-eighties," or perhaps even for "women," would have had very different connotations.

It thus became clear in the interviewing process that outside leftist, feminist, and "race-cognizant" communities, my question was closing more doors—and mouths—than it was opening. No matter how much I was learning from the refusals to speak, I needed to alter my approach. I felt caught in a dilemma: should I restrict my interviewing to radical communities or become more covert in my approach? (The possibility of appearing to be "non-discriminatory" by interviewing women of color as well as white women and then not using the interviews was suggested to me but seemed neither respectful nor appropriate.)

Next I tried a few interviews with a more indirect approach, saying, "I'm interested in women's life histories." (I approached only women whom I already knew to be white and organizations that I knew to be monoracial.) Since I wanted to address questions about white women and race via life histories, this phrasing of the question was not entirely false, but it altered the ordering of my priorities. This was, in a sense, a retreat back into the blank-faced persona.

In three interviews I conducted under this "life history" rubric, the problems of a covert approach loomed large. First, I had to find a way to bring questions about race difference into the discussion. This was often awkward, since race is not usually an issue by means of which white women order their accounts of their lives. Second, the experience brought home very sharply the assumption implicit in this formulation that interviewees are simply "data," and not "thinkers" or "readers," that my covert approach would never be exposed, for example, by an interviewee picking up this book in a bookstore. Further, the approach foreclosed the possibility of interviewees' engaging analytically with the issue of race. And it also represented a withdrawal from the feminist goal of sharing power by sharing information.

Eventually, a series of strategic compromises and reformulations resolved the situation, at least provisionally. First, with the help of intermediaries, I was able to avoid addressing racially diverse groups of women in order to ask to speak with white women in particular. (For example, colleagues in other research sites engaged in projects very different from my own and friends in a diverse range of workplaces approached white women on my behalf and arranged for me to contact them.) Second, I reformulated the overall question with which I approached the women in a way that stayed close enough to my purpose to make an interview possible, but that was not so threatening as to foreclose speech: "I'm interested in whether you have had contact with people of racial or cultural groups different from you, and whether you see yourself as belonging to an ethnic or cultural group." In this context, I could explore my concerns, which, of course, did include those expressed in that question. As a compromise, this mode of posing the question in a sense "translated" it into a slightly different discourse on race. At the same time, it was a retreat from the goal of sharing my concerns, in my *own* mode of thinking about them, with all the women I interviewed.

Interview and Dialogue

Ironically, if my own race–cognizant view of racism as an environment and body of ideas into which all white people are inscribed was unhelpful in approaching white women whose primary discursive repertoire was color- and power-evasive, *within* the interviews it was crucial in enabling and provoking speech for women across the whole discursive spectrum. Central to my dialogical method were the ways in which I offered information both about myself as inscribed within racism and about my analysis of racism as systemic as well as personal. In effect, I broke the silence of the blank-faced interviewer in order to facilitate the breaking of silence on race by a diverse range of white women.

My interventions in the interviews took a range of forms. In interviews with women whose discourse was more like my own (feminists, Marxists), explaining my analysis enabled us to debate, as peers, issues of theory and strategy about racism. Additionally, exchanging stories of personal experiences (about involvement in interracial relationships and communities, for example) would not have been possible had I adhered to a more

removed or ostensibly objective self-presentation. I also used myself at times as a source of validation or shared misery with regard
to the internalization of racist ideas or feelings. This, it seemed to
me, was particularly crucial given the shame associated with racist
feelings in a society that has repressed rather than abolished them.

The following interview fragments explore in more detail other
ways in which my own interjections functioned. The first example involves a story I told several women about my childhood
in the north of England. The story encapsulates the racial structuring of white women's material environments and the intersection of race with class, and also indicates that white women may
have a range of feelings toward racial Others. In a sense it gives
"permission" to talk about seeing difference:

> I grew up in an almost all white suburb. But to get into the city, we
> would drive in the car through much poorer neighborhoods than ours,
> where there were many more people of color, from South Asia, Africa,
> and the Caribbean. As a small child, I would look out of the car
> windows, both fascinated and afraid of the poverty, [of] the dinginess,
> and of the different racial groups I saw, the cracked sidewalks, the
> secondhand furniture stores, and so on. I was just learning to count at
> that time and would keep a tally on my fingers of how many whites
> versus people of color we drove past.

My story sometimes reminded women of similar kinds of experience. One woman reciprocated with a description of feeling
afraid in a Black neighborhood of Los Angeles and began to speculate about where she had been given the clues to feel fear. Even
a response like "We never went to *those* places! There was no reason to do so!" would tell me something about social distance in
the racial mapping of that woman's childhood.

Another mode of interjection involved my bringing an analysis
of racism into the interview in order to enable speech. The following excerpt illustrates the effectiveness of the strategy. Evelyn,
a self-styled conservative in her fifties, but one who nonetheless
views herself as "not a prejudiced and biased person," talked toward the end of the interview about who her friends were:

> RF: One final question, and then that's probably about it. And again, it
> sort of goes back to what I was saying about how I see, when I think
> about white women and race and contact with different ethnic groups,
> different racial groups. I know that for myself, I was raised in a very
> white, 99.9 percent white environment—

EVELYN: Mhm.

RF: —and I also know that, the way that my life is set up, and probably the way most people's lives are set up, the people that you spend time with are usually people in the same income bracket, and the same—

EVELYN: Mhm!!

RF: —type of person. So I was wondering if that was the same for you? Is it the case that your friends are mainly in your same income bracket and mainly in your same racial group or ethnic group?

EVELYN: It's probably true. But I don't think it was done out of choosing, I think that it just—well, you have to have a sense of having something in common in the first place—

RF: Right.

EVELYN: And with women generally the first thing is, are you married—then you have something in common. Do you have children—then you have something in common. And then it's a question of the husbands—can they talk to one another? And so it's true, most of our friends, they do have, certainly economically we're about the same level, most all of them are college graduates. A great many of them are engineers, businesspeople. It's true, but I don't think that we do it out of—deliberately. I think it just happens to be the way our lives all fall together.

RF: No, that's why I phrased it the way I did.

EVELYN: Yeah.

RF: Because a lot of times, I think that if I asked somebody that question, they would feel challenged—

EVELYN: Yes.

RF: —criticized by the question. Which isn't my intention, because what I'm real interested in is just I think things shake down that way.

EVELYN: Mhm, mhm, I think they do too.

RF: And with me, it's been that way in the past, in terms of that my friends have been white people.

EVELYN: Mhm.

RF: And I don't know if that's been true of you, that your friends are—

EVELYN: Uh, I have one friend that's an Argentinian. (Laughs) Where would I meet all these other people, you see? And so, as I say, it isn't anything that's done deliberately, I think it's our circumstances.

RF: Right.

EVELYN: And there again, when you have friends, friends are people that you can talk to, that can understand why you feel a certain way about a certain thing, you have something in common. And it wouldn't make any difference if they were black, green, yellow, or pink. It just

happens—that—they—[tails off and throws up her hands]. We have
friends of different *religious* backgrounds—atheist, staunch Catholic, and
just as many that are Protestant. And also Republicans *and* Democrats.
Now *there's* a difference. (Laughs)

In this conversation, I approached the question of the racial
makeup of Evelyn's friendship group cautiously, prefacing it with
an analysis of why she might *not* have friends who are people of
color. When I finally, as it were, popped the question, Evelyn's
response was phrased within a discourse on race that was different
from my own, emphasizing her fear that the absence of people of
color in her friendship group might be viewed as an act of intentional racism. The conversation continued with a "battle of the
discourses," as I continually reemphasized an analysis of monoracial friendship groups as socially constructed, in order to make
a safer discursive space for Evelyn to say who her friends were.

This encounter yielded a great deal of information. First, Evelyn was anxious not to be thought racist or, in her terms, "prejudiced," but felt that might happen at any moment. Second, she
did *not* have friends of color, with the possible exception of an
Argentinian (and it is not clear whether or not Evelyn viewed her
friend as a person of color). On the contrary, she felt an enormous
sense of social distance between herself and people of color
("Where would I meet all those people?"). Third, her discourse
collapsed into illogicality as she raised the need for similarity in
terms of marital and parental status as reasons why she might not
get along well with people of class and race positions different
from her own—rather, potential commonality by virtue of marital and family status were overridden by social distance and a
sense of irreducible difference. Fourth, use of the phrase "Black,
green, yellow, or pink" is, I suggest, a euphemism or strategy for
avoiding race: it shifts attention away from color differences that
make a political difference by embedding meaningful differences
among nonmeaningful ones. Again, the assertion of differences
that she can live with—Republican versus Democrat, Catholic
versus Protestant—stood in as quasi substitutes for race. By contrast, "white," "race," and other racially explicit terms seemed to
be taboo words that Evelyn avoided using. Finally, it is interesting
that when she was asked about friends, Evelyn assumed friends
were female.

In short, in the exchange with Evelyn I learned a great deal about the circumstances of her life, about how she conceptualized racism, about the profound sense of social distance and difference Evelyn did feel in relation to people of color, and about how race difference and racism structured her experience as a white woman. And I do not think I could have done so without very carefully constructing the question and the discursive space in the way that I did.

Another example illustrates the ways that my own "caughtness" in the relations of racism limited my speech and my abilities as an interviewer. Here, Margaret Phillips described an incident in which her son, who had joined the Rastafarian religion, brought home a Black friend to stay overnight, without Margaret's knowledge. Analytically, what is interesting here is not my speech, but my silence:

MARGARET: It's very hard on his father, because he's a very traditional businessman, and he's fairly conservative in his politics. I'm pretty liberal in my politics. So within our family, it's—we've kept it light, it hasn't gotten too heavy, but they [the kids] know we're in different camps. The kids seem to be more liberal. . . .

But [my husband] has gotten more liberal, and we have had [my son]'s friends over, who are Black, and we like doing that, we're comfortable with that, when we know ahead. But we don't like it when he springs it on us. One night he got a call in the middle of the night, and I went in to awaken him, and this face turned around—this head of dreadlocks—this face turned around, and it was a Black face, in his bed. And, you know, in the middle of the night—I was so totally confused. So that kind of thing is very hard, if somebody brings home friends, and that triggers something. I wouldn't say fear, but caution—I mean, there is something in my upbringing that makes me say—mainly because my son would bring somebody that he didn't know. I mean, if you had someone in your home you didn't know, you'd always feel a little cautious.

RF: Mhm.

MARGARET: If you didn't feel—

RF: Sure.

MARGARET: —anyone knew them.

RF: Sure.

MARGARET: So that was pretty offensive to us, and we started setting limits around that.

RF: Yeah. Yeah.

MARGARET: So we've been through a variety of experiences around this, as you can imagine. But one grandmother took to it not well at all and the other grandmother was just here with [my son's partner] for the first time and bent over backwards [to be accommodating].

Telling the story, Margaret was very distressed, almost, it seemed, to the point of tears. She did not, however, elaborate on her confusion or say what she thought had happened, who the stranger was, why it had been so terrifying to encounter a Black face in the bed when she expected her son's white face to turn toward her. My response here seems to have been largely reassurance, the implication being "Yes, I understand."

Over the several years since the interview took place I have reinterpreted this story in several ways. One possiblility is that while at a conscious level Margaret was doing her best to accommodate her son's and his friends' differentness, at night, at her most vulnerable, she was overwhelmed by it. Another possibility—and this was my earliest interpretation—is that for a moment Margaret imagined that her son had turned Black, echoing an element of an older racist discourse wherein it was thought that color "rubs off"—that white people who associate too closely with people of color will take on their color. Third, it could indeed have been that the appearance of a stranger—any stranger—in a son's bed would be disquieting to any mother.

In any event, it would have been interesting to explore the point further, for clearly there was something important to be learned from the incident about how Margaret felt about her son, his Rastafarianism, and his Rastafarian friends, and possibly something of what is repressed, frightening, or shameful in white women's feelings about race. My response, ostensibly protecting her from further exploration of the incident, was perhaps designed to protect me as much as Margaret. For it is also possible that, rather than the content of Margaret's "racial unconscious," the incident generated the return of something repressed in mine, crystallized part of what is shameful for *me* about white race consciousness. As another white woman, I felt, or perhaps projected, that shame, and therefore colluded in keeping it repressed by not asking Margaret any further questions about the incident. Instead, I followed her lead when she shifted the ground away from the racialness of the incident. Reading this transcript, removed from the interview, I can see myself working from within the discourse

I am seeking to challenge, maintaining one of the silences I am setting out to break.

Experience and Memory: An Interview Is Not the Telling of a Life

> The raw material of oral history consists not just in factual statements, but is pre-eminently an expression and representation of culture, and therefore includes not only literal narratives, but also the dimensions of memory, ideology and subconscious desires.[7]

As James Clifford says in introducing a collection of essays and experiments in the "new ethnography," "Ethnographic truths [and, we can add, all other research accounts] are inherently partial, committed and incomplete."[8]

What does it all mean, anyway, when the talking is done, the microphone cable is rewound, and the tapes are labeled and transcribed? What is the status of an interview narrative? An interview is not, in any simple sense, the telling of a life so much as it is an incomplete story angled toward my questions and each woman's ever-changing sense of self and of how the world works.

Several times during the interview process, I experienced what I called tip-of-the-iceberg moments, when something a woman said would remind me of the enormous amount that was not being expressed. For example, toward the end of one interview, a woman who presented herself as a person for whom race and culture had been background issues until her early twenties suddenly made passing mention of dating a Mexican fellow student in high school. The questions here are, first, how might race or cultural difference have constructed the relationship and, second, what was at stake in this particular woman's prioritizing of events? Why had this relationship not featured prominently in her telling of her life? I frequently witnessed the eruption of memories about race and culture in the course of interviews, as well as finding clues to what remained forgotten. Early in one interview an older woman suddenly remembered sharing her childhood neighborhood with a priest who was famous for his racist and inflammatory radio broadcasts. Having told me about him, the woman said, "I had no idea I was going to say that, it just came out!" What remains forgotten: one woman could not remember whether the gay bars where she used to live, in Atlanta, were integrated; another could not recall whether her high school had been desegregated before or after she left it.

The working of memory is complex, political, and idiosyncratic. Luisa Passerini suggests that memory presents different levels during an oral–history interview, one being what she refers to as an " 'all-ready' memory, stereotyped, revealing general views of the world," and another "more directly connected with life experience."[9] This distinction may usefully be applied to apparent "contradictions" in white women's narratives, where, for example, a woman might say that she did not notice race differences when she was growing up and elsewhere describe incidents in which she made decisions on the basis of an awareness of race.

Interviewees were multiply positioned in relation to these life narratives. On the one hand, they were coproducers of the narratives. On the other hand, they were observers, both of their environments and of themselves as they retold and reevaluated what had gone before. This reevaluation was frequently an explicit component of the narratives. And if interviewees' relationships to the text were complex, so is mine. As the interviewer, I too stand as a coproducer of the narratives. At the same time, I am an observer, of the lives described and of the mode of telling them. What makes interview narratives readable, analyzable, open to questioning and critique—in effect, "writerly," in Roland Barthes's terminology[10]—is that they contradict themselves and each other. They are self-reflexive, and they confirm as well as contradict other accounts of the social world outside of the project. In a wider sense, they intersect with other local and global histories. In the chapters that follow, I have tried to analyze the narratives in all of these ways: in terms of their internal coherence and contradiction, in relation to each other, and in the context of a broader social history.

3

Growing Up White: The Social Geography of Race

My family was really very racist. It was just a very assumed kind of thing.
— *Patricia Bowen*[1]

Ever since I was a baby, Black people have been around, the person who taught me to walk was a Black woman, that was a maid for our family . . . pretty much all throughout my childhood, there was a maid around.

— *Beth Ellison*

I was so unaware of cultural difference that I probably wouldn't have noticed they were different from me.
— *Clare Traverso*

The main things I remember . . . are some friends. . . . The Vernons were two sisters and they had a little brother too, just like our family, and they were Black. And the Frenchs . . . they were white.
— *Sandy Alvarez*

I never looked at it like it was two separate cultures. I just kind of looked at it like, our family and our friends, they're Mexicans and Chicanos, and that was just a part of our life.
— *Louise Glebocki*

This book begins with childhood, looking in detail at five white women's descriptions of the places in which they grew up and analyzing them in terms of what I will refer to as the "social geography" of race. *Geography* refers here to the physical landscape—the home, the street, the neighborhood, the school, parts of town visited or driven through rarely or regularly, places visited on vacation. My interest was in how physical space was divided and who inhabited it, and, for my purposes, "who" referred to racially and ethnically identified beings.

The notion of a *social* geography suggests that the physical landscape is peopled and that it is constituted and perceived by means of social rather than natural processes. I thus asked how the women I interviewed conceptualized and related to the people around them. To what extent, for example, did they have relationships of closeness or distance, equality or inequality, with people of color? What were they encouraged or taught by example to make of the variously "raced" people in their environments? *Racial* social geography, in short, refers to the racial and ethnic mapping of environments in physical and social terms and enables also the beginning of an understanding of the conceptual mappings of self and other operating in white women's lives.

The five women upon whom I focus in this chapter do not represent the full range of experiences of the thirty women I interviewed, and the landscapes of childhood will in fact be a recurrent theme in this book. Rather than taking these particular narratives as representative in their content, I draw on them here to begin the process of "defamiliarizing" that which is taken for granted in white experience and to elaborate a method for making visible and analyzing the racial structuring of white experience. This method, it seems to me, takes the question of white women and racism well beyond that of the individual and her beliefs or attitudes to something much broader and more grounded in the material world. For it becomes possible to begin examining the ways racism as a system shaped these women's daily environments, and to begin thinking about the social, political, and historical forces that brought those environments into being.

All five of the women in this group were between twenty-five and thirty-six years old at the time of the interviews, their childhoods and teenage years spanning the mid-1950s, 1960s, and early 1970s. One woman, Beth Ellison, grew up middle class, the other four—Pat Bowen, Clare Traverso, Sandy Alvarez, and Louise Glebocki—in working-class homes. Pat grew up in Maryland, Beth in Alabama and Virginia; Sandy and Louise are from the Los Angeles area, and Clare is from a small town outside San Diego, California.

These women's stories all bear the marks of an era of challenges and transformations in terms of race, racism, and antiracism. Sandy's mother, for example, was a political activist involved in struggles for integration. By contrast, as we will see, Beth's mother was ambivalent in the face of challenges to the racial status quo in her all-white, middle-class neighborhood. All five women spent at least part of their childhoods in racially desegregated schools, indicative of the effects of the civil rights movement on the patterning of children's daily lives. As will be abundantly clear, however, the women's material and conceptual environments were shaped in complex ways by long histories of racism. Regional histories also differentiated the racial and ethnic landscapes of these women's childhoods. Thus, for southerners Pat Bowen and Beth Ellison, the people of color with whom they had contact were mainly African American (or, in the language of the time, Black). Clare Traverso grew up on the U.S.-Mexican border, in a town with Native Americans and Mexican Americans. And both Sandy Alvarez and Louise Glebocki grew up in racially heterogeneous (Latino, Asian, Black, and white) working-class Los Angeles neighborhoods.

As adults, these five women were also distinctive in the extent to which they had thought about, or acted on, antiracism. Two of them, Sandy Alvarez and Clare Traverso, taught in high schools whose students were predominantly Asian and Latino; for each of them, teaching was to some extent tied to social change. Thus, for example, Sandy had tried (with limited success) to raise faculty consciousness about racism, and Clare had worked to make student literacy a vehicle for empowerment. Louise Glebocki was active in a left party. And while neither Pat Bowen nor Beth Ellison described herself as an activist, both had thought a great deal about the interracial dynamics with which they had grown up. In addition, Louise and Sandy were both in long-term primary relationships with Chicano men. One of the five, Beth, was lesbian, the others heterosexual.

These women were, then, unusual in certain ways, both politically and in their life choices. Their accounts of childhood, however, resonated with those of more conservative interviewees, and, like the others', their experiences ran the gamut from explicitly articulated and de facto segregation to what I will refer to as "quasi integration." There was, then, no predictive relationship between ways of growing up and adult perspectives. (Indeed, even Sandy, whose mother was an active integrationist, described her sister as having become "racist" in her adult attitudes.)

Race was, in fact, lived in as many different ways as there were women I talked with. Nonetheless, patterns emerged as I analyzed the interviews. I clustered the childhood narratives around four types or modes of experience, not because each narrative fell clearly into one or another mode, but because there were enough common threads to make the similarities worth exploring, and because the contrasts between modes were significant enough to require analysis. Of the four modes, one seemed at first to be characterized by an absence of people of color from the narrator's life, but turned out, as I will suggest, to be only *"apparently* all white." Second, there was a racially conflictual mode. Third, there were contexts in which race difference was present, but unremarked, in which race difference functioned as a filter for perception while not always being consciously perceived. Finally, some white women described experiences I have interpreted as quasi-integrated, that is, integrated but not fully so, for reasons that should become clear below. One of the five women I focus on in this chapter is drawn from each of the first three modes and two from the quasi-integrated group.

Beth Ellison: An "Apparently All-White" Childhood

Many of the women whose childhoods were apparently all white shared suburban middle-class childhoods. Beth, born in 1956, grew up in a white, middle-class, professional suburb in a town in Virginia. Today, she describes herself as a feminist. She is an artist who makes a living as a retail worker. Beth said of her childhood:

> I was born in Alabama and spent my real early years in New Orleans. I was five when we moved to Virginia. I remember living in a professional subdivision, our neighbors were all doctors and lawyers. . . . It was a white neighborhood. . . . The only specifically racist thing I remember from growing up in Virginia was when a Black doctor and his family moved into the neighborhood . . . at that time I guess maybe I was fourteen and I still didn't think about racism . . . I wasn't interested in politics . . . but I vaguely remember neighbors banding together to see if they could keep this family from moving in and I remember thinking that was disgusting, but I was more concerned with my life and being a young teenager.

In the telling of this incident, racism is categorized as "politics," and as separate from daily life as a teenager. Beth's self-description in this sense highlights a key difference between whites' experience of racism and the experience of people of color: racism is frequently pushed to the forefront of consciousness of people of color, as a construct that organizes hardship and discrimination.[2]

The statement that the only *specifically* racist incident was the attempted exclusion of a Black family from the neighborhood suggests a view of racism as limited to willed, concerted activity. Yet the very existence of a neighborhood whose residents are all white itself bespeaks a history of racist structuring of that community. Elements of that history might include both the "redlining" of neighborhoods by realtors to keep Black people from buying property in them and also the economic dimensions of racism that would place affluent neighborhoods beyond the reach of most Black families. The incident that drew Beth's attention to racism was, in short, only the tip of the iceberg.

There *were* Black people not too far away, for Beth says:

> I saw a lot of Black people around . . . on the street and . . . in class and downtown, but . . . I don't remember there being many Black and white people hanging out together, I just don't remember seeing that. And also I didn't pay real close attention to it, either. . . . Now that we're talking about this, I remember seeing a lot of Black people around, and I remember not really hanging out with them . . . it wasn't any kind of conscious decision but it was just not what I did.

With or without a conscious decision, Beth's experience of friendship and community was racially structured in multiple ways.

Beth said that there were no parts of town that she avoided when she was growing up. In her hometown in Virginia, the poorest—and Black—part of town was on the way to the downtown record and bookstores, and Beth traversed it regularly. So, unlike some other women in the "all-white" group, Beth did not perceive people of color as a threat or a group to avoid; rather, their presence or absence was not a salient issue.

If Beth felt no anxiety, however, her mother seemed to oscillate between what Beth called a "humanist" belief in at least a limited integration and the sense that she needed to keep her children apart (and, in her perception, *safe*) from Black children and adults. This is illustrated in Beth's description of school integration, which for her began in fifth grade:

> I would have been about ten when schools were desegregated [in 1965]. I don't remember anyone in my family being upset about it, or my mother trying to withdraw me from school or anything. . . . I was . . . a little bit excited about it because it was something new. . . . My mother tried really hard to be—she's kind of a humanist, so I don't remember her saying anything like "Don't hang out with Black kids."

But later, in high school, Beth was involved in an incident in
which she was pushed up against the wall of the gym changing
room by a Black girl. This resulted in her parents moving her to
a segregated private school. Beth comments:

> We didn't talk about it at the time, but as I look back on it now . . . it
> seems evident to me that they did this because it wasn't a school where
> there would be, uh, what they might consider rowdy Black girls for me
> to have to contend with.

Beth's mother showed a similar ambivalence on the question of
residential integration. On the one hand, Beth did not think her
mother had taken part in the effort to keep the Black family out
of her neighborhood. Her response was very different, however,
when Beth, at twenty, moved to a poor, racially mixed part of the
same town:

> I do remember my mother being really concerned and I don't know if
> that's because there were a lot of Black people living there or because
> it was an extremely poor part of town where you'd be more inclined to
> be ripped off . . . [but she] wouldn't let my younger brother come
> visit me.

So Beth grew up in a context in which Black people were the
"significant others" of color, and where race and income were
intertwined. Being white and middle class meant living somewhere different from Black people. The social distance between
white and Black people—which was considerable—was produced and reproduced through the conscious efforts of white
people, including Beth's mother and neighbors, and through the
more diffuse effects of the interplay of the class structure with racism. White people like Beth's mother deliberated over the per-
missibility and safety of living in the same terrain as Black people,
seemingly projecting their fear or dislike of Black people when
they made such decisions.[3] Less visible here are the forms of white
people's personal and structural violence toward African Americans that marked both residential and school desegregation and
the period of civil rights struggle in general.

In any event, Beth received mixed messages. Her environment
was shaped by at least three factors. First, there was a preexisting
arrangement of racial segregation and inequality, reproduced, for
example, by the all-white private school. Second, Beth's mother's
verbal messages about segregation espoused ideas about equality

or what Beth called "humanism." Third, and contrasting with her humanism, there were Beth's mother's actions in response to Beth's experiences and choices, which, as Beth tells it, frequently leaned in the direction of segregationism and hostility toward Black people. The result was that, without trying, Beth could continue to live a mostly racially segregated life.

For Beth, the structure of racial inequality was at times simply lived in; at other times, it was both lived and seen. If the consequences for *herself* of a racially structured environment were not always obvious to Beth, however, the impact on others of race and class hierarchy was at times very clear. She said of the two communities she knew well as she was growing up:

> BETH: In [the town in Virginia] it seems like it was mostly poor neighborhoods where Black people lived, but there were also a lot of poor white people that lived there too. But in [the town in Alabama], there was a Black part of town and a white part of town. There was the rich part of the white part of town, the middle class, and then the poor white section. And then there was shantytown, and it was literally shacks.

> RF: So the shantytown was really the Black part of town?

> BETH: Yeah . . . these tiny little shacks that looked like they'd been thrown together out of plywood and two-by-fours. The difference was incredible, because you could drive for one minute in your car and go through rich, beautiful neighborhoods to . . . what looked squalid to me.

Comparing Beth's words here with her memories of her own neighborhood, it is striking that Beth was much more sharply aware of racial *oppression* shaping Black experience than of race *privilege* in her own life. Thus, Beth could be alert to the realities of economic discrimination against Black communities while still conceptualizing her own life as racially neutral—nonracialized, nonpolitical.

For Beth and the other women who grew up in apparently all-white situations, there were in fact at least one or two people of color not too far away. It is in fact conceptually rather than physically that people of color were distant. In this regard, one startling feature of several descriptions of apparently all-white childhoods was the sudden appearance in the narratives of people of color as employees, mainly Black, mainly female, and mainly domestic workers. What is striking here is not the presence of domestic workers as such[4] but the way in which they were talked about. For, oddly, these Black women were *not* summoned into white women's accounts of their lives by means of questions like "Were there any people of color in your neighborhood?" or "Who lived in your household when you were growing up?" Rather, they arrived previously unheralded, in the context of some other topic.

Black women domestic workers appeared in Beth's narrative when I asked her if she remembered the first time she became conscious of race difference, or conscious that there were Black and white people in the world. Beth responded that her first consciousness of race as a difference was when she was about four years old, when her mother chastised her for referring to a Black woman as a "lady." Here, of course, we are seeing race not just as difference but as hierarchy. Beth said:

> Ever since I was a baby, Black people have been around, the person
> who taught me to walk was a Black woman, that was a maid for our
> family . . . pretty much all throughout my childhood, there was a maid
> around.

She added that, although she had not really noticed at the time, she realized now that when her mother remarried, the family stopped employing anyone to do housework. Thus Black domestic workers, despite involvement in Beth's life on the very intimate level of teaching her to walk, seemed on another level to have been so insignificant as not to have merited mention earlier in our conversation. Nor had she noted their departure from the household after a certain point in her life.

The forgotten and suddenly remembered domestic worker recurred in several of these white, middle-class childhoods. Tamara Green, raised "solidly middle class" in suburban Los Angeles, said:

> I totally forgot until I just started thinking about it—we had
> housekeepers who, all but one from the time we lived in California,
> were Latin American, Mexican, Colombian, Honduran, Salvadoran.
> There was one British Honduran who was Black. And I had a close
> relationship with one of them.

Why is the story told in this particular way? It may be the status of domestic workers from the standpoint of white middle-class women, or the status of people of color from the purview of a white and middle-class childhood, that made these women invis-

ible and stripped them of subjectivity in the landscapes of childhood.[5] But whether or not it is race per se that determined how
the domestic worker of color appeared in the interviews, it is primarily through employer-employee, class-imbalanced relationships that women from apparently all-white homes encountered
women of color. If not themselves in positions of clear authority,
these white middle-class women must have seen their parents in
such positions, able to summon and dismiss the racially different
Other at will. It is perhaps in this sense of control and authority
that the home was indeed all white, and the neighborhood similarly so.

Patricia Bowen: Race Conflict and "Segregation"

> I grew up in a town that was semi-southern . . . a fairly small town, and
> pretty much in a working-class family. The town was very racist, it was
> very segregated. Everyone was aware of race all the time and the races
> involved were pretty much white and Black people.

Patricia Bowen grew up in Maryland in the 1960s, in a town
where race conflict and racism were in the forefront of daily life.
Pat described her town as "segregated," yet, as we will see, she
and her family had more interaction with people of color (specifically, Black people) than either Beth or Clare (whose narrative
follows). Segregation, in Pat's experience, was a complex system
of interactions and demarcations of boundary rather than complete separation. In fact, Black and white people lived close
together:

> [We] lived on a street that was all white, and there were no Black people
> on that street. But the back of our house—our front door faced an all-
> white street, the back door faced an all-Black street. . . . It was
> completely separate.

The boundary between white and Black was thus very clear. And
differences between the streets were also evident to Pat: the houses
on the Black people's street were poorer, more "shacky" (her
term), and there were more children playing outside.

In this setting, both the presence and the absence of Black
people were sharply indicated. They were very noticeably absent
from the street in front, yet in some sense almost more visible
than whites, given the children playing in the street beyond the
back door. Added to this sharp distinction was a feeling of fear:

> We were kind of told that it wasn't safe to walk down the Black
> street. . . . [Black children would] yell at you . . . I never got hurt but
> [they] threatened you a little bit. . . . So I grew up learning that Black
> people were dangerous.

Pat never came to any harm on the "Black street," and in fact
often used it as a shortcut: the idea of danger was introduced by
adults and by the threats (apparently never carried out) of the
Black children, but in fact Pat went in fear rather than in danger.
As an explanation for the threats, Pat suggested that the Black
children "weren't used to whites walking through"—yet it sounded
as though Pat and her friends routinely cut through the street.
One is tempted to interpret the situation as another aspect of
boundary demarcation, or as a gesture of turf maintenance on the
part of Black children frustrated at their treatment by their white
neighbors. In any event, in Pat's experience, difference, opposition, and threat lived right on the back doorstep.

As Pat describes others in her family, however, it seems that
for them the issue was not fear so much as maintaining a complex
balance of association with and differentiation from Black people.
Black and white people used the same stores. As the person in
charge of the household, Pat's grandmother took care of shopping. As a result, Pat explained, her grandmother knew many of
the Black women in the other street. She would chat and even
visit their homes but always maintained a separateness:

> PAT: She'd tell me proudly or just very self-righteous, "Well, you know,
> I would never sit down when I go in their house. I would go over and
> talk to them, but I wouldn't sit down." You know, because to sit down
> would imply some equal relationship and she wouldn't do that. They
> would come up to the back door.
>
> RF: Instead of the front door?
>
> PAT: Yes.

This elaborate and contradictory boundary maintenance was
undertaken by other relatives, too:

> My uncle was pretty young . . . , a teenager when I lived there. He and
> his friends would kind of play with boys who were Black, but again
> they didn't really consider them friends in the same way . . . Black
> culture was really cool, they would imitate them all the time, and the
> funny thing was they spoke exactly like them . . . it was pretty much
> the accent something like they had anyway. The way they danced was
> really cool and everyone listened to Black music all the time . . . , but at

the same time there was this "niggers, niggers, niggers," it was this weird contradiction.

The direct teaching Pat received from family members about racism was equally mixed. On the one hand, she said:

> My mother was more liberal . . . so she would always tell me not to say 'nigger,' that Black people weren't any worse than white people.

On the other hand:

> I remember this one incident. . . . When I was about eight or nine and walking with my uncle down the street and kind of mutually bumping into a Black woman. I just said "Excuse me," and he said, "Don't ever say excuse me to a nigger. If you bump into them or they bump into you, it's always their fault." And I said, "How is it their fault if I bumped into them?"

Notice here Pat's resistance or at least her puzzlement in the face of explicitly racist socialization. Like Beth, Pat was not always an unquestioning recipient of her environment.

The potential for complexity in responses to racially structured environments was dramatized in Pat's descriptions of two relationships she had with young Black teenagers in her junior high school years:

> There are some things about friendships that I developed with Blacks at that time that are kind of interesting. There were two in particular that I really remember. One was a guy in my junior high . . . who was kind of a leader, very charismatic person, and he started hassling me a lot, he wanted to pick on me and he would tease me and kind of threaten me, pull my hair or whatever and I was terrified of him. This went on for a while and then one Halloween my friends and I were out trick-or-treating—we were teenagers and were tagging along with the little kids. . . . We saw him with a friend also trick-or-treating and we laughed. It was a kind of bonding because we were both these obnoxious teenagers out trick-or-treating, trying to get candy with the kids. So I had a feeling he kind of really liked me after that. . . . The relationship kind of switched from him threatening me to being a real friendly relationship. I wasn't afraid of him any more.
>
> But the way that got played out is a lot of jokes about racism acted out, like he would pretend to threaten me or tease me in front of people, like Black and white people who were there, and I would play with him back, and everyone would be nervous and thought a fight was going to break out. . . . It was something where we would never really talk or become friends, but it was a neat little thing.

And Pat had a similar experience with a Black girl:

> She was a very, very large woman and she would pretend to threaten me
> sometimes and I remember some Black girls going "ooh" because I was
> much smaller than she was. We'd play around with that.

In playing with the segregation system like this, Pat and her
friends were taking at least a small step toward subverting it. By
acting out their roles as enemies but not really fighting, they signaled that they knew what they were caught in; the dramatization
was a kind of stepping aside from their assigned roles, although
this did not, of course, change them. For Pat, one could say that
this kind of play involved *acting* being white simultaneously with
being white.

However, white people's fear of people of color—which played
a part in many narratives—involved another, much less self-
conscious inversion of social reality. For if Pat's African American
friends were playing with the racial order by pretending to
threaten her, that threat itself inverts the institutionalized relations
of racism wherein African Americans actually have much more to
fear from white people than vice versa. Commonplace as is white
people's fear of people of color, and especially of Black people, it
is important to step back from it and realize that it is socially constructed and in need of analysis. I will return to this issue later.

Most of the time Pat and others around her lived out the rules
of segregation without subverting them. The same girlfriend with
whom Pat "played" racial tension also experienced it directly in
an incident that Pat described:

> There were three of us that hung around together, . . . Janet, who was
> Black, and my friend Sandra and me. Sandra—again, like I had this
> whole liberal interpretation I got from my mother about Black people
> and race. Sandra was just more—"nigger"—she would whisper that
> word and things like that—yet we were both friends with Janet. . . . I
> remember one night—this is really an awful, painful thing—we were at
> Janet's house just hanging around, she was drinking Coke out of a can
> and she passed it to my friend Sandra, and Sandra . . . said no, and we
> all knew it was because she wouldn't drink out of a can after a Black
> person, but yet this was our friend that we hung around with. I
> remember Janet just looking really sad, but also accepting, like it hurt
> her. . . . I guess it never occurred to me not to drink the Coke.

Pat, Sandra, and Janet were all around twelve years old at the time
of their friendship. It is worth noting that Pat did not state the

race of her white friend, Sandra; as is often the case, white stands for the position of racial "neutrality," or the racially unmarked category (see chapter 7). Pat further commented on this incident that "we never really talked about race, it was just too taboo a subject."

Taboo or not, race difference and racism seemed never to be far from the forefront of Pat's experience. Her life was structured very visibly by race hierarchy. Curiously, however, segregation bespoke the presence rather than the absence of people of color. This might partly have been a result of the fact that Pat was working class: Pat pointed out that middle-class whites in the town would probably have had less contact with African Americans than she did, and in fact one can speculate that, had Pat been middle class, the racial social geography of her childhood might have resembled Beth's.

Boundary demarcation of physical space—being in the same street or house, sitting or standing, making physical contact, sharing a drink—seemed to be of major concern for the white people Pat described, probably precisely because of the proximity of white and Black people in the context of an ideology and practice of white superiority. However, boundary maintenance was an issue in other women's stories too, evidenced, for example, in Beth's all-white neighborhood. In addition, as I will discuss in the context of other narratives, the taboo on interracial sexual relationships, possibly the most intimate form of refusal of racial boundaries, came up in conversations with many of the women I interviewed (see chapters 4 and 5).

Clare Traverso: Race Difference as a Filter for Perception

In contrast to this very clear and immediate awareness of race difference, the situation described by Clare Traverso was a complex mix of noticing and not noticing people of color. Whether Clare saw people of color as different from or the same as herself was at times also unclear. Clare was born in 1954 and grew up in a small, rural town not far from San Diego. The town, said Clare, was

kind of like a redneck town, actually. . . . Very conservative politically. People off to themselves, don't want to be bothered with government or politics or other people, love to drink beer and drive around and stuff like that.

Clare's parents were "fundamentalist Christian, but not moral majority" people who had moved to California from South Dakota with their children. Clare, the fifth child of six, was born in California. Describing how her time was spent as a child, Clare explained:

> We lived sort of off into the hills. We didn't really go into town much. . . . The amount of times I went out to eat before I went to college was maybe five times. . . . See, my parents had more traditional values from the Midwest—always saving money and . . . we never went on vacations. I went on two, but they were back to South Dakota to visit my relatives.

Consequently, aside from school and, later, church-related activities, Clare spent a lot of time during her early years playing on the land around her family's house. Nonetheless, she was able to describe the racial composition of the town:

> The town itself is located right next to an Indian reservation. . . . There was also a small Mexican American population that went to our high school, but I would say probably no Blacks. Maybe one or two.

One may note that Clare's standpoint here is clearly different from that of the African American townspeople themselves, for whom it would be impossible to confuse existence with nonexistence. What Clare's cloudy memory on this point perhaps indicates is the lack of importance accorded to Black people in the community by whites.

Clare's first contact with people of color was when she began traveling on the school bus. At that point, her response, like Pat's, was fear:

> The bus I rode, there were these . . . Mexican American families, lived on the hill across from us, so they rode our bus, and they always had the reputation for being really tough. And I was really scared of this one girl, I remember, because she used to get in fights with this other girl.[6]

Clare speculated that her fear was probably bolstered by her brother, who was in class with one of the "tougher" Mexican American boys. Again like Pat's, Clare's fear did not come from experience of personal attack so much as from a sense of different behavior perceived as louder or rowdier than her own:

> They used to yell, flip people off—I came from a more sheltered environment. My parents never did things like that.

In a sense, the explanation—my *parents* never behaved that way—suggests that, unconsciously, a cultural explanation is being advanced for the difference in behavior: it is placed in the realm of things taught. Although the fact that this group was Mexican American is clearly a part of the anecdote, once the children were off the bus and in school, Mexicanness became less important as a feature of conscious differentiation:

RF: So your [kindergarten] class was all white?

CLARE: I'm pretty sure it was—probably—oh, wait, I had one little friend, Ralph Vasquez. Their whole family was Mexican American, my sister went through school with one girl in that family. . . . But I never really thought of them as, like, different from me. I don't think I was aware of them being culturally different

A similar pattern appeared in Clare's description of her Native American schoolmates later on in school. On the one hand, she said:

I was so unaware of cultural difference that I probably wouldn't have noticed they were different from me.

On the other hand, she remembered Native Americans in school as a distinct group, noting that they were in the remedial classes. Differences were thus both seen and not seen, or perhaps seen but only partially. Race difference entered into Clare's conscious perception of her environment only on those rare occasions when it carried a real or imagined threat to herself (as when she was afraid on the school bus). The ways in which racism did seem to cause hardship for students of color, by contrast, were perceived only dimly, accessible to memory but not remembered as having made a strong impact on Clare at the time. For, presumably, racism accounted for the location of the Native American students in remedial classes and, more indirectly, perhaps for their intragroup fights too.

The composition of Clare's friendship group in high school further supports this picture of a daily life that was in effect patterned by race: structured around the student council and a church youth group, it was all white. What shaped Clare's descriptions of all three groups—whites, Mexican Americans, and Native Americans—was on the one hand the absence of a conscious conceptualization of cultural and racial difference per se, but on the other hand, the *experience* of a racially structured environment, not understood as such at the time. In sum, Clare saw individuals in her immediate community through a racial lens, but did not consciously see race, cultural difference, or racism.

Clare came to awareness of all three concepts as she grew older but, interestingly, in relation to communities other than her own:

> CLARE: In sixth grade I started learning Spanish and learning a bit about Latin culture, Latin America. My awareness of race came through that rather than Mexican American people.
>
> RF: So what did you learn about Latin America?
>
> CLARE: Pyramids, music, sometimes we'd listen to the radio. I was fascinated by the Aztecs and the Incas.

Latin America thus appeared to Clare as a site of more real or authentic cultural difference, and as the proper adjunct to learning Spanish. Cultural difference was at a distance and in the past rather than nearer to home. At the same time, in a contradictory vein, Clare commented that Spanish seemed like the appropriate language to study in school, rather than German or French, "because we were living around and across the border from people who spoke it."

If Latin culture was conceived as being far away, it was clear that the Spanish language was closer at hand. In this nearer context, though, difference referred to social inequality more directly than to cultural difference. The Mexican border was less than a two-hour drive from Clare's home, and for some, although not for Clare's family, border towns like Tijuana were places to visit on day trips. Clare *did* visit across the border in rather different circumstances, as described in the following story. Note the implication that Mexican Americans or Chicanos somehow do not really count as members of a Latino, Spanish-speaking culture. Again the issue is one of the perceived inauthenticity of Latinos on the U.S. side of the border:

> CLARE: Even though I had Spanish in high school, I didn't really speak it—once when we went down to Tecate at Christmastime to give away clothes and we spoke a little bit of Spanish to real people who spoke it. . . . This Spanish teacher I had . . . every year they used to collect all these clothes and bring it down and give it away to people in Tecate. I think we did that twice. And you'd give away the clothes to people, the poor people there.
>
> RF: So how do you do that?

CLARE: You just walk up to people and say, "Hey, do you need something?"

RF: Just like that?

CLARE: Yeah, it was kind of weird, really. . . . We would walk around—and, yeah, we had trucks or cars or something. . . . Our teacher knew someone there. I think he knew the mayor. . . . I felt really odd about giving things away like that, even though they didn't have anything and I know they needed things. They needed food and clothes. You could tell by the way their houses were, just like little shacks, really—dirt floors . . . I remember feeling a real contrast between myself and them. . . .

RF: Do you remember any comments, from your parents, or from school?

CLARE: I'm sure they thought it was good. . . . We all felt happy that we'd helped poor people out.

In this incident Clare was unwittingly inscribed into the power relations involved in any act of charity. While the sharing of wealth in almost any form is of course useful, here the process was controlled entirely by the givers. The receivers were dependent on the mercy of the schoolchildren who, at their teacher's behest, walked the streets asking, "Do you need anything?" This power imbalance may in part have accounted for Clare's feeling that something was not quite right about the situation. In going to Tecate, Clare became starkly aware of the imbalance of resources on opposite sides of the border. But it was not clear from our conversation how, if at all, this imbalance was explained to her. It is likely that in this context the United States would be identified as generous and "good" rather than as partially responsible for Mexico's poverty.

Remember that this expedition took place in the context of learning a language. As adjuncts to the language, Clare was taught about ancient and distant *cultures* (exemplified by her fascination with the Aztecs and Incas), along with present-day, physically nearer *poverty*. This pattern replicates the classic colonialist view of the conquered society: a view of past glories and present degradations (from which, within a colonialist ideology, it is the conqueror's duty to save the poor native).

Further, authentic difference of any kind was placed firmly outside Clare's home community. Asked about the possibility of practicing Spanish with Mexican American fellow students, Clare

was unsure whether any of them spoke Spanish. She summed up
this contradictory situation thus:

> I think I was so—like I say, we never went to Mexico, we never had
> contact with other races, really, and if they were there I wasn't aware
> that they were from another race, I mean vaguely, only looking back on
> it.

Toward the end of high school, social studies classes analyzing
global inequality and her sister's involvement in the movement
against the Vietnam War gave Clare a political outlook and a set
of values that she felt were more "liberal" than those of most
people in her family and hometown. Again the focus was largely
outside her immediate community, however. The same was true
of the process whereby Clare began to see *herself* as a culturally
specific being:

> I went away to college [in Minnesota] and I met . . . all these people
> who had a real sense of "I am Swedish," "I am Norwegian." And then
> when I went to [stay in] Mexico. That was the two strongest things, I
> think.

The social geography of race for Clare differed from Beth's in
the greater number of people of color she encountered and the
absence of the racially divided employer-employee relationships
in the family. Her story also differed from Pat's in that racial difference was not in the forefront of consciousness, nor was there
visible ongoing conflict.

One feature common to all three stories is white women's fear
of people of color. As I have suggested, this fear needs careful
analysis, both because of its prevalence and because it is an inversion of reality. In general, people of color have far more to fear
from white people than vice versa, given, for example, the ongoing incidence of white supremacist terrorism around the United
States, which targets African and Asian Americans, Latinos, Native Americans, and Jewish Americans (in addition to gay men
and lesbians); and the problematic relationship with the police that
leaves many communities of color with, at the very least, a sense
that they lack legal and physical protection.

White people's fear of people of color is an inversion that can
be contextualized in a number of ways. Most importantly, it must
be understood as an element of racist discourse crucially linked to

essentialist racism, or the idea that people of color are fundamentally Other than white people: different, inferior, less civilized, less human, more animal, than whites. Further, U.S. history is marked by many moments when the power of racist imagery constructing men of color as violent, dangerous, or sexually threatening has been renewed, as rationale or pretext for white hostility, in the context of political and economic conflicts between particular communities of color and white Americans. Thus, for example, a key aspect of white women's fear of Black men has to do with the persistent, racist image of the Black man as rapist. As Angela Davis has clarified, the production of this myth took place alongside the abolition of slavery and efforts by Black and white people toward reconstruction of the southern economy and polity along more racially egalitarian lines. The lynching of Black people was a means of social and political repression; accusations of rape were used as alibis for what were in effect politically motivated death squads. A discourse ostensibly about threat or danger was in fact a rationale for repression or control.[7]

Similarly, it was in tandem with white, "nativist" movements for immigration control and economic protectionism that, from the late nineteenth century into the first decades of the twentieth, first Chinese, then Japanese, then Filipino male immigrants were represented in the white-owned press as sexually lascivious and physically violent.[8] Most recently in the United States, in the context of the Los Angeles rebellion of May 1992, newspaper and television reports once again described African American protesters as "savage," "roving bands," engaged in a "feeding frenzy" of looting. More generally in the present, I would further speculate, white people's fear of men and women of color may have to do with the projection or awareness of the anger of individual people of color at white racism.

Beyond these few examples of contextualization, white people's fear of people of color and the distinctively gendered dimensions of it require far more extensive discussion than is possible here.[9] It is also crucial to ask what "interrupts" or changes white people's fear of people of color: for those who are not afraid, what made, or makes, the difference? I do not know how to answer this question, but I register it here as an important one for us as white women to address.

Quasi Integration: Sandy Alvarez and Louise Glebocki

Sandy Alvarez and Louise Glebocki both grew up in contexts that I choose to call quasi-integrated, which is to say, seemingly or apparently integrated. I qualify "integration" in this way because it seems to me that true integration would require a broader anti-racist social context than existed in the United States while Sandy and Louise were growing up. It might involve, for example, that no area of physical space be marked by racial hierarchy and that racist ideas be entirely absent—a situation that is impossible in the United States as it is presently constituted. As Sandy's and Louise's narratives show, neither woman's life circumstances in any sense placed her outside the system of racism. Their experience of close peer relationships with men and women of color nonetheless marks them off from the women I have discussed so far.

Both grew up in working-class families in Los Angeles. Sandy was born in 1948. She teaches English as a second language, in a high school. Her husband is Chicano and she has two small children. Louise was born in 1958. She cleans houses, not a job she enjoys but one that she feels is "OK for now." She described herself as always learning, growing, and active. She and her partner of seven years were about to get married at the time of the interview. Like Sandy's husband, he is Chicano.

Sandy Alvarez

Sandy said of the neighborhood where she lived before she was five years old:

> The main things I remember . . . are some friends. . . . the Vernons were two sisters and they had a little brother too, just like our family, and they were Black. And the Frenches . . . they were white. . . . I'm only mentioning race because of this interview . . . as a kid it wasn't until I went to elementary school that I really became aware that these people were different races. Before that you just played with everybody.

From the beginning, Sandy had friends from various ethnic and racial groups. At five, she moved to a community, still in Los Angeles, that was, in her words, "equal thirds Japanese, Mexican, and white, with two Black families," and her friends reflected this mix. Sandy says that she played with Japanese boys and with the only girl in the neighborhood, who was in Sandy's terminology "Anglo." Her school friends were Mexican and white. Her "crushes" (again to use her word) and boyfriends were Anglo, Mexican, Guamanian. A Black woman who was Sandy's neighbor is to this day "like a second mother":

> [She] is one of my dearest friends. She always thought of me as her
> daughter. She never had a daughter, and couldn't have any more kids.
> She really loves me and I really love her, and it's a real close relationship.

Looking at the differences between Sandy's experience and Beth's, the first and obvious precondition for Sandy's more racially mixed childhood is that people of color and whites were living nearer to each other. In addition, people responded to physical proximity in a particular way; it need not have led to the mixed friendship groups Sandy describes. The complex relationships between Pat and the Black children in her neighborhood contrast with the visiting back and forth between the Vernons and Sandy's household. The Vernon children would often stay overnight at her house.

The other major difference between Sandy as a child who grew up "integrated" and the other women I interviewed is her parents' standpoint. I asked Sandy what her mother thought of her having friends who were Black. She responded:

> Well, my mother is really—she's a radical, politically. . . . The church
> we went to . . . the community had turned primarily Black and it was
> an all-white church and [my parents] were really into helping to
> integrate the church.

Clearly, Sandy's mother was a woman unlikely to object to her children having Black friends—and for preschoolers, parental cooperation is key to social interaction. Less obvious but also extremely interesting was Sandy's awareness that her childhood was in this respect unusual, so that she cited her mother's activism to account for it. Given that it took work to integrate the church, Sandy's parents may well have been different from other whites in the neighborhood. Later in the interview, Sandy made explicit her sense of being different:

> I don't know that a lot of people have had the integrated experience that
> we've had growing up, where it wasn't just our acquaintances but our
> real good friends and all our peers were of different races.

How are race and cultural difference conceptualized in this context? As she suggested earlier, Sandy felt that it was not until she was about six that she became aware of racial differences between herself and her peers. She explained:

> In second grade . . . there are just two pictures in my mind, and I just remember a Black boy, about my age. I don't remember if he was just one of the things that made me aware . . . I just remember becoming aware different kids were different races. And this one girl that I'll never forget. I was really aware she was culturally different, because—she may not have been Mexican, she could have been Filipina, I don't know which culture—somehow I think she was Mexican because the neighborhood was about a third Mexican. But she'd wear her hair up in a bun, and, um, she must have been Asian, because she had those big chopsticks in her hair and in the playground she fell down and one went right inside her skull and they had to take her to emergency hospital. And, uh, I was just aware that was a big cultural difference, that I would never wear those in my hair.

Here, the specifics of cultural difference are perhaps more imaginary than real in any substantive sense. Sandy, drawing on her early memories and perceptions, did not know to which ethnic group the little girl belonged. The key here is not whether Sandy could answer this question correctly but her struggle as a child to make some sense of cultural difference. The two points to note here are, first, that Sandy was registering how cultural and race differences shape appearance and experience; and, second, that Sandy's awareness that her schoolmates and friends were culturally and racially different did *not* evoke fear, as it did for Clare and Pat.

It was not until many years later, Sandy said, that she was conscious of others seeing her as white and therefore belonging to a privileged group. When I asked her whether her awareness of race changed as she grew older, she said:

> SANDY: As you grow older you see how others perceive you, look at yourself. Before that you just act, you are who you are. In that sense [here she mentions a recent adult experience of feeling judged for being white] that's the only change.
>
> RF: So in junior college and at university you were still "acting," rather than thinking about how you were acting?
>
> SANDY: Yes.
>
> RF: At any point in your life did you think of yourself as white?
>
> SANDY: From elementary school on up I guess I was aware of that.

Here, strikingly, whiteness is described as having been noted without any negative or positive charge—in contrast with most contexts, where white either stands for superiority or is neutralized and assumed. Elsewhere—and this may be the most common experience for young white feminists of the 1980s—"white" is a concept learned simultaneously with a negative connotation of privilege (see chapter 6). For Sandy in this early period, however, "white" or "Anglo" merely described another ethnic group. One cannot help but see this as connected to the multiracial peer context within which she experienced her ethnicity: one in which, at least within the confines of home, elementary school, and the neighborhood, racial and ethnic identities were not hierarchically ordered.

However, it is important not to present a falsely utopian picture of Sandy's experience. Although her friendship groups were racially mixed, from preschool to college, she pointed out that there was racial tension and division elsewhere in the schools she attended. Nor was she immune to racist ideology. For example, she told me that a Black male school friend had asked her out on a date. She explained that she did not accept because she could not bring herself to face the stares she knew they would receive as an interracial, especially as a Black and white, couple. Sandy was not convinced by the myth that says only "bad" white women date Black men, but she was afraid to challenge it in public.

In other words, growing up in a racially mixed context did not mean that racism was absent, nor that the environment was not racially structured. Rather, Sandy was placed in a specific relationship to race difference and racism.

Louise Glebocki

Louise Glebocki, who was born in 1958, did not come from a family that used the languages of integration or antiracism, but she grew up with a more thoroughgoing connection with a community of color than the rest of the women I interviewed. Like Sandy, Louise described growing up in Los Angeles. Having spent her first six years on the East Coast of the United States, Louise, with her mother and two older sisters, came west, moving

into a barrio, basically around all Spanish-speaking people. . . . Besides Mexicanos, the others that lived there were poor whites. . . . It was just a poor, small community.

Right from the start, Louise and her sisters began having boy-friends. And more of Louise's boyfriends and female friends were Mexicano, or in other terms Chicano, than white:

> LOUISE: I remember I had a white boyfriend and then a Chicano one.
> But more I started hanging around more with the Chicanos. But both—
> always.

> RF: How come you hung out more with the Chicanos?

> LOUISE: To me they were more—at that point I did have white friends
> too. I don't know, there was just something real honest about them, and
> real friendly, and real close relationships formed, I remember, around a
> couple of girlfriends I had. Just visiting their families was a really nice
> atmosphere—kind of like ours. Because for a white family, while we
> were poor, we grew up [around] a lot of people. We had a lot of
> relatives in the L.A. area. It was always a lot of activity, and hustle and
> bustle. And a lot of times I guess, among the whites, even if they were
> poor, it was kind of like more snobby, more uppity.

In short, Louise viewed Chicano families as similar to her own, rather than different from it. Louise was also commenting here on class and people's perceptions of themselves. She suggested, in ef-fect, that there was a link between class position and cultural style, linking her own working-class position with a liveliness shared with Chicano families. The suggestion is that other poor whites acted differently, aspiring to a style of life associated with a higher class position. Louise preferred the Chicanos' way of life, viewing it as more down to earth, more honest, and more like her own. Of course, Louise's words are adult ones: it is hard to know ex-actly what form these thoughts would have taken in the con-sciousness of a younger person.

In fact, Louise's extended family was not only similar to the Chicanos, part of it actually *was* Chicano. For as Louise explained, a number of her mother's sisters and brothers had Mexican Amer-ican partners:

> RF: Did it feel to you like you were in a bicultural family, or a family
> with two cultures? . . .

> LOUISE: I never looked at it like it was two separate cultures. I just kind
> of looked at it like, our family and our friends, they're Mexicans and
> Chicanos, and that was just a part of our life.

More than any of the other women described here, Louise had a childhood in which a community of color played a central role.

The following description from Louise's narrative underlines three things: first, the closeness of Louise's connection to Chicano or Mexican American culture; second, the fact that at the same time, Louise and her relatives were clear that she was white; and third, the extent to which white culture remained, at least linguistically, Louise's point of reference:

RF: If you would go to your aunt's house or your uncle's house, would there be things about how their house was and how they raised their kids, things that they would have on the walls or would do, that came from the fact that it was a partly Mexican and partly white household?

LOUISE: Yeah. Like I remember my aunt, she was married to this Mexican dude. And his background was really, *strongly* into the whole Mexican scene. . . . He was real strong in terms of what he was. I mean, he would never want to be anything else but Mexican. And he had a real strong "machismo." He had something like thirteen kids in his previous marriage. . . . And she really took all that in. In fact she's still constantly like that . . . her attitude is, well, a woman should be a woman, and in her place—the whole mentality was, I don't know, really a trip.

But I remember like, with these relatives, the Chicanos, they would always joke around, you know, around us being Polish, and white. There would be a lot of joking about it and stuff, oh you know, "You honkies gotta learn more" and stuff.

And in terms of their house? They'd play a lot of Mexican music, and a lot of regular music, and have stuff on the Indians up on the walls, and from Mexico.

There are interesting contradictions and complexities here. On the one hand, Louise said that she did not conceptualize the two cultures as separate, yet it is clearly possible for her to do so descriptively. The sense of Chicano culture as more sexist (assuming that "machismo" connotes sexism in Louise's usage of it) is jarring, given Louise's statement that Chicano culture was better, more "in tune with reality." The distinction between Mexican and "regular" music suggests that the dominant culture remained the reference point in her description. However, Louise was also conscious of her whiteness in this description, as, it seems, were her Chicano relatives. The use of the usually negative "honkies" to describe Louise and her white family members suggests that no one lost sight of the wider context of race conflict, either. "Taming" the word *honkie* by joking about it suggests a context in which it has been possible to situationally subvert and play with external hierarchies.

Curiously, despite this mix of relatives on her mother's side of the family, Louise's father had very different ideas, including, as Louise put it, "racist tendencies." For example:

> My parents had been saving money, and they wanted to buy a
> house. . . . I'm pretty sure one of the things my dad really emphasized
> was . . . a nice, white community.

Although the family moved to a white section of a small town in the Los Angeles area, their situation did not change much

> because our school just ended up being pretty poor, and the majority
> was Chicanos, and a lot of them were people who had just come over
> from Mexico, so there was a lot of Spanish-speaking people. And there
> was a whole section of whites, too, but it wasn't this pure, middle-class,
> white area, it was once again a real mixture.

Through school and into adulthood, Louise continued to be close friends with Chicanos, as much as or more than with whites (see chapter 5). But like Sandy, she may well have been unusual in this, for she described increasing racial and cultural conflict among students throughout her school career:

> When we were in elementary school, everybody was together, playing.
> By junior high, things started really dividing up, into groups of people.
> Hey! By high school—to me, the school system really helped set it
> down. You had your sections. By that time, you had a whole section of
> these white racists that were into surfing—very outspoken on being
> racist. I just started seeing a whole lot of divisions—a whole lot of
> different lifestyles coming together and just crashing. . . . Low
> riders, . . . gangs. Things started becoming more segregated, more
> separate.

Louise described the "surfers' " attempts to recruit her to their side, and her refusal to move over: "I saw myself with pride as an antiracist white."

She also saw herself as Polish, identified as such by her surname:

> We had to put up with . . . a lot of racist, Polish jokes, but I looked at
> it—I just laughed, you know, I just looked at it like, "It doesn't bother
> me! I feel great!"

In Louise's life, then, despite her own connections to Chicano culture, explicit racial conflict was as visible in her environment as in Pat Bowen's in Maryland. Louise responded to it, though, by means of a much more explicit antiracism.

Despite the extent to which Sandy and Louise grew up with close ties with Chicano (and in Sandy's case, also Black and Asian) people as well as whites or "Anglos," there are reasons to argue that experiences like Sandy's and Louise's represent only a partial or qualified integration. Nor can they be anything else in a racist society, if racial integration is taken to mean the absence of race hierarchy and racist ideas. In fact, Sandy's was an integrating family rather than a family living in an integrated environment. This was also true for two of the other women whose childhoods were marked by what I call a quasi integration. Their parents were also radicals, and both of them felt it necessary to offer this fact to explain a state of affairs they know to be abnormal (although desirable) in a racist society. All of these women encountered racial hierarchy and racist mythology once they were outside a limited, protected space.

Conclusion

In all of these narratives, landscape and the experience of it were racially structured—whether those narratives seemed to be marked predominantly by the presence or the absence of people of color. This is of course not to say that race was the only organizing principle of the social context. Class intersected with race in differentiating Pat's and Beth's relationships with Black communities and as part of the context for the quasi-integrated experiences of Louise and Sandy. Controls on sexuality link up with racism to create hostility toward relationships between African American men and white women.

Once a person is in a landscape structured by racism, a conceptual mapping of race, of self and others, takes shape, following from and feeding the physical context. Thus, for example, Sandy experienced the term "Anglo" initially without any negative or positive connotation; Clare both saw through the lens of racial stratification in her own environment *and* did not perceive racial stratification as such. Even the presence or absence of people of color seemed to be as much a social-mental construct as a social-physical one: recall the invisible African American and Latina domestic workers in some apparently all-white homes.

This analysis has some implications for a definition of racism. First of all, it clarifies and makes concrete some of the forms—some subtle, some obvious—that race privilege and racism may

take in the lives of white women: educational and economic inequality, verbal assertions of white superiority, the maintenance
of all-white neighborhoods, the "invisibility" of Black and Latina
domestic workers, white people's fear of people of color, and the
"colonial" notion that the cultures of peoples of color were great
only in the past. In this context, it would be hard to maintain the
belief that race only affects the lives of people of color. Moreover,
racism emerges not only as an ideology or political orientation
chosen or rejected at will but also as a system of material relationships with a set of ideas linked to and embedded in those material
relations.

The racial structuring of white experience as it emerged in each
of these narratives is complex. It is contradictory: the two women
most explicitly raised to espouse racist ideas, Beth Ellison and Pat
Bowen, found moments and situations, however fleeting, in
which to question the racist status quo. Conversely, Sandy Alvarez and Louise Glebocki, raised to find ways in which to challenge racism, were nonetheless not outside its reach: racism as
well as antiracism shaped their environments, and both women
drew at times on white-centered logics in describing and living
their lives.

These women's accounts of their environments were also mobile. All five indicated in various ways that, with hindsight, they
had become more cognizant of the patterning of their earlier experiences: phrases like "now that we're talking about this I remember" and "I was so unaware of cultural difference that" signal
both lack of awareness of racism *and* moments of recognition or
realization of it. "Experience" emerged here as a complicated concept. As the narratives showed, there are multiple ways in which
experiences can be named, forgotten, or remembered through
changing conceptual schemata.

Later chapters will return to the landscapes of childhood in the
context of other discussions; this chapter has by no means ex-
hausted the range of ways in which white women conceptualized
their environments, nor, in particular, the ways generation shaped
both material and discursive relations. Race shaped the lives of all
the women I interviewed in complex ways, at times explicitly articulated and at other times unspoken but nonetheless real.

4

Race, Sex, and Intimacy I: Mapping a Discourse

[In Detroit in the 1940s] it would have been a horrible thing to marry someone of a different race, or someone Catholic, even. . . . [In Oregon in the 1980s] Henry still thinks his son married a slant-eye!

—*Irene Esterley*

[In Maryland in the 1970s] . . . in high school you're taught really strictly what to do and not do around sex. I mean, it's bad to be a slut, anyway. But [for a white woman] . . . to have sex with a Black man is like being the worst slut in the world.

—*Patricia Bowen*

Interracial sexual relationships have been and remain a controversial terrain in the United States. This chapter and the next focus on interracial primary relationships as idea and as material reality. Examining the discourse on interracial relationships or, as one might more accurately state it, *against* interracial relationships (since it seems to me that there is at this time no popular discourse specifically *for* them) brings into sharp relief a range of issues key to comprehending the impact of racism both on white women's experience and worldview and on social organization more broadly. The *racialness* of constructions of masculinity and femininity are apparent in this discourse, as are the construction of race difference as "real," "essential," and based on "biology" and the construction of racial and cultural groups as entirely and appropriately separate from one another.

Examining these issues provides an opportunity to examine the relationships between individual subjects and discourse. In the same way that, as I argued in chapter 3, there is no way for white women to step outside the reach of racism's impact on the material environment, here I show that, while white women can and do challenge racist discourses, engagement with them is inevitable, in the literal sense of that term. In this chapter I will analyze white women's words about masculinity, femininity, and the discourse against interracial relationships. In chapter 5 I will reread the discourse in relation to the narratives of white women who were actually in interracial relationships. This provides a second opportunity to think more generally about discourses, for it shows how the discourse against interracial relationships, while certainly affecting these women's lives and those of their partners and children, neither adequately described nor fully contained them.

This exploration also indicates the ways in which earlier historical moments continue to shape present-day experience and subjectivity. The women I interviewed spoke at times of change or progress with regard to the social acceptability of consensual interracial relationships and child rearing. And it is indeed the case that both are now more prevalent, and certainly more clearly legally protected, than they once were. However, it was striking, in reading these narratives, that elements of today's discourse came into play well before the twentieth century.

Interracial sexual relationships have been a charged aspect of American culture, politics, and law since the beginning of Anglo settler colonialism. Marriage between whites and men or women of color was either actually illegal or not constitutionally protected for most of the past four hundred years. The first antimiscegenation law (which is to say, law against marriage between white people and people of color) was enacted in Maryland in 1661, prohibiting white intermarriage with Native Americans and African Americans. Ultimately, over the next three hundred years, thirty-eight states adopted antimiscegenation laws. In the nineteenth century, beginning with western states, antimiscegenation statutes were expanded to outlaw marriages and sexual relationships between whites and Chinese, Japanese, and Filipino Americans. Not until 1967 did the U.S. Supreme Court declare antimiscegenation laws to be unconstitutional.[1]

A thorough analysis of the ban on "miscegenation" is beyond the scope of this book, but a brief discussion provides a context for the analysis of women's narratives that follows. Controls on interracial relationships are most fruitfully examined by means of simultaneous attention to the *cultural* dimensions of racism, that is, racist belief systems, and *structural* racism—the organization of social, economic, and political hierarchies along racial lines. In cultural terms, Anglo colonizers of what was to become the

United States brought with them arguments for white racial superiority articulated in the language of Christianity.[2] These were
succeeded by, and absorbed into, so-called scientific racism,[3] and
biology- and evolution-based theories of race hierarchy. Each in
turn laid the foundation for antimiscegenation laws on the grounds
of essential difference between groups defined as racially different from one another. Consonant with the notion of essential
difference was the idea of "mongrelization" as the dread outcome of interracial sexuality and procreation. Historian Reginald
Horsman, for example, describes the concern of some Anglo-
Americans at the time of the Spanish-American War about the
negative effects of incorporating the "mongrel race" of Mexicans
into the United States.[4]

This insistence on essential difference and hierarchy coincided,
in different ways at different times, with the efforts of white
Americans to establish and maintain economic and political control: assertions of racial difference and superiority were the grounds
for Euro-American claims for economic and political advantage.
Analysis of the part played by Anglo and other European *cultural*
systems in the legal prohibition of consensual interracial relationships is thus, while necessary, insufficient without simultaneous
exploration of the economics of racism. For, clearly, interracial
sexual activity (much of it coercive) did take place. Those who
insisted on the inherent racial inferiority of Native Americans also
asserted that, to the extent that Native Americans had made any
advances toward civilization, this was the result of "race-mixing"
with Caucasians.[5]

It is well documented that in the context of the slave economy,
white plantation owners frequently raped the Black women who
were their slaves. It is equally well documented that legally, and
in contrast with the patrilineal reckoning of descent for the non-
slave population, the children of interrracial unions between slave
owners and enslaved women were themselves slaves.[6] Although
one may assume that slave owners used rape as a means of wield-
ing power and obtaining sexual pleasure, the economic dimension
of the prohibition on miscegenation was also evident: sexual in-
tercourse with enslaved women—in the context of matrilineal descent laws for enslaved people—produced more slaves. Thus, as
much as laws prohibiting *legitimated* unions across race lines drew
on cultural dimensions of racism, such laws also served to ensure
the continued existence of an enslaved population and to restrict

membership in the group with economic and political power. One may also assume that, since white claims to a right to appropriate land (vis-à-vis Native Americans) and to be free rather than enslaved (vis-à-vis African Americans) were racially defined and justified on grounds of inborn superiority, marriage and procreation across racial lines would in fact threaten the power structure itself.

The linkage of cultural racism with economic and political control is equally clear when one examines the circumstances in which antimiscegenation laws were applied to Chinese, Japanese, and Filipino men in the United States in the nineteenth and twentieth centuries. Megumi Dick Osumi, analyzing this process in California, points out that in all cases, the passage of antimiscegenation laws was integrally linked to the activity of Euro-American groups committed to economic and political exclusionism. California's antimiscegenation statute, enacted in 1850, was extended in 1880 to "prohibit the issuance of a license authorizing the marriage of a white person with a 'Negro, Mulatto, or Mongolian.' "[7] In 1905 the law was strengthened further, this time not only declaring marriage between whites and "Mongolians" illegal, but also declaring extant marriages void. Next, in 1933, in the context of legal and political debate over the racial classification of Filipinos and the original intent of the 1905 law, Filipinos ("Malays" in the terminology of the time) and whites were prohibited from marrying, and in this case too, already existing marriages were declared void. Not until 1948 were antimiscegenation laws declared unconstitutional in California.

The antimiscegenation laws accompanied other Euro-American efforts—by labor unions, "nativist" ("antiforeigner," pro–Euro-American) organizations, the press, elected representatives, and the judiciary—to restrict Asian immigrants' access to jobs and to settlement in the United States. The first extension of the law to include prohibition of white-Chinese marriage came on the heels of an economic decline in California; white working people blamed the lack of jobs on Chinese immigrant men brought to the United States by business owners as a source of cheap labor. Antimiscegenation laws were passed in a broader context of anti-Chinese racism; and two years after the antimiscegenation statute was passed in California, the federal Exclusion Act prohibited any immigration of Chinese laborers to the United States. In 1884, that act was extended to exclude the wives of Chinese male immigrants. Taken together, these laws placed massive restrictions on the development of Chinese communities in the United States. Osumi summarizes the situation thus: "The anti-Chinese movement attempted desperately to prevent the procreation of a second generation of Chinese, thereby insuring that the 'Chinese problem' would eventually disappear."[8]

An almost identical pattern of events shaped the simultaneous enactment in 1906 of immigration controls and antimiscegenation laws with regard to Japanese laborers, this time alongside school segregation statutes separating white from Asian children. (Between 1906 and 1920, Japanese women followed male immigrants to the United States, so that by 1920, Japanese women made up over one-third of the Japanese American population).

Given the exclusion of Chinese and Japanese labor, agriculturalists turned next to the Philippines for a source of cheap labor. And for a third time, the same coalition of labor, nativist, press, and legislators who had fought for immigration control once again marshaled anti–Asian sentiment. Once more, in the context of economic depression, attention was focused simultaneously on immigration control and on antimiscegenation laws—so virulently that two race riots were incited by white men enraged at Filipino men socializing with white women. Extension of antimiscegenation laws to Filipinos involved debate over whether Filipinos were, like the Chinese and Japanese, members of the "Mongol" race and thereby included in existing statutes. Even before the California judiciary concluded that Filipinos were not Mongols but "Malays," bills were introduced to the state legislature explicitly prohibiting "Malay"-white marriages and retroactively voiding marriage licenses granted earlier. Thus, as we saw was the case in African Americans-white marriages, Asian-white interracial marriage and childbearing also were perceived as threats to a power structure in which race, class, and gender were linked.

Integral to this set of linked discursive, economic, and political histories were constructions of masculinities and femininities along racially differentiated lines. Foremost was the construction in racist discourses of the sexuality of men and women of color as excessive, animalistic, or exotic in contrast to the ostensibly restrained or "civilized" sexuality of white women and men.

Key instances in this discursive history are the stereotypic figures of "Jezebel" and "Mammy," linked to the sexual abuse and economic exploitation of African American women during the time of slavery and in its aftermath.[9] Work by African American critics and others has brought increased attention to the origins of the myth of the African American man as sexual aggressor or "rapist" in the years immediately following slavery, as white men sought rationalizations for continued repression of Black men and women.[10] It is striking that in the context of the nativist movements against Asians, racist constructions of Asian men as lascivious and predatory also emerged. In short, given male dominance within white culture, the "protection" or "salvation" of white women and their supposedly civilized sexuality from men of color and their "primitive" sexuality has been the alibi for a range of atrocities from genocide and lynching to segregation and immigration control. Ironically, the success of anti-Asian immigration laws in excluding Asian women from the United States, which created "bachelor" communities of Asian and especially Chinese men for much of the late nineteenth and early twentieth centuries, led to an inversion of the construction of Asian masculinity from "hypersexual" to "undersexed" or "effeminate."[11]

As Peggy Pascoe points out in her analysis of interracial marriage in the western United States, the focus of antimiscegenation laws on some racial groups more than others further reveals the extent to which the imperative was shoring up white and male economic power as much as preserving white racial purity. For, in addition to laws affecting African Americans,

> laws were applied most stringently to groups like Chinese, Japanese and Filipinos, whose men were thought likely to marry white women. They were applied least stringently to groups like Native Americans (who were inconsistently mentioned in the laws) and Hispanics (who were not mentioned at all), groups whose women were historically likely to marry white men.[12]

Further, Pascoe points out, court records reveal numerous cases in which the families of recently deceased white men sought to annul the marriages—often very long-lived—of those men to women of color who stood to inherit their property.[13]

Given this history and the relative newness of definitive legal ruling *against* the prohibition of interracial marriages, it is perhaps not surprising that interracial relationships and parenting was a contentious area in the narratives of the women I interviewed. The 1967 Supreme Court ruling that outlawed legislation against interracial marriage was enacted during their lifetimes. In this chapter and the next, the traces of history emerge time and again, in both blatant and subtle ways. Most visible are the stereotypic descriptions of men of color, and in particular of African American men, as sexual aggressors or as "supersexual" beings, of white men as self-chosen "saviors" of white women, and of white women in relationships with men of color as sexual or social transgressors. More subtle, but nonetheless significant, is the mention of Asian men as less sexually threatening, and of both Asian and Latino men as more acceptable than African American men as partners for white women; this is also, I suggest, linked to this history. Equally, a more generalized hostility or skepticism toward interracial relationships, on the (tautological) grounds of their social unnaccceptablity, while ostensibly more "modern," rests, as I will argue, on assumptions of total difference between members of different racial groups.

In the late twentieth century, interracial relationships are no longer illegal in any state. The number of visible, consensual interracial partnerships has increased steadily.[14] But there is, I suggest, still a discourse against interracial relationships circulating in the United States that, while clearly not the same as that of the seventeenth, eighteenth and nineteenth centuries, nonetheless bears the traces of the history of antimiscegenation laws.

The current discourse against interracial relationships includes the following elements. First, it entails a range of racialized masculinities—images of what it means to be a man differentiated by race and class and drawing at times on the racist stereotypes of the nineteenth and early twentieth centuries. Second, femininity is also racialized, and here my focus is on *white* femininity: white women who choose interracial relationships are presented as sexually "loose," sexually unsuccessful, or (at the least negative) sexually radical. Third, the discourse generates a view of interracial relationships as transgressing fixed racial or cultural boundaries. Linked to this, a fourth element views children whose parents are racially different from one another as "mixed" and therefore doomed not to fit into the social structure as it is currently constituted. These four elements presuppose a fifth, the idea of "race" as a fixed and essential axis of differentiation, and a sixth, the idea of cultural differences as absolute and tied to "race" and biological belonging. The seventh and final element of this discourse is the hierarchical ranking of the essential nature and character of racial and cultural groups.

In this chapter I will examine these discursive elements in detail, both through their direct expression as part of the belief systems of some of the women I interviewed and less directly through the experiences of white women as "targets" of the discourse. Looking at interracial relationships and the attitudes that surround them provides the context for examining how white women are "answerable" to this and other racist discourses, whether or not they choose to be. In other words, whether or not an individual woman chooses to participate in reproducing a racist discourse, the discourse has an impact on her life. The women I interviewed were engaged with the discourse against interracial relationships in a range of different ways. At times they actually espoused elements of it; at other times they described themselves as having *in the past* espoused elements of it. At times they described succumbing to the pressure of the discourse, even when they did not themselves endorse it (as, for example, when Sandy Alvarez refused a date with an African American friend because she could not face the public attention they would attract). Some of the women described experiences of public hostility or, worse, familial rejection because of their own disregard for the discourse. Finally, some described how they or others had specifically gone out of their way to challenge the discourse (Sandy, for example, suggested that her mother would have been proud if she had gone out with a Black man: "Aha! See—she's showing everyone"). But at the same time, lived experience continually exceeded and interrupted the discourse. Tracking a discursive environment shows us how inhabiting it is not a matter of individual choice, any more than is the case for material conditions. Rather, subverting it and transforming it both are long-term, collective projects.

Racialized Masculinities . . .

The images of interracial sexuality and relationships held by the women I interviewed and their choices of partners made visible the ways constructions of masculinity in their narratives were differentiated by race. These constructions ranged from the simplistic, stereotypic, and blatantly racist to others that were more positive, more complex, and clearly grounded in intersubjective experiences.

The most repetitive and explicitly derogatory images focused on African American men and white women in relationships with them. Images of African American men were frequently blatantly racist, echoing older stereotypes. For example, Chris Patterson, who was born in 1955 and raised in a white middle-class community on Long Island, said that she had learned the stereotype of the African American man as "rapist" early on. Describing her experience of school desegregation, she says:

> CHRIS: The Black boys—I was just scared to death of them, figured they wanted to be sexual with me.
>
> RF: Why did you feel that?
>
> CHRIS: I think, a stereotype I'd learned.
>
> RF: Where from?
>
> CHRIS: Books, TV, *To Kill a Mockingbird,* we studied it in school a lot. . . . [We learned] that there were parts of the country where things aren't so rosy—the South, that had slavery and the thing that happened there all the time was that Black men wanted to rape white women.

It is ironic, even tragic, that at the very moment when Chris first met African American students as peers, she simultaneously encountered the stereotype of the Black male rapist. It is unfortunate too that, while teaching Chris and her classmates that racism was a feature of the "distant" South, her teachers apparently failed to provide a perspective that would counter this particularly pernicious image of Black men.

Chris also described a much later incident that had pushed her to think again about another, closely linked element of racist discourse. Living next door to a young Black couple, Chris had often heard shouting and the sounds of physical violence, which she assumed had been initiated by the husband, despite the fact that he otherwise seemed "gentle." Through overhearing discussions between the couple and the wife's father, Chris eventually discovered that the woman had started the fights and that the husband was not, after all, physically violent:

> It was a really intense realization about my assumptions that he was a "big, Black brute." . . . Finding out turned me around. I'm glad it happened to me.

Despite her own perception of her neighbor as gentle, it was all too easy for Chris to draw on stereotypic constructions of Black masculinity as aggressive and violent and femininity as passive and nonviolent until her assumption was finally overwhelmed by the weight of countervailing evidence.

While Chris was with hindsight aware of the stereotype *as* a stereotype and able to gain critical distance from it, others continued to think within racist parameters. Thus, Lisbeth Poirer, only twenty-one at the time of the interview, claimed that white women had good reason to be afraid of Black men because "let's face it, they are only a few generations out of the jungle." The contradictions embedded here are both fascinating and appalling. First, Lisbeth's extreme youth contrasts with the centuries-old element of racist memory. Second, the statement is of an extreme type most clearly associated with Klan or neo-Nazi rhetoric or more generally with racial conservatism. But Lisbeth considered herself politically progressive—in fact, she and I had met at a fund-raiser for Central American feminist groups! Even more startling was her next comment: "Who knows whether that's really the reason. I only just thought of it." Evident here is the "naturalizing" process that serves to conceal the constructedness of all effective ideological systems. Thus the image of African Americans as "primitive," "natural," "uncivilized" seemed to Lisbeth to be an idea that originated with her rather than one of the oldest racist lines in the European lexicon.

Similarly, Evelyn Steinman's choice of an animal metaphor in speaking of Black male paternity drew directly on the nineteenth-century "scientific" racist ideologies: she described the white daughter of a family friend as having children "sired" by a Black man. Implicit in the concept of "siring" is a construction of Black men as *only* sexual. It denudes fathering of any social, familial, or nurturing function, and even of pleasure, connoting only sexuality directed toward reproduction. Ironically, "siring" is historically a better description of white men's sexual relationships with Black women than of Black men's relations with white women, for this was precisely the mode of sexual activity through which *white* slave owners "fathered" Black children. Here as elsewhere, then, racist ideology involves inversion of social reality.

The women at times described situations in which white women *and* men of color appeared to be dealing with one another in terms clearly linked to racist constructions of masculinity. Pat Bowen, for example, grew up in the 1960s in a small Maryland town where the Black and white communities were unequal and highly demarcated (see chapter 3). There, as Pat described it, the stereotypic image of Black men as sexual threat was typically encoded in the "body language" of an African American man passing a white woman in the street:

> A lot of times if you were walking down the street—I'm a young white girl and there's a Black man—he would drop his head and not look at you, it was a very subtle kind of thing, like, "I'm not looking at you, don't worry."

Also encoded here, perhaps, is African American men's awareness of the history of white male assaults on them—notably lynchings—for allegedly looking at or speaking to white women.

Two other figures in the "discursive family" that constructs the African American male sexual aggressor are the white man as savior and the white woman as victim, or she who needs to be saved. (Invisible in this scenario is the African American woman, who has historically been a much more frequent target of assault, and not by Black men but by *white* men.) In fact, two women who were in relationships with African American men described experiences in their high school years of white men attempting to "save" them from their partners. Debby Rothman spoke about an incident in Berkeley in the early 1960s:

> I remember [my boyfriend] and I touching each other in school, and a teacher pushed us apart. He shouted, "What would your mother say if she saw you?" I told him my mother wouldn't like *him* pushing me.

Jeanine Cohen remembered being accosted, with her Black partner, in the street by a drunken white man brandishing a bottle and shouting, "Take your hands off her."

It is significant that in both instances it was a white *man* who challenged the couple, echoing a tradition in U.S. racism, established as far back as the time of slavery, in which white men cast themselves in the role of protectors who must defend the honor of white women from Black men. Beyond the United States, the colonial "sexual division of labor" with respect to racism and male domination was identical. White women are viewed both as objects of white male protection and as people unable to control their own sexuality. In either case, white women and nonwhite men are to be kept apart, by white men.[15]

Although the women I interviewed spoke out of different degrees of critical consciousness, for most these images were part of the received environment, such that they had to respond either *to* or *through* them (or both). Thus, even Debby Rothman, who somehow managed for a number of years *not* to know about the image of Black men as "supersexual," found the image coming to claim her later. Debby described the beginning of her relationship with her African American boyfriend, in high school:

> I remember him saying something about my wanting the excitement of going with a Black man, that they were supposed to have big penises. I was shocked. This was the first time I'd heard [it]. Of course, he didn't believe me.

While it was Black masculinity that was most explicitly and frequently constructed negatively, other modes of being a man were also spoken about, at times explicitly and at times in more subtle terms. For example, Chris Patterson said that, while she was afraid of both white men and African American men, she was *not* afraid of Asian men. This makes a statement about the construction of several racially demarcated types of masculinity where, crudely put, some masculinities are stereotypically construed as more aggressive or threatening than others. (All three stereotypes are in their own way objectifying and limited in their perception of actual, individual men.)

Finally, though, it is important to note that not all of these women construed Black masculinity negatively, nor in terms of physical or sexual hyperactivity. Frieda Kazen, for example, spoke of her partner's tendency to suppress rather than act out frustration and anger. And Helen Standish explained that she and her African American partner had broken up because she was more interested in sex than he was.

Depictions of masculinity were marked by class as well as race. A mode of white masculinity marked by both was at stake in Margaret Phillips's description of her husband's "anguish" about their son's involvement with Rastafarianism and his relationship with a Jamaican woman, Kadedra. The Phillips family was wealthy: Margaret's father owned a large business in the Midwest, and her husband was the senior partner in a firm of stockbrokers.

> MARGARET: I believe it's important to strike out in a new direction. Not be a clone of your parent. My husband doesn't agree! He would love to have his son settled in and doing the business thing, and thinks he'd be very successful at it, and it's very painful for him to watch our son.
>
> RF: Yeah, you mentioned that before—

MARGARET: And on the racial issue, he said something that might interest you—because it's hard for him not to accept our son's girlfriend, who's Jamaican, in a personal way—he really likes her. But just to accept the fact that his son, the only person carrying on his name, is going in such a new direction. His children might be biracial. That just doesn't feel good to him.

I think it's an ego thing for my husband, although it's a traditional ego thing. But, you know, he would like to see his son carry on.

RF: In his footsteps.

MARGARET: Ye-es. Somewhat. In his style. And the people he meets— he's always meeting people starting new companies in the high-tech industries, and they are young often. Very talented, skilled, well-trained people. They're thrilling! They are the creators, they're the business world, but they are the adventurous ones, they are brilliant and dazzling and exciting. And he looks at these people, and he could really see his son in that place. He has a good education, and he has a lot of energy and style. He *could* fit into that. But he's really gone in such a different direction.

Brilliance, dazzle, the spirit of adventure in the entrepreneurial world, good use of good training, being the progenitor of descendants *within* the racial group: these emerge as the dimensions of a form of white upper-class masculinity to which, it was expected, Margaret's son would conform. And it is not only Margaret's *son* who is affected by his rejection of the style of business-class masculinity held out to him. In rejecting it, he compromises his father's ego and perhaps even his father's masculinity, particularly in relation to his father's role as head of an ongoing descent group. It is, of course, crucial that the father's fear is not that his son will fail to have children, but that the children will not be white. And it is also important to note that travel to Jamaica, intimate connection to another culture, community, and religion, and partnership outside one's natal culture, are not the kinds of "adventures" that qualify this son to inherit his father's male identity. Masculinity emerges here as a product of class and race as well as gender and involves reproduction and repetition of what has gone before.

While Margaret Phillips spoke admiringly of white masculinity, other women's descriptions of white masculinity were geared to explaining why they had turned outside their ethnic group in seeking a partner. Thus, at the opposite end of the class spectrum, Louise Glebocki, who grew up in a working-class, poor, white and Chicano extended family, had had all of her primary partner-

ships with Chicano men. I asked Louise why she had mostly chosen Chicano boyfriends throughout her school years:

> LOUISE: When we moved [to a new neighborhood in Los Angeles] I had
> a mixture [of friends], whites and Chicanos, but from that point on—
> third grade—I never liked a white guy. I liked a couple of Hawaiian
> guys that I was seeing for a while, but mainly I just started seeing
> Chicano guys. That was more what I lived for, what I liked. I never
> liked a white guy. (Laughs)
>
> RF: How come?
>
> LOUISE: Um—
>
> RF: Kind of a weird question, but—
>
> LOUISE: I just liked the way, like, um, the Mexican guys looked, I liked
> their color, and their personalities, and just their knowing a couple of
> languages. I don't know. White guys, to me, especially from back
> then—I'm going to get married in a couple of weeks—we've been
> together for seven years, so we decided we're going to do it—
>
> RF: That's great!
>
> LOUISE: But now, especially since I started hanging around in the last
> couple of years with the punk movement, I started seeing that if I was
> single I'd maybe go out with some white guys. But up until a couple of
> years ago, it was like, they were just too, um, I don't know, I didn't like
> them. Just not my style. Until I started seeing these punk youth that
> were kind of like wild, and rebellious. The kind of people I like.

Later, Louise described meeting her current partner, also Chicano:

> When we first met, we were both radical. We still are, but we were both
> really working closely with the same organization. . . . I wanted to find
> someone that would have a liberating feeling towards women . . . I was
> tired of relationships where these guys were coming from this macho
> kind of bullshit. . . . And what was interesting when we first started
> seeing each other was that he was so much—and he still is—pretty
> consciously into breaking all chains of women's oppression. And I was
> holding onto a lot of them in such a big way. *I* was the one who was,
> kind of like, "God, can't he be a *little* macho?" It was really funny. I
> liked it, but at the same time, it was really different.

Here, modes of masculinity are being described and associated
with particular ethnic groups. In describing Chicano masculinity,
Louise began by naming physical characteristics. However, in her
suggestion that more recently she has imagined the possibility of
dating white men (that is, has encountered modes of white masculinity more appealing to her), stylistic and social attributes

emerge as definitive. For among white punks, says Louise, are the characteristics of rebelliousness that she had hitherto only associated with Chicano men.

Is there any difference between the description of masculinity in which Louise valorized Chicanos and those in which others excoriated African American men? First, of course, Louise's description is positive rather than hostile, and second, her preference goes against, rather than for, the dominant group. But white women at times actually drew on elements of racist and colonial discourse in order to praise communities of color (see chapter 7). Yet Louise's description was more complex, more conscious of variation within cultural groups and—probably a decisive factor—was based on shared lives and experiences. Her characterizations of both Chicanos *and* white punk men were rich in content, more reminiscent of Margaret Phillips's descriptions of white upper-class men than of Chris, Evelyn, and Lisbeth's one-line comments on African American men.

. . . and Racialized Femininities

Gender and sexuality, just as much as racial identity, emerge as relational categories in these narratives. Like masculinity, femininity was constructed in ways differentiated by race and culture; at the same time, femininities were constructed *in relation to* masculinity. As in the discussion of maculinities, there are two dimensions to explore here. One is the crudely stereotypic and mainly derogatory imagery that attaches to white women involved with men of color. The other is the more complex and nuanced way in which modes of living white femininity were consciously or unconsciously articulated, embraced, and rejected in the context of white women's partnerships with men of color.

The complexity of this matrix of coconstruction of masculinity and femininity through the lens of race was expressed well by Dot Humphrey, who described the range of responses when she adopted her daughter, Frances, the child of a white mother and a Black father, in 1969. Dot explained the events leading up to the adoption:

DOT: When my husband [who is white] and I were married, my second child was a girl who died five days after she was born. She weighed four pounds and six ounces, and my son had only weighed four pounds and twelve ounces. At that point I felt I really wanted another child . . . and

I wanted a girl. . . . I didn't want to get pregnant again, because my son had been premature also. . . . The woman upstairs . . . said that she knew a woman who was going to have a racially mixed child who went to a public prenatal clinic and that *she* knew a woman who was going to have a racially mixed child who was going to give it up for adoption and the adoption agency backed out. And the baby was going to be born in six weeks, and that she was looking for someone to adopt it.

RF: The adoption agency backed out because the child was racially mixed?

DOT: No. . . . Because they couldn't get the signature of the father.

After meeting the mother and spending time with her through the last few weeks of her pregnancy, Dot and her husband adopted the baby. Because Dot's baby had died only six weeks earlier, Dot was able to breast-feed her adopted daughter:

DOT: One of the parts that was interesting was, at the time, I was living in Washington, D.C., in an area that was—two blocks away was an area that was almost entirely Black, it was a very militant Black neighborhood where there was a lot of politics coming out of. . . . It was quite amazing when I would go out with my husband, who is blond and blue-eyed, and I would be nursing this child, and everyone viewed him as a cuckold. (Laughs) Like I'd had this secret affair, gone and had this baby, and now here was this father to this child that was a different color. That was sort of interesting. Or that Black men—I had a lot of experiences in the park, for example, where Black men would view me as a white woman that they could get more from. Because I had a Black baby so I must have been easy. . . . I've had that experience quite a few times, even recently. I've been a lesbian for so long that [it] always takes me by surprise.
    And then the feeling of being in the line in [the supermarket] and have Black women be hostile. I've experienced that too. Less [so] in more recent years. But there was a certain period in the early seventies when that was especially true. In Washington, D.C., and New York.

RF: The idea being that you are taking away a Black man from the community?

DOT: Mhm. . . . And I don't really know how white women view it. They are much more covert in their reactions.

One striking feature of this story is the disjunction between the actual events leading up to Dot's and her husband's parenting of Frances and the narratives that are subsequently written by observers onto the tableaux of mother, father, and child and, later, mother and child. (It is important to remember that I am drawing on Dot's account, for I do not, of course, have access to those who actually observed her.) First, Dot's sexual activity and by association her husband's masculine prowess (his ability to retain sole rights to his wife's sexual activity) were called into question. Next, assumptions were made about Dot's past and future sexual choices: Dot was erroneously assumed to be heterosexual and, in particular, heterosexually active with African American men. Finally, Dot was written into a script in which she was seen as complicit with an unnamed Black man who deserted his own community to join the white community in partnership with a white woman (thereby conjuring images of this imaginary man's own sexual practices and commitments).

The biological presuppositions implicit here are also worth noting: it is assumed in all of these imaginary scenarios that sexual union is the only route to parenting and that children are always genetically linked to their parents. The social and physiological dimensions of parenting, in short, are viewed as inseparable. Further, the physiological sex act that (apparently) leads to parenthood is viewed as inseparable from sexual choice on two dimensions—race and gender. Through this reductive thinking, Dot, as the parent of a Black child, was viewed as necessarily the potential social and sexual partner of African American men.

Like the negative stereotypes of African American men, images of white women in relationships with men of color frequently reduced them entirely to sexual beings. Patricia Bowen's description of an experience in her final year of high school in San Francisco in the mid-1970s encapsulated both the hostile view of white women in relationships with men of color and the racism that underlies it. Since Patricia had just moved from Maryland to San Francisco, the anecdote also captured a kind of culture shock:

One white friend of mine introduced her boyfriend to me and he was Black, and I was just kind of shocked. In [my home town], that just would not be done. . . . I know this sounds really racist. It *is* really racist. In high school you're taught anyway really strictly what is OK to do and what not to do around sex. And what we got really strongly is for a woman to have sex with a Black man is like being the worst slut in the world. I mean it's bad to be a slut anyway, but with a Black man it's *so* degrading. So I had a bit of a feeling when she introduced her Black boyfriend, like surprised that she wouldn't be embarrassed to do that. It was like she was giving herself away. Not so much surprised that she would be with him—well, I suppose that was there too—but surprised that she would feel no hesitation about introducing him to me. That she would be so open about it, I guess.

Here the prohibition on Black-white relationships intersected with control of young women's sexual activity in general: "the worst slut in the world" indicates that there were, in fact, other kinds of "sluts," or rather other controls on female sexuality. Signaled within the story was an indication that Pat's point of view (relationship to the discourse) had changed over time, for she interrupted her story to analyze it ("This sounds really racist"). At the same time, her standpoint remained white-centered, so that she said "for a *woman* to have sex with a Black man" (my emphasis) when presumably she meant "for a *white woman*."

Another element of Pat's story was the idea that her friend should feel embarrassment or even shame for being involved with an African American. Other narratives, too, articulated the idea that white women signal either inadequacy or perversion through interracial relationships. The two most politically conservative women I interviewed, for example, expressed this point of view, one saying that she couldn't help wondering what was wrong with "those" women that meant they couldn't get a white man, and the other referring to the daughter of a friend as "clearly having a *thing* for Black men." All of this is, of course, deeply racist, for the notion of a compromised, hypersexual, or perverted white femininity makes no sense without the counterpart from which it follows: the construction of Black masculinity as a deviation from an unnamed, but clearly non-Black, norm. Also underpinning the view of interracial sexuality as deviant is the idea of race differences as essential, biological differences—an idea to which I will return later.

Chicano-white relationships produced some equally hostile responses in the minds or experiences of these women, suggesting that white femininity can be "compromised" by association with Chicano as well as African American men.

Louise Glebocki remembered a time when she and her partner, a Chicano, visited a shopping mall soon after moving to East Oakland:

> Some Black dudes, a young Black dude, said, "Man, we don't like that shit," talking to [my partner], "a pimp with a white girl." It was like, "Oh my God, is this what we're going to have to face, living here?" And then some of the kids were all tripping out: "A mixed couple! How funny!"

And Sandy Alvarez, now married for many years to her Chicano husband, confided:

> I will be real honest with you. Before I got married, I wasn't sure if I could handle being looked at all the time. But either it's changed or I have, because I don't notice it any more. I knew I shouldn't feel this.

Sandy's distinction between knowing and feeling—"I knew I shouldn't feel this"—exemplifies the ambivalence that appeared repeatedly in the narratives of white women caught historically and psychically in a discourse on race that they rejected politically and intellectually. I will return to this point later.

Less derogatory but nonetheless signaling exceptions to the norm were a range of images marking white women in interracial relationships as different. Chris Patterson, speaking in the context of several years of desegregated schooling, said that white girls who dated Black students had seemed to her "radical, more cool, smoked cigarettes more, seemed freer of those kinds of things." Although she was not so thoroughly negative, Chris certainly viewed such girls as divergent from an implicit white, female norm: risqué, other than average, perhaps less bound by a range of social controls other than sexual ones, and, in general, "on the wrong side of the law." (There was no mention here of Black girls dating white boys, nor of how Black male students who dated white girls might have been viewed.)

The construction of white femininity in the narratives was not, however, entirely confined to the production and impersonal application of stereotypic images. Its other axis involved white women themselves acting to choose or reject relationships and simultaneously to choose or reject forms of femininity.

Speaking of a three- or four-year period of personal transformation, Louise described different modes of female behavior, all enacted within Chicana/Chicano communities, and the male roles that corresponded to them:

> LOUISE: I guess I changed. . . . Back when I was more into the low-riding scene, it was kind of like, you are supposed to be more "girly." . . . [Later] I realized I had been almost upholding women's oppression, by some of these backward ideas.
>
> RF: Like, what kind of backward ideas?
>
> LOUISE: Well, it was always real contradictory because at one point, I was, like, real rebellious, a revolutionary young woman. But at the same

time I held onto, like, a guy should have this "macho," and a woman should be "girly." That kind of thinking.

RF: "Girly" in clothes and stuff?

LOUISE: Yeah, and just more kicking back, letting him deal with the situations and stuff. Even though I was always real vocal. In fact it got me into trouble sometimes, because I wasn't supposed to speak up. It was constantly contradictory. . . .

   A lot of it had to do with where I lived. It was a lot different than, say, living up here [in Berkeley and Oakland]. When I first came to Berkeley, just for one day when I lived down there [in Los Angeles]— oh my God, I hated it. I thought people were so *weird* and *uncool*. It was like—you have to act a certain way, if you're cool, you know what I mean? You have to have a certain style and class, you know. . . . Everything had to be a certain way back there, you know. Your pants had to be *starched*. If you had a low-rider car, the girl *always* sat in the middle, and the guys on the side. Sometimes I'd see people just all bunched in—my God—a guy sitting near a guy! . . . It was just really different. And I hated it at first—"Yuk!"

It is clear here that femininity and masculinity are coconstructed: for every female role or action that Louise described, there is a corresponding male one. A transgression of norms for one also compromises the other; there is perhaps an element of homophobia in Louise's remembered revulsion at the idea of two men sitting close together. Masculinity and femininity, then, keep one another in place. There is also a marked difference between Louise's more complex and varied description of Chicano masculinities and femininities and the simplistic, unidimensional images of men of color and white women quoted earlier. A key reason for this richer description, it seems to me, is that Louise was describing events in which she herself was an active participant rather than an outsider or an observer.

As we know, Louise later set out to find a partner who would endorse her commitment to nonsubordinated female roles—a partner with "a liberating feeling towards women." Less self-consciously, Suzie Roberts also chose a partner who, among other things, had the potential to free her from a form of femininity very much tied to her own class and race. In Suzie's story, we see again the coconstruction of masculinity and femininity, for, as Suzie switched from a white, upper middle class partner of her own age to a Mexican partner twenty years her senior, her options as a woman shifted in some ways. As we will see, also striking is the extent to which her options as a woman stayed the same and perhaps in some respects even shrank in scope.

Suzie was born in 1954 and grew up in a middle-class household in Los Angeles. By the time she finished high school, her family had moved to a beach community, still in Los Angeles and still largely middle class. Suzie and her (white) high school sweetheart moved in together, still in the neighborhood, when they started college. Suzie's boyfriend was the son of wealthy parents, and both sets of parents supported the match:

> SUZIE: But it was like we were playing house or something, because we lived in a house that his parents owned, and we had the furniture that his parents owned, and we got married, and my mother, she was very happy with the way things turned out for me, because it just seemed so cute and nice. But I was really unhappy, I wanted to get away from that area, I wanted to see other places, I wanted to come to school up here [the San Francisco Bay Area]. He didn't want to, he wanted to stay close by. So I had this real unhappiness, because I felt real stagnant and inexperienced. I just wanted to see more. And then I met—this is interesting—I met a Mexican man who I ended up going to Mexico with. And seeing the world and finding myself (laughs) and all those things that you are supposed to do when you are twenty years old. So—and he's the father of my kids. So that's what I did when I was twenty.
>
> RF: How did you meet him?
>
> SUZIE: We were living next door to him. He was a bachelor, living kind of a fast life, and it really fascinated me. And I kept giving warning signals—"I wanna go to Mexico, I wanna do this, I wanna do that"—to the guy who was my husband, and he was just real disinterested in that, so I just ended up doing it, going. At this point in my life, it's painful to talk about, and to think that I really did this.
>
> RF: How come?
>
> SUZIE: Um, 'cause it was mean. (Laughs)
>
> RF: How you did it?
>
> SUZIE: Yeah. Just taking off like that. I didn't tell my parents, and my parents flipped out, totally. And I thought—the guy I went with, his name's Rodrigo, my parents hated him beyond words. They just didn't want to have anything to do with him. And for a long time I thought it was because he was Mexican. And then in our later years together, I realized what an ass he was, and I could see what they meant. For one thing, he was twenty years older than I was.

On the surface, the images of cuteness and playing house sit oddly with Suzie's view of her life as stagnant and unhappy. Perhaps

what links them is the way in which not only were Suzie and her
husband following directly in their parents' footsteps, it was
Suzie's parents and in-laws who produced the stage set on which
the young couple would in a double sense play out their adulthood. In leaving, Suzie rejected one set of things that "you are
supposed to do when you are twenty" (marry, settle down, em-
ulate an older generation) in favor of another. Thus, Suzie both
rejected the mode of femininity set out for her and spurned the
mode of masculinity represented by her husband.

Suzie's husband was, in her words, "a very benevolent person.
Everybody loved him. He was a doll. The perfect man." By comparison, Rodrigo was "exciting":

> At the time, I guess he played the father role, he had this—you know,
> he had a language, he had his people. I became very close to his mother
> and his whole family.

Ironies abound here, as marrying, growing up, and taking on the
roles of the previous generation became infantilized as "play,"
while stepping away from those roles became "real," the means
to self-discovery. It is curious, too, that as she stepped away from
the "play house" of her marriage, Suzie was in a sense further
infantilized by her connection to a partner who "played the father
role." The "unreal" and the "real" switched places here as Suzie
left her "real" life (in the sense of a life consonant with her age,
class, and race) for a life that felt *more* real, more interesting, and
more apt to produce an intensity of feeling precisely because it
was *less* real, less rational and predictable.

This story is not only about gender and sexuality, but also
about race and culture. For, of course, before Suzie left she already
had a language, a family, a people, a mother and a father. She
received from Rodrigo all of those things, but replaced and in a
new form. Suzie's sense of her own home base as a noncultural or
"empty" space is linked to a historically specific way of viewing
dominant versus subordinate cultural groups in which the latter
become more marked, visible, and at times enticing to white
outsiders precisely as a result of their subordinate status (see chapter 7).

When Suzie and Rodrigo returned from Mexico, after only six
weeks, Suzie went to her parents, apologized, and asked them to
take her in while she decided what to do next. But her parents
were furious with her, given their hostility to Rodrigo, their hurt

at her abrupt and unannounced departure, and perhaps also her rejection of the future they had expected of her. Suzie felt that she had no choice but to stay with Rodrigo.

In terms of femininity, "difference" emerged here as the same in a new guise. Suzie never once imagined herself able to survive outside a familial or marital context, feeling that, given her parents' rejection, she *had* to go with Rodrigo. (Her youth as well as her gender no doubt contributed to this feeing.) In addition, Suzie became a "wife" once again and, as she had with her young husband, lived a life that intimately involved her partner's parents. And, in much the same way that she felt her husband had single-mindedly acted on his own interests and desires rather than taking hers into account, Suzie realized with hindsight that Rodrigo had done the same. In the sense that she had quickly left her young husband but stayed with Rodrigo for six years, Suzie was perhaps even more confined in the second relationship than in the first. What made this "same" relationship "different," then, had little to do with gender per se, and everything to do with class, race, and culture. Through a shift, not in *how* she enacted her femaleness but in *where* she enacted it—and, ironically, by stepping into a family that was subordinate with respect to race, class, and income—Suzie experienced excitement, adventure, joy, and liberation.

Border Infractions and Shifting Ground: Images of Interracial Couples and Children

Given the range of hostile images of men of color and white women in relationships with them, it should come as no surprise that the interracial (heterosexual) couple per se also evoked negative responses. Comments about interracial relationships, as distinct from the individuals who participated in them, however, hinged less on constructions of femininity and masculinity than on racial or cultural differences, viewed as absolute, determining, and, for many, crucial to maintain. Interracial relationships frequently presented an affront to family unity, and an interracial child an affront to cultural belonging.

The women I interviewed frequently framed their comments about interracial relationships and childbearing in terms of concern over the welfare of the parties concerned: the couple or the child, some argued, would experience neither cultural belonging nor societal acceptance—but there was considerable slippage between those arguments and more "old-fashioned" images of essential biological difference and hierarchy among racial groups.

Some of the women located their own ideas and their assessments of social acceptance of interracial relationships within national or regional histories. Irene Esterley, for example, commented that in her German Protestant girlhood in Detroit in the 1930s and 1940s:

> It would have been a horrible thing to marry someone of a different
> race, or someone Catholic, even. . . . It's hard to imagine how far it's
> come. . . . As long as they [the interracial couple] live in a big city, they
> are all right, but if they lived in a provincial community it would be a
> big problem.

Irene here invoked the idea of progress over time, equating the city with greater advancement and possibly also with greater autonomy from extended families and communities.

Like other women, Irene moved back and forth between explicitly derogatory images of interracial couples and ostensibly pragmatic concerns over social acceptance. Thus, in recounting a conversation with her husband, Irene tried to excuse or explain her cousin Henry's attitude toward his Chinese American daughter-in-law:

> [My husband] said, "Henry still thinks his son married a slant-eye!" and
> I said, he lives in a small town in Oregon and he feels that way because
> he knows the children are always going to be different—and not even
> different as Chinese—they are going to be half. I don't think it'd be as
> hard to be all Chinese as it is to be half Chinese in an all-white, rural
> city, because they don't fit either place. They don't have a culture they
> can identify with. To me, that's the problem.

As Irene moved her attention away from Henry to the community's relationship with his children, the grounds of his (or her) objection to the relationship also changed. Irene's "defense" of Henry was confusing, for his ostensible concern for his grandchildren's welfare sat uneasily with his objectifying descriptions of his daughter-in-law.

Irene's anxiety about bicultural children ("half Chinese") was shared by others. Twenty-eight-year-old Marty Douglass argued this point strongly:

> The only thing that bothers me about interracial relationships is the kids
> that are produced—that poor child! The Japanese American girl I used to

know was outcast by both cultures. . . . You see a Black and white couple together and they have a child, and you know the whites'll say "ugh" and the Blacks'll say the same. As a matter of fact, I used to work for a couple—he was Black, she was white. They had kids, but by previous marriages. They didn't make their own and I thought, "That's great!"

Despite a professed and perhaps actual concern with the social questions of group and community belonging, Marty's feelings arose out of a discourse that constructs groups and communities in biological terms. For it is biological makeup rather than, for example, residence, socialization, or experience, that is seen to determine group participation. "Chineseness," "Blackness," and "whiteness" are within this conceptualization states of being that cannot be socially constructed or socially achieved, but only physiologically ascribed. Linked here is a notion of wholeness or purity: the "half" or "mixed" person, it is suggested, does not belong anywhere. Implicitly, then, biology is seen as underscoring culture, and an argument is being made that race is an essentially biological difference.

In fact, the concept of a racially "mixed" person is an odd one. Even if it made sense to subordinate the social dimensions of humans to their physiological states, genetic matter and its combining are highly complex. The notion of a racially "mixed" individual brings forth a simplistic and entirely erroneous image of two pots of paint (or blood!) stirred together, so that a "half Chinese" person is exactly twice as Chinese as someone who is "a quarter Chinese," and so on.

As we will see in chapter 6, both Irene and Marty also argued that race differences are essentially unimportant. As Irene put it:

The more you meet different kinds of people, the more you realize people are all the same: there is no difference.

Confident assertions of common humanity stumble over the questions of marriage and procreation. The very fact of noticing the racially mixed child contrasted with these women's insistence on the similarity of all people whatever their race. Neither insisted that the "mixed" individual is essentially "the same" as everyone else; both were anxious about the fate of biracial children.

Ginny Rodd, a working-class grandmother in her late forties, explained the extent to which she had rejected the segregationist practices of her childhood in rural Alabama in the 1930s. Simultaneously, she stated her limits:

> GINNY: Black people would ride in the back of the bus, had different restrooms, and couldn't eat in the same cafeteria as a white person. When I went into town with my husband to buy my kids some clothes—it's funny, I guess you're raised like this—if you see Black people touch anything, you won't buy it. I don't know why.

> RF: Because that's how you're raised?

> GINNY: Yes. But since I've got older and especially since I've come to California, I always—never taught my kids that. I said I didn't want them to marry into it, you know what I mean. But as far as being friends, I've had Black people in my house. . . . To me, they're like me or anyone else, they're human.

Here Ginny contradicted herself: in rejecting the idea of interracial marriage for her children, she is viewing Black people as, precisely, *not* like her and everybody else. The boundary between white and Black people shifts but remains intact: from a position of full avoidance of shared space, Ginny will now allow Blacks into the house and into the friendship circle, but not into the family and not into the bodies of family members via sex or procreation.

Ginny also raised the issue of children:

> RF: Do you think [interracial marriage] causes problems for the couple?

> GINNY: Mostly it's not so much for them as for the children, because they are half and half. I have a friend right now who married . . . a Black guy and had a baby with him, and she can't go with a white guy [with whom she was in love] because he would mistreat her son. . . . She didn't want to marry into the Black again but said she felt she had to, because of her son. . . . And that's where I don't think it's right because the kids have to pay for it. . . . I've seen too many little kids has to pay for something their parents has done. . . . When the kids get older and are ready to marry, they can't get a Black or a white, because they are mixed.

This brief statement is dense, contradictory, and worth detailed analysis. Although it is ostensibly a story about the suffering of children, much of it concerns the experiences of Ginny's friend, an adult white woman. Superficially at least, it is curious (although perhaps not unheard of) that a woman who has lived with and borne a child with a Black man could then fall in love with someone who is explicitly and perhaps even violently racist. Through Ginny's story, there is, of course, no real access to the friend's subjectivity. But from Ginny's viewpoint, it is the white woman who was suffering privation here. Her life was portrayed as irrevocably changed by the existence of her "half-and-half" child. Now trapped, so to speak, in the Black community, she has, one could almost say, become symbolically Black while simultaneously remaining white.

Ginny's story then shifts back to the child, who is viewed as paying for the parents' actions: the parents are seen to have incurred a debt, or perhaps sinned—for Ginny's phrase sounds very much like the biblical injunction that "the sins of the fathers will be visited on the sons." (It is interesting, in this regard, that one of the few things Ginny remembered being told by her parents about Black people was that "When Adam and Eve sinned, they had a Black child.")

When Ginny speculated briefly on the historical context of her feeling against Black-white relationships, she nonetheless chose not to change her stand. She noted that although her daughter's husband is, in her words, "part Spanish" (Spanish, here, is a euphemism for Mexican Filipino—one that is premised on the valorization of the white or European over the indigenous parts of her son-in-law's heritage):

GINNY: I still wouldn't want [my children] to marry Black. I don't know why.

RF: So you feel differently between Black and Spanish?

GINNY: Mmm. But I mean, if he was full Spanish, I don't know about that. If they could speak English it may be all right, I guess. But I don't know why. Maybe because they [Blacks] were always slaves—but it's like I said—we brought them over, or our ancestors did.

Here, Ginny alluded to the political dimensions of her own and African Americans' shared history: slavery, it is suggested, connotes inferiority and, therefore, unfitness to marry whites. The next moment, though, Ginny pointed to white complicity in perpetuating this status: "we brought them over."

While Ginny described herself as being more accepting of "Spanish"-white relationships, this might be an after-the-event rationalization for the fact that her daughter's husband is of Filipino-Latino heritage. Ginny's view of interracial relationships is complicated, and the terms of analysis shift constantly from biological to cultural to social to historical grounds and back again. But this shifting takes place around a fixed limit point. For contradictory as her analysis is, her conclusion was firm: Ginny was not in favor of Black-white sexual or marriage relationships. Here, the notion of a taboo—with its connotations of a firmly held belief or conviction not necessarily amenable to rational argument—is apt.

In Ginny's narrative, the image of the "mixed" child rejected by both sides was subsequently supplanted by the rejection of the child by one side—the white. That the child should be accepted as Black rather than white fits in with a cultural and legislative history that constructs whiteness as a biologically pure category. The desire for racial purity and the power to enforce it by defining out people of diverse ancestry have in fact largely been preserves of white Americans.[16] In common parlance, a person whose parents come from two different ethnic or racial groups will be identified by reference to the nonwhite, subordinate, named, or marked group rather than the dominant and therefore normative white heritage: "She's part Native American" and "I'm half Jewish" have a much more familiar ring than "She's part white." Only if all of a person's ancestry is nonwhite will the whole be listed, as in "She's Puerto Rican Chinese."

A lack of attention to racism is thus implicit in the view of both the racially mixed child and the interracial couple as "rejected by both sides." True, an interracial couple may face opposition from both sides, although I heard more tales of rejection by white families than by families of color, and at the same time I heard several tales of warm acceptance by families of color. Perhaps an even more important quesion is whether opposition from a family of color should be viewed as exactly mirroring that from white families, or whether each should be set within different, but linked, trajectories.[17]

The failure to mention racism signals an absence of any sense that interracial sexuality, and perhaps life in general, are politicized terrains. All these stories, rather than holding society responsible for the problems of "mixed" children or adults, blame the parents. Likewise, while Ginny, Irene, Marty, and others all noted and applauded progress toward greater acceptance of interracial relationships and "mixed" children and adults, none cited any reasons for this change, viewing it rather passively as a natural process (perhaps as part of an inevitable march of civilization?). In contrast, as the next chapter will show, women actually in interracial families frequently drew attention to the impact of racism on their relationships, on their partners, and on their children.

A key theme of these conversations about interracial sexuality is the setting and marking of boundaries. This took two forms: addressing the degree of proximity permissible between white and nonwhite people, and assessing "degrees of difference" between whites and people of color. In the latter regard, it was striking that, in contrast to a discourse on masculinity that was most explicitly hostile to African American men, these women seemed at times to be equally negative about all interracial relationships, and especially about the fates of all interracial children. At the same time, some did argue that there were degrees of racial difference. Thus, Ginny Rodd had accepted her "part Spanish" son-in-law, but still strongly objected to white-Black marriage. Evelyn Steinman, a political conservative around Ginny's age, pondered this question too, agreeing that "people" find white-Mexican relationships easier to accept than white-Black ones. Comparing both with white-Asian relationships, she said:

> It's funny that the stigma always seems to be with Blacks and . . . to a certain extent the Chicanos, the Mexicans. Those seem to be the two, because people will accept a mixed marriage between an Oriental and a Caucasian much more readily . . . I guess because the skin tones are more similar . . . and maybe—it's a known fact—Orientals are bright people, the brightest in the world, if you want to categorize them intellectually.

Degrees of similarity and difference are in the eyes of the beholder, constructed by a history of ideas. Tested against reality, the idea that all Asians are intelligent (a stereotype, though not a derogatory one) would not hold up any better than the idea that the degree of similarity of skin color between white, Asian, Chicano, Black, and Native American people is fixed. Moreover, its social meaning is the more important question here, because there is no a priori reason why color (the factor Evelyn Steinman cites) should be a significant factor in the choice of a sexual partner.

Closely connected to the question of boundary marking is the concept of purity; its opposite, impurity, is implied in anxiety over racially "mixed" children. And purity, in its turn, implies difference, not just of experience or of culture, but of essence, or being. It is an anthropological truism (but perhaps a misleading one) that this kind of boundary marking might be understood as a "universal" attribute of cultures, based on groups' tendency to consolidate their own identity in contrast and opposition to others.[18] This formulation obscures more than it explains, however, since it does not ask why, here, "race" comes to serve as a criterion of differentiation. Culturally specific rather than culturally universalist arguments are, it seems to me, more useful in this regard.

An explanation of contemporary racial boundary marking in the United States must look in part to the historical context sketched at the beginning of this chapter. Centuries of economic, legal, political, and cultural processes reinforced one another to produce and maintain white-initiated, selective hostility toward interracial relationships. Since 1967, interracial relationships have been definitively constitutionally protected, but, as in other spheres of life, legal protection does not by any means have a direct or immediate impact on cultural norms. Interracial relationships symbolically challenge the boundaries of communities structured by race and culture—but more than that, publically acknowledged and socially sanctioned interracial relationships challenge a hierarchical structuring of racial and ethnic communities that supports an economic hierarchy organized in part along racial lines.

The previous chapter, on what I called the social geography of childhood, indicated the infrequency of close, nonhierarchical interactions between people of color and white people in the United States. Given a society that is more racially segregated than (quasi-) integrated, and given the generalization that people tend to find sexual and marriage partners within, rather than outside, their class, community, and religious groups, it is perhaps not surprising that interracial relationships are the exception and not the norm. In the narratives discussed here, however, such relationships are not merely exceptional. They are a focus of anxiety, disapproval, and taboo. Alongside concerns about the social and cultural problems that racially "mixed" couples and children may experience are arguments that turn (implicitly or explicitly) on notions of essential, irreducible differences between racial groups.

In this chapter I have shown some of the ways in which white women are inscribed within the discourse on interracial relationships, at times speaking unself-consciously from within the terms of the discourse; at other times analyzing the extent to which they were raised with, but now reject, its assumptions; and on occasion analyzing their own incapacity to think outside a universe of discourse that they recognize as premised on racism. In the following chapter, I shift from talk *about* interracial couples to talk *by* the white members of interracial couples. While the discourse against interracial relationships is part of the context for these women's experiences, their experiences also further a critique of the discourse.

5

Race, Sex, and Intimacy II: Interracial Couples and Interracial Parenting

[In San Francisco in the 1980s] there was no way we could escape from the outside world. It was like the outside world was in our bedroom. . . . Racism was in our bedroom.

> —*Jeanine Cohen*

[The] hardest thing to deal with is his constant awareness of his race. It's not a conflict, but something that you have to feel with that person. . . . He's so aware in everything he does, feels judged. This whole thing racism does to people—I have to share that. It's not a burden, but something you can't lift off and be free of.

> —*Sandy Alvarez*

When I had my kids [in Sacramento in the early 1960s], I'd be put into wards with Latina women and Black women because of my name. Which was fine, but I just thought it was really interesting!

> —*Donna Gonzaga*

We've been together for seven years now. We're always constantly growing, together. We always love, a lot of times, the same thing, in terms of music, food, culture, entertainment, friends, everything. We're constantly growing, in that kind of way.

> —*Louise Glebocki*

In this chapter I reexamine the terrain of race, sex, and intimacy from the point of view of white women in primary relationships with partners or children of color. Their stories provide a different perspective on the discourse, both underscoring its impact on white women's experience and further revealing the complexity of white women's relationships to it, but also foregrounding elements less visible from the "outsider" perspective. These narratives also bring into sharp relief the context of racism in which interracial relationships take place.

Border Infractions: Rejections, Negotiations, Symbolic Resolutions

In chapter 4, I argued that hostility toward interracial relationships hinged on constructions of racial and cultural differences as absolute, and of families and communities as monoracial and monocultural. It is not surprising that most of the white women in heterosexual interracial relationships spoke of family pressure against them, often applied early in the couples' relationships. Several had relatives who refused to attend their weddings, and others spoke of being "disowned." Both gestures have high symbolic value, and both, I suggest, are geared specifically toward symbolic resolution of the contradiction posed by the arrival of a nonwhite addition to an all-white family.

Refusing to attend a wedding suggests a refusal to witness and thereby endorse the public entrance of a stranger—here a stranger of the "wrong" kind—into the family fold. The public nature of the occasion may be crucial. As Frieda Kazen talked about her marriage in the early 1970s to an African American man, for example, it became clear that her mother's private and public behavior were at odds. Frieda's mother, and all her mother's relatives, refused to come to the wedding, while her father and his family did attend, but:

> My mother called every day the week before the wedding to see if there was anything I needed. After the wedding there was no more she could do, so she accepted it.

Once they were married, Frieda and her husband visited her parents frequently ("Sundays, we often went to my parents' house and then to his"). Here, the public-private dichotomy is dramatically illustrated and an apparent rejection of Frieda's husband seemed to have been rescinded immediately after the ceremonial proceedings were over. Although Frieda commented that "it wasn't pleasant" for her husband, she also noted that her mother was "nice to him, to us."

It is also worth looking closely at Frieda's account of the substance of her mother's objections to the marriage. Frieda noted that she and her mother had argued before "over the same thing." From the context, this seemed to mean dating and socializing with African Americans. "But," Frieda added, "getting married is rather different." Her use of the phrase "*is* rather different" rather than "*was* rather different" suggests to me that she was making a normative statement, that Frieda shared her mother's assessment of interracial marriage as a violation of a cultural norm, though she obviously responded to it differently. The importance of group and ethnic boundaries was indicated in Frieda's speculation that her mother's family would have liked her to marry a "conventional Jewish man." Marriage to any non-Jew might have provoked concern, but Frieda viewed it as a more specifically targeted opposition, saying, "My mother's people . . . were more uptight, racist." "Uptight" here suggests a tightly defended group boundary, an inflexible adherence to cultural norms. Finally, interracial marriage was linked with other activities assessed as marginal by Frieda's mother:

> My parents were afraid of what would happen to me because I was nonconventional. My mother has never liked me traveling in left circles.

Marrying a Black man may thus have been viewed by Frieda's mother as a "left-wing" act (compare Chris Patterson's childhood view of white girls who dated Black boys as "radical" or "cool").

Being "disowned" at times carried financial consequences. Margaret Phillips, from an upper-class family, said that she almost lost the inheritance of a large piece of land as a result of her son's choice of a Jamaican partner. She explained that her father unexpectedly threatened to reapportion the land among other (male) family members immediately after being informed by Margaret's mother of their grandson's "transgression" (Margaret's term). While her father did not explicitly mention it as a factor, Margaret saw the two events as almost certainly connected.

Beyond its economic aspect, the act of disowning makes the statement that "you are no longer my child," a symbolic severing of genealogical ties to a family member who has, in the parents' eyes, joined the "wrong" genealogical group. Like refusing to publicly acknowledge a marriage, disowning attempts to resolve a perceived contradiction or impossibility—the tying together of two groups seen as utterly separate—by rejecting and symbolically "unwhitening" the white family member. As elsewhere, a biological view of race difference lurked within these dramatizations of the impossibility of a white/nonwhite connection. This was evident in the disapprobation Dot Humphrey faced when she adopted a child who is racially mixed:

I knew my parents wouldn't like it. They didn't. They've never treated her the same as they treat my son, partially because she's Black and partially because she's adopted. The two together make her way out there.

"Way out there" is apt: Dot's daughter was viewed as irremediably distant and different, impossible to incorporate within the boundaries of the family.

The impact of actions like these on the women I interviewed depended on the quality of prior family relationships. For women not close to their families, rejection might cause amusement or anger, but not too much pain. For others, though, continued negotiations with the family over invitations (or noninvitations) to family gatherings such as weddings and Thanksgiving dinners were extremely painful. For Suzie Roberts, who, at the time of the interview, was in a relationship with an African American man, such events caused confrontations with some family members, anxiety and questioning about the honesty of others, and feelings of divided loyalty in relation to the family on the one hand and her partner on the other. Suzie's story of her sister's wedding (which took place just over two years before our conversation) spelled out the complexities:

SUZIE: My parents came up for the wedding, they met Vince, and they flipped out (laughs) completely.

RF: Did they know he was Black before they met him?

SUZIE: [No] . . . I just don't talk about those kinds of personal things, I don't talk about my boyfriend with my parents. . . . It was just that my sister invited him to the wedding, so his name was on the invitation. About two weeks before the wedding, my dad met Vince, and then about a week later, he wanted to have a private talk about this. I was really taken by surprise. I know they really freaked out when I was with Rodrigo [her children's father, a Mexican man], but he was such a jerk that I thought, well, that's why they freaked out. But I'm older now, I'm my own person, and I did not expect them to flip out at the *sight* of somebody!

RF: So what happened?

SUZIE: My dad took me out for coffee . . . and said, "You know, it's going to upset your mother when she sees Vince." . . . He was trying to tell me that when we choose partners that are so different from ourselves, it alienates people we love. And that it was alienating him and my mother for me to be doing this.

RF: So how did you respond?

SUZIE: I was really angry, . . . controlled, . . . crying. . . . I just said I felt like I'd grown up in a real void, there was no sense of coherence within our family, we all couldn't stand each other, I mean, all we did was fight. . . . I told him I really resented that, and whenever I find somebody with a strong family background, it's important to me. I kind of lashed out, and said some really low things about the way I'd been raised. . . .

Anyway, my dad asked me to not bring Vince to the wedding, because it would be upsetting. And he also intimated that my sister hadn't invited Vince. That I had just assumed. . . .

So I was angry, I went home, and I had a real hard time. I didn't know if my sister really had not meant to invite Vince . . . [or] had talked to my dad about it behind my back. I talked a little bit about it with Vince. I said, "Why don't we just not go? I won't go and you won't go." And then he thought I was being a big—what's the word?— no backbone. I was just giving up and wasn't standing up for myself, and that I didn't respect him enough to bring him. So I got it from him. He was telling me he couldn't count on me when things were rough, that he'd never be able to count on me. I still didn't know about my sister. So I called her up. It took me a few days to even get the courage. . . . She just told me, "Suzie, Vince is invited to the wedding. We invited him because we wanted him to come, and don't even think any other thing." . . .

The way it all turned out was, we came to the wedding. Vince and I had a nice time. . . . My parents really did an avoidance thing with us. They weren't around that much. And it went OK.

But Suzie described a huge conflict that took place "all under cover" after the bride and groom had left because a friend of Suzie's sister took charge of the cleanup and thereby offended Suzie's mother. The friend was a lesbian and, according to Suzie, her mother had a "feeling, there was something she didn't like about her."

After the wedding Suzie's parents took the family out for dinner but didn't invite Suzie. Her oldest sister, who had stayed at Suzie's apartment for the wedding, left on bad terms after Vince stayed overnight there:

SUZIE: She kind of walked around the house being hostile, and left on a really sour note, just saying, "You people in the Bay Area are crazy. And I'm never coming up here again!" . . .

RF: Do you think that was because of Vince?

SUZIE: I think it was, three-quarters of it. But she was also pretty pissed at this woman who'd "taken charge."

> I still to this day haven't unraveled what went on. . . . It took me a
> long time to get over that, feel forgiveness at all.

About two weeks after the wedding, Suzie's father wrote to her, apologizing, but after reading the letter once, she put it away in a drawer, unable to think about it further:

> He got much more personal than he'd ever been, and he told me a story
> about when I was a little girl, and how I was independent and able to be
> my own person, and how he hadn't been able to see that until now.

Although the confrontation over the wedding brought her relationship with Vince into the open, Suzie still lived a painful double life:

> This last Christmas was really hard, because of that, too. Because I
> wanted to see Vince, I wanted to spend time with him. But my parents
> were staying with [my sister], so I had to go [there] and see my parents,
> and then I'd come home around ten and call Vince and he'd come
> over. . . . I felt like I was having an affair. And he wasn't involved at all
> in anything I did or the kids did, during their vacation.
>
> I feel like I'm an impostor, with my family and with Vince. I'm just
> trying to please everybody. . . . For my parents I'm being a unit, a
> single person, who isn't able to talk about anything having to do with
> my feelings or my personal life . . . and then with Vince, I'm pushing
> him out of—just to protect everybody I'm keeping him out, too. And
> not being fair, or truthful. I just feel like a big phony.

A particular constellation of family expectations gives shape to this situation. In beginning her story, Suzie described herself as not having an emotionally intimate relationship with her parents, so that the question of her "boyfriends" never came up. However, Suzie's father took his discovery of her relationship with Vince very personally, speaking of being alienated (cut off, driven away) and upset. Suzie responded with the counteraccusation that there never *was* a family closeness from which she could now alienate her parents. But there is ambivalence here, both on the father's side and on Suzie's: Suzie's father, whatever *his* sense of the family's closeness (and we have only Suzie's assessment of it), felt within his rights to protest Suzie's relationship with a Black man, and to try to stop her from bringing him to a family occasion. Like the strangers and schoolteachers we met in chapter 4 who attempted to "save" white women from their partners of color, Suzie's father saw an interracial bond as grounds for suspension of a norm of nonintervention. For her part, Suzie, although she was angry, continued to try to please and protect her family as well as her lover, at considerable emotional cost to herself.

Suzie and her father shared an assessment that there is a contradiction between participation in the family and participation in an interracial relationship. (Of course, while the father viewed this as reasonable, Suzie did not; both, then, felt themselves to be in the right.) Suzie twice described her relationship in terms of her "personhood," as opposed to her family membership. Thus, Suzie said that as "my own person" she did not expect her parents to "freak out" in relation to this, her second interracial primary relationship. Her expectation, then, was that family intervention should cease with maturity. Her father placed Suzie in a trajectory in which she had *always* been independent, her own person rather than the family's person, using this realization to make Suzie's behavior intelligible. The implication here is thus that the interracial relationship would be inexplicable had Suzie not been different and autonomous in relation to the family. And it was perhaps with this in mind that Suzie's father questioned whether his other daughter could really have invited Vince to the wedding.

As in other stories, it was a formal demonstration of family solidarity, a wedding, that precipitated the crisis. Suzie's parents, consciously or unconsciously, felt that an African American man had no place in that group. His presence was conceived as upsetting not only to Suzie's mother, but also to the patterning of the occasion and that of the kinship group. Unable to prevent the couple's participation, the parents found an uneasy resolution to the contradiction he represented, symbolically making the couple absent by avoiding direct contact with them. And in another moment of symbolic resolution, Suzie was stripped of kinship when her parents excluded her from the "family" dinner after the ceremony.

This story offers some interesting crosscurrents and parallels between interracial and lesbian sexuality. Suzie's mother and her oldest sister (not the marrying one) were apparently disturbed by Suzie's partner *and* by the lesbian friend of the bride. Both strike a discordant note in the context of a white, heterosexual norm. Suzie's sister's parting shot—"You people in the Bay Area are crazy"—may refer to the San Francisco area's well-established and well-known gay and lesbian community, as well as to other aspects of its radical history. The appellation "crazy" connotes a perceived loss of rationality, control, and normalcy in behavior and an evaluation of both interracial and lesbian sexuality in these terms. The struggle over inviting the partner, Suzie's enforced double life, her pretended singlehood, and the family's claiming the right to approve or disapprove not the partner's character but the mode of sexual practice itself are fully parallel to the experience of many gay men and lesbian women.

Suzie took upon herself the burden of resolving these contradictions, attempting to maintain connections with both her partner and her family. Her pain and anxiety are clear in her tears, her dread of telephoning her sister, and her sense of guilt and failure. (There is stress and pain for the partners, too. I focus here on white women and their families because it is the women with whom I talked about these family dramas.) Suzie's attempt to resolve the conflict amounted to splitting herself: posing one moment as a family member without a partner and the next as a partner without a family. No wonder Suzie felt as though her life was based on pretense!

There is an element of blaming the victim in Suzie's father's claim that Suzie was "alienating those she loves." For, of course, it was her parents' evaluation of the relationship, rather than Suzie's actions, that gave rise to their feelings of alienation. Suzie had no doubt that it was Blackness per se that her parents objected to; her previous partner was "a jerk," but her father reacted at the mere sight of Vince. Regardless of personal attributes, Blackness constituted irremediable, alienating difference. In this context, Suzie's attempts to "protect" everybody were complicated: who was being protected, and from what? It is tempting to argue that, among other things, Suzie was protecting her parents from feeling the effects of their own prejudice.

Both Suzie's and Frieda's stories make interesting comparisons with the accounts of the possible fates of biracial couples offered by the women I quoted in chapter 4. On the one hand, the basic elements of the discourse are same: the marking of boundaries by symbolic actions; the insistence on an immutable difference and distance between white and nonwhite groups to the point where white relatives, confronted with boundary infractions, responded by placing their daughters *outside* the kinship group; a view of interracial relationships as socially unacceptable; anxiety about the fate of white women who get involved in them; and a view of those women as morally reprehensible or (the other side of the same coin) radical.

But on the other hand, in these accounts of actual relationships one sees evidence of flexibility and room for maneuver that contributed to making the relationships viable. Even in the generally disapproving families there was complexity and fluidity. Thus, Frieda's mother came to accept the relationship, at least in private. Suzie's family was divided, her parents' hostility partially offset by her sister's acceptance and support.

Racism: The External Force

In stark contrast with the language of the discourse against interracial relationships, white women in relationships with men or women of color named and discussed racism: its impact on their partners, its "rebound effect" (my term) on the women themselves, and its impact in structuring the relationships.

Interracial partnerships frequently heightened white women's awareness of societal racism. Donna Gonzaga, born in 1944 into a working-class family, met and married Ernesto in her final year of high school. As a man of Portuguese heritage, Ernesto might otherwise have been considered "white," but his skin was dark, and in Donna's words, "My mother saw me as marrying a Negro." And as Donna spoke of her life with Ernesto, it was clear that Donna's mother was not the only one to view him as a person of color.

In any case, Donna was aware of the disparities in their situations:

> DONNA: His mother was on welfare, and he was one of five kids. So even though I was working class, having a hard time, I just really saw a certain kind of cultural difference and class difference, by virtue of their ethnicity.
>
> RF: Did you know that it was their ethnicity that was connected to that?
>
> DONNA: Yeah, I did. Because I knew I was poor too, but I knew it was different and I knew I had more advantages than Ernesto did. And he knew it. There was a way that he was attracted only to white women because he wanted out of his situation. . . .
>
> He was on probation when I met him. The police—the probation officers—were coming to our house every month for the first couple of years that we were together. . . . And the police would come to his mother's house. I just had never been around so much . . . police

involvement and interference, and so much "system" stuff, you know, and I just felt it had to do with the fact that they were Portuguese and dark-skinned.

Donna's involvement with a partner positioned differently in the racial order of the United States brought into sharp relief both his situation and her own. In blaming racism rather than Ernesto's family for their high levels of involvement with "system stuff," Donna differed from her mother, who was embarrassed to be linked to a family on welfare. By contrast, Donna translated the welfare connection into another instance of state intervention.

Louise Glebocki also answered in the affirmative my question about whether she thought her close connections with Chicanos gave her a different perspective on things. She offered as an example the fate of her boyfriend:

> They put him in a mentally retarded class, . . . where people got high all day and partied. And in fact he's not very stupid. He ended up graduating from college. . . . But that was the direction they put a lot of people. Basically to a large extent they had your life already worked out—"You are going to be a janitor. You're going to work on cars"—because they had a lot of auto mechanics [classes] for the Chicano guys and the poor whites. And for the women, "You're going to be a good housewife."

In effect, close relationships with people of color created a particular social geography for these women, bringing an intimate connection to racial oppression. As working-class white women, Donna and Louise both had personal experience of economic hardship and inequality. Both made an explicit connection between class and race as axes of hardship—but both insisted that racism had a specificity of its own, so that the working-class people of color they met were even worse off than their white counterparts.

In a middle-class context, Frieda Kazen also brought up the issue of racism, noting that her African American partner and his (also Black) co-worker were "never promoted, not going anywhere." Further underlining the importance of the issue, Sandy Alvarez interrupted my questions about cultural differences to emphasize that:

> [The] hardest thing to deal with is his constant awareness of his race. It's not a conflict, but something that you have to feel with that person. . . .

He's so aware in everything he does, feels judged. This whole thing racism does to people—I have to share that. It's not a burden, but something you can't lift off and be free of.

Racism: The Rebound Effect

In suggesting that racism "rebounds" on white women in inter-racial relationships, I am thinking of a force that owes its existence and direction to an earlier aim and impact, yet retains enough force to wound. The impact of racism on white women is prem-ised on, and shaped by, its effects on their significant others of color; but though it is related, the impact is neither identical to nor merely a weaker version of the original impact: it is qualita-tively new. And while it is hard to measure pain, it is safe to say both that the racism that rebounds on white women has spent some of its force in the original impact it made on their nonwhite partners *and* that white women nonetheless feel its impact.

A first example of rebounding is the experience of sharing or empathizing with a partner's pain. As Cathy Thomas put it: "Even if our experience is secondhand, it's still our experience." Cathy argued that white women not in close contact with people of color have less impetus to examine their unconscious racism:

> They live in a white community; they don't live in a mixed community
> so they don't have to deal with, you know, loving somebody who
> might in fact really want to go off someplace and cry, or might want to
> kick your teeth in for a [racist statement]. They are not exposed to that.

Beyond empathy, racism directed toward partners also had a material impact on white women's lives. Donna, for example, de-scribed the harrowing experience of her husband's being in a se-rious car accident in rural northern California in the early 1960s:

> DONNA: They wouldn't put him in the ambulance, they wouldn't take
> him to the hospital for a very long time, until the bile started coming
> out of his mouth, because they didn't know what he was. . . .
>
> RF: So, like, if he was Black, they wouldn't take him to the hospital?
>
> DONNA: Right. They didn't know which hospital to take him to. . . .
> They eventually took him to a general hospital, to where they take
> people who don't have insurance [which he did, Donna said later]. . . .
> And they left him on the emergency table until his insides were coming
> out of his mouth. He had a hole in his duodenum. I got up there and
> they had finally performed some kind of surgery. But he almost died.

Donna explained that her husband's condition actually deterio-rated after surgery, when he developed bedsores and other com-plications. She finally brought him back to their home city, where he was operated on for a second time and eventually recovered. She had learned something from the incident:

> There I was, pregnant with my second baby, and I was at that time twenty years old. So that was a real lesson around racial stuff.

Here, although the discriminatory practices of the health care sys-tem were not actually directed at Donna, they nonetheless had an impact on her. In other instances, Donna was, in effect, treated as a woman of color:

> When I had my kids, I'd be put into wards with Latina women and Black women, because of my name. Which was fine, but I just thought it was really interesting!

Of course, these women's departures from their own racial posi-tions and identities were symbolic or temporary: they were not permanently "unwhitened." Were Donna to return to her unmar-ried name, for example, she would not be placed in hospital wards with women of color.

Finally, a white woman's relationship with a person of color may be invisible to people who don't know her well, and this produces its own ironies and frustrations. Cathy Thomas, for ex-ample, told me about a racist comment that was made to her:

> You wouldn't believe this white woman, what she said to me. *She didn't know who she was talking to.* (Emphasis mine)

Racism: The Pressures Within

Given the racialized matrix of U.S. society, it is not surprising that race and racism affect the internal dynamics of primary rela-tionships. The women I interviewed did not, however, talk about straightforward replication of racist hierarchies—stereotyping, emotional or physical abuse of people of color by whites—but raised more complex issues. One was the struggle to relate as in-timates and equals in a society that refuses either possibility. In a second dynamic, problems in the relationship were played out in racial terms. A third scenario was the (impossible) desire to resolve or transcend individuals' differential positioning as persons of color or white, in the context of intimate relationships. Surrounding all these dynamics were varied political moments and environments. I will look at three relationships in detail here, two that took place in lesbian feminist contexts where racism was being addressed in specific terms and a third, heterosexual relationship that was set against the earlier backdrop of the shift in the 1960s from an "integrationist" rhetoric to the language of Black Power and separatism.

Jeanine Cohen spoke to me about her eight-year relationship with a Black woman, Lucinda, which took place in the late 1970s and early 1980s:

> Here I was relating to another woman, and she's a woman of color. And the impact that had on our dynamic wasn't because of, necessarily, what we were doing between each other, but because of what was going on out in the world, and what that was doing to us. And that's where it hurts. . . .
>
> I'm trying to think of something specific. I think that it's generalized because of what we both brought into our situation on the basis of what is going on out there in the world, and each of our individual relationships to it. You know, my guilt, her anger.

Here Jeanine clarified the impact of external social context on the internal working of the relationship. "My guilt, her anger" came not from personal actions but from their being white and Black, and aware of societal racism.

A second form of external pressure arose in choosing social networks, for these too were shaped by a racially divided social structure. Jeanine said that there was a question

> JEANINE: . . . for both of us, you know, moving in what circle? It's like, in a Black circle, it's unacceptable—
>
> RF: —to be a mixed couple?
>
> JEANINE: Yeah. On some level. And, it's like, in that circle, then, feeling like I didn't exist. In a white circle, it's all the trappings of racial privilege that for her could be very frustrating.

The problems named here express two sides of the same coin: on the one hand, the race privilege of white people; on the other, the anger of people of color, who may reject white people in response to racism and race privilege. Given this context of inequality, Jeanine remembered

sometimes feeling that she could never really be open to me, because I
was a white person. The way sometimes [in past relationships] I felt I
could never really open myself because the person I was relating to was
a man.

The parallel here is, of course, between racism and sexism, between white people and men as representatives of the oppressor
class, regardless of their individual characteristics. Jeanine described the extent to which race consciousness became heightened
for her, so that at times she felt

JEANINE: . . . very tuned into her reality, . . . sometimes more than my
own, you know, of like, how she was experiencing the situation. And a
lot—and there, I think, is another element of guilt—taking
responsibility for it. It's like, we'd go into a situation, if it was all white,
I'd feel acutely uncomfortable—for her. . . . And I'd want to protect her
from the impact of that situation. I'd want to make it all right for her,
basically. Oh, God.

RF: But you couldn't.

JEANINE: No. It was so intense.

For Jeanine and Lucinda, it was clearly impossible to operate as
racially neutral individuals: given a racially structured environment—and their sharp political awareness of it—race politics
were threaded through the two women's lives with an intensity
that seemed painful for Jeanine, even as a memory. Jeanine's sense
of guilt or responsibility for all-white environments she did not
create suggests a process of shuttling back and forth between selfhood and group membership. As Jeanine analyzed her relationship with Lucinda, she pointed to the ways her own personality
and ethnicity shaped her responses to racial pressures:

JEANINE: I played out this very maternal role anyway in our
relationship, and that, sort of, just fed into it, it was, like, another
aspect. But, yeah, it was ridiculous. . . .
    I think it's also my own stuff around being responsible for the world,
sort of. Very Jewish—

RF: And very female, too.

JEANINE: Yeah. That's true.

Beyond being "Jewish" and "female," perhaps Jeanine's guilt and
sense of responsibility in response to racism were also shaped by
her feminism. Her response was "female" in that socialization into
"caring" roles often creates in women a heightened capacity for

empathy, an ability to, in Jeanine's words, "tune in" to the reality of loved ones and dependents. Women are also, of course, encouraged to be protectors and caregivers. The contradiction—what in Jeanine's words was "ridiculous"—was the impossibility of Jeanine as a lone individual protecting her partner from the weight of racism, a long-standing and pervasive social reality.

Jeanine's reaction was "feminist" in the sense that, for feminists, the personal is also political. This means, for one thing, that one's very sense of self and personhood are seen as socially constructed and, for another, that one has the responsibility to work for social change with, and as part of, groups with whom one shares ascribed characteristics and social positions (whether simply as women or, more recently, in more restricted identity groups: working-class women, Latinas, white women, and so on). It was, perhaps, this sense of the ultimate inseparability of the individual from the group that created Jeanine's feelings of guilt and responsibility.

Jeanine was, however, able at least part of the time to maintain a distinction between the racism of the wider culture and her own responsibility. She said:

> When [Lucinda's] anger and frustration about racism started coming out at me, I would challenge her, and say, "When I am directly racist towards you, fine. But when I am not, I'm not going to be the target for your anger and frustration."

Jeanine's ability to make this distinction depended on a complex political analysis of racism as a societal and an individual issue. By contrast, for Debby Rothman, only a teenager at the beginning of her eleven-year relationship with Stuart, her African American partner, this kind of analysis was absent. As a result, Debby felt that accusations of racism became a cover for problems in the relationship and that the fear of, in her words, "feeding others' racism" kept her in the relationship longer than she would otherwise have stayed. Debby and Stuart began dating in high school. Both were part of a racially mixed (Black, white, Asian), rebellious, and politically active friendship group: "Beatniks were beginning to fade and the hippies hadn't quite come in yet. It was all fomenting in that group." After high school they moved in together. Stuart was drafted and sent to Vietnam; he returned suffering from what sounds, from an outsider's perspective, like post-traumatic stress disorder. Debby described the eleven-year sweep of the relationship:

> There were times when, in the early days, when we were still involved with this group of friends, and it felt so right. I really enjoyed it. In no way, shape, or form, at fourteen, was I thinking of getting into a long-term relationship. I wanted to have fun, have a boyfriend, do teenage type things, all of that, and it rather rapidly got into something much heavier than that, in a very overpowering sort of way.
>
> I felt very much that I had entered an alien world, distant from my family. . . . Their world seemed so attractive to me. I really yearned for just doing fun things, and laughing and having fun as a family, going to a concert or a movie, whatever. We hardly ever went anywhere, because he was growing paranoid, particularly after he came back from Vietnam. He hardly ever left the house. . . .
>
> I felt a combination of fear, I felt sorry for myself, I felt really caught up in something that I had to get out of. . . . In the beginning, standing together against the world, suffering together, was part of the romance. But later when things got really bad, I lost that.

Thus far, this story of a deteriorating relationship does not appear to be specifically racialized. Debby's "alien world" did not stem from racial or cultural difference but from her partner's mental ill health. The partners could well have been two white people or, for that matter, two Black people. What "racializes" this story is the extent to which the couple's consciousness of racism shaped their responses to the situation. Debby said that, for both of them:

> It was hard to separate the individual problems from the societal or racial ones. The racial problem was obvious—it was obvious that we couldn't even talk about relationship problems without it taking on racial tinges.

Although the relationship ultimately became physically violent, Debby said:

> There was no question that, not just to leave, but even to deal with the problems was made a racial issue. Asking to be treated better was like asking to be treated better because I'm white.

Here, either one partner or both defined the situation in terms of Debby's "racism." But elsewhere, Debby assessed her situation in relation to a broader definition of racism. For example, part of Debby's feeling of alienation and distance from her family and others came from her choice not to confide in anyone about her problems. She explained:

> Part of not talking to people was a racial thing. I was afraid it would fit
> into people's beliefs that these things can't work, or that Blacks are
> terrible people, or whatever. There was a sense of having to protect him,
> protect the idea of this. I was very, very conscious of that.

In other words, Debby's awareness of hostility toward interracial couples made her feel that a great deal rested on the success or failure of the relationship, beyond its meaning for her and her partner. As with Jeanine and Lucinda, one senses here that it was difficult to avoid relating as representatives of racial groups.

The changing style of antiracism further complicated the picture:

> When I first met Stuart and his group of friends, integration, freedom
> rides were the big thing. . . . Equality and integration were the key
> words. . . . While Stuart was in Vietnam, the Black Power movement
> was growing, things were changing. It was difficult for both of us to
> deal with. He was torn between betraying his race and finding it difficult
> to accept more violent expressions of hate. . . . Things in the Black
> community—he was attracted to it, but it was not part of his
> upbringing as a man to throw his girlfriend or her family to the winds.
> He was going through all kinds of things. I think it would have been
> amazing if the relationship had worked out, given our age and the
> circumstances.

Once again, gender intersected with race in shaping a relationship. Stuart felt torn, it appears, between competing modes of antiracism and racial belonging and their implications for appropriate male behavior. Beyond this, his emotional and physical abuse and Debby's effective acceptance of it fell into a stereotypic male-female pattern. Similarly, Debby's desire to be protective, whether of her lover or of the ideal represented by their partnership, is a distinctively female one. These gendered patterns intersected with the politics of racism and antiracism.

Cathy Thomas's story unfolded two decades later and was equally a part of its political moment. Cathy's relationship with Miranda, a Chicana, happened in a place and time—the San Francisco Bay Area in the early 1980s—when feminism, and the lesbian-feminist community with which Cathy identified, were being increasingly criticized as "racist." Women of color were collectively making their voices heard in feminist communities, rejecting the predominance of white women in the feminist movement, articulating an analysis of racism, and celebrating their own colors and cultures.

As we talked, Cathy described her attempts to come to terms

with this critique both during the relationship and after it ended. The two women had broken up about six months before our discussion, when Miranda left Cathy for a Chicana. Cathy's description of her involvement with Miranda was slanted by the context of the interview and therefore only a partial telling. Nonetheless, it became clear that the relationship had been the grounds for an attempt to resolve both Cathy's and Miranda's questions and ambivalences about their racial positioning. Cathy described the reasons they were drawn to each other:

> The reason that Miranda and I fell in love so deeply, and one of our greatest bonds, was that for some unknown . . . reason both of us have a stake in working out our trips about race. Because she was raised basically . . . in a Mexican household, grew up as a Chicana in East L.A. and had an incredible cultural wealth, including her native language. . . . She also had a really ambitious mother, who is really . . . into the trappings of a successful American life. So basically, in some ways she was raised to be a good white girl, and to never stand out as a Mexican, to be able to mix with white people and stuff like that. And . . . because I have such a long, broad streak in me about being responsible, racially, in whatever contorted or mixed-up way, I did definitely get word about it as a kid that I was responsible somehow, or at least involved in racial things. So we had a lot of motivation to work through it.

Cathy described Miranda as having been raised within a Mexican cultural context, yet also encouraged to fit into the dominant white culture. Cathy put it strongly: the notion of Miranda being made into a "good white girl" suggests concealment of a Mexican cultural self in exchange for potential gains in class position. Miranda's struggle seems, then, to have been connected with the question of who and where to be, culturally.

Here Cathy alluded only briefly to her socialization regarding race. Earlier in the interview, though, she talked about a childhood in which her father had been verbally very racist, while her mother had from time to time placed Cathy in situations where she was intended to help people of color. For example, as a seven-year-old, Cathy had been given the task of teaching reading skills to an adult Mexican man supervised by Cathy's father at work. The notion of a "contorted or mixed-up" sense of responsibility referred to Cathy's feeling, as an adult, that her "helping" projects had been inadequate and even patronizing.

In her early twenties, as a lesbian feminist, Cathy had been, she said, outspoken and politically confident—a confidence about

which she had later become disparaging. Her ideas were challenged first by students of color at the university she attended,
leading to new realizations about her racial position:

> [I thought] I had the line on everything. And then I found out that I
> didn't. . . . I started to see that just because everybody didn't talk like I
> did, it didn't mean they didn't have anything to say. And the reason
> maybe they didn't talk like I did was because I *did* talk like I did. And so
> I started to learn about apportioning space and stuff like that. And that
> was all tied in with learning about the world being made up of more
> than one kind of person, i.e., white. It was all in the same lesson.

Encapsulated here is a recognition of one way in which white
women may dominate feminist discourse, setting the terms and
mode of discussions and not providing conceptual or auditory
space for the viewpoints of women and men of color. Thus, if
Miranda brought to the relationship a need to work through the
politics and cultural meaning of being Chicana, Cathy was becoming more conscious of the position of dominance associated
with being white, as well as continuing to grapple with the question, carried over from childhood, of how to be "responsible"
with respect to racism.

The response to these combined trajectories was, Cathy felt in
retrospect, not a good one. Part of Cathy's attempt to resolve her
relationship to racism, as a white woman, was to become as involved as Miranda in living out day-to-day aspects of Chicano
culture:

> It's a little indicative of where we were in our respective places about
> race, and exactly how we identified, because the first time Miranda
> played salsa for me, I really grooved on it. And she admitted to not
> having listened to it very much. But pretty soon, that's all the music we
> were listening to. We ate a lot of Mexican food. We spoke a lot of
> Spanish. I was signed up, culturally. I was like I was at my mother's
> knee.

Cathy suggested here that in some ways Miranda was learning
about Mexican culture alongside Cathy, but for the most part,
Cathy viewed herself as learning from Miranda, not vice versa.
The maternal analogy evokes a process of resocialization that, at
the time, felt total to Cathy. But the process of immersion
brought new problems, both for the relationship and for Cathy.
Having grown up in California, Cathy began to learn Spanish in
high school. From Miranda, Cathy gained a working knowledge

of the language—as she put it, again using a maternal analogy, "at her knee." Cathy's ability to speak Spanish came to epitomize a dynamic whereby Cathy's increasing "fluency" as a Chicana of sorts threatened Miranda's sense of her own cultural authenticity:

> I think she started to feel like that was maybe threatening her, maybe undermining her definition of who she was. It was the only thing that made her different from me in the way she was brought up. We were brought up similarly along class lines, in terms of our parents really getting into telling us what fork to use, . . . how you eat with the rich and how you mix among them and they can't tell who you are.

Reading between the lines of Cathy's account, it seems that, given Miranda's concerns about having been urged to "assimilate," the similarity that Cathy sought to create ran exactly counter to the sense of difference that Miranda needed to maintain.

There was no reciprocal sense in which Miranda consciously learned and adopted aspects of Cathy's ethnic background. By the end of the relationship, Cathy and Miranda were able to articulate consciously their feeling that in a society where white culture is dominant, such a move would have felt tantamount to Miranda assimilating to white culture—and this in a political context where the cultural singularity of Chicanos and other people of color was being cherished and celebrated in defiance of "assimilation." From Cathy's point of view:

> I was so completely eclipsed by the enormity of [Miranda's] reality, and it was so psychologically important to me to discover what her reality was about, that the notion I might have one was completely invisible.

Why was Miranda's culture, her "reality," so encompassing for Cathy? And why was it psychologically important for Cathy to try to inhabit it? The answers, I believe, have to do with Cathy's particular response to the political moment of feminist antiracism in which she was participating (see also chapter 6). The end of the relationship brought with it a retrospective sense of the impossibility, for Cathy, of "living as a Chicana." She read to me an entry from her journal from just after the breakup:

> This second identity, this adopted culture of mine was falling away from me, lying at my feet in a thousand pieces, exposed for the illusion it must be. . . . And here I am again, just another alienated middle-class white girl with no culture to inform my daily life, no people to call my own.

The words *second* and *adopted* suggest that Cathy was something else previously. The vision of her adoption of Chicanahood as an illusion rather than a real option suggests, once again, that biological belonging determines cultural belonging. But Cathy's statement that, as a "white girl," she has "nothing"—no culture, no people—in a sense undoes the biologism. To see "whiteness" as "nothingness" is to see "whiteness" as a cultural void (see chapter 7 for further discussion of this point) and to reject white culture and white racial positioning. This rejection, both emotional and political, follows from Cathy's recognition of the racially dominating aspects of whiteness in general, and from her feminist consciousness in particular. Regarding the lesson she learned about "apportioning space" to people of color, Cathy said, "I learned it too well, and completely moved over." In transferring these lessons into the relationship, Cathy said that her commitment was

> to let [Miranda] go as far as she wanted to in describing her experience, in describing what racism is about because she had never really been given leave to talk about it, or think about it. . . . And I sort of traded any kind of loyalty I had to myself or to my ethnic attitudes for the ability to go with her on that leg of the trip. . . . I wasn't supposed to go because I'm white . . . but basically I did go, . . . because I loved Miranda, and I wanted to support her. And I knew what she was doing was true.

Corresponding to the need to "apportion space" differently was Cathy's desire to give her partner conceptual space for describing her experience and describing racism. The notion of a "traded loyalty" speaks to an idea that to be white is inevitably to be racist and, further, to have no part in the process of examining or challenging racism. Cathy acknowledged that, by avoiding connections to other whites, she could occupy a liminal or exceptional space (my words) as "the only white girl with her head worth talking to" (her words). By contrast, to connect herself with whites would be to share responsibility for their racism, which would in turn expose the potential of hers. In a different form, this raises an issue present in Jeanine's and Debby's stories: each sensed a very present link between herself and white people as a group.

Further, a dramatic inversion seemed to have taken place in Cathy's worldview. Rather than just qualifying her earlier feeling that she "had the line on everything," at this later point she saw herself as by definition "wrong": the truth lay with Miranda and other women of color. In another act of inversion, Cathy described herself in her journal as "middle class"—a reduction of her status as a woman who, although she was college educated, grew up in a home that was actually upper working or lower middle class, rather than simply "middle class" (the latter implying greater class privilege).

Cathy, like Debby and Jeanine, described an attempt to withstand and respond to racial inequality in the context of an interracial relationship. All three relationships were marked by the wider social context of racism, and "local," radical analyses of it. The women and their partners shuttled back and forth between a sense of themselves as partners in a dyad and identification as members of larger racial, ethnic, and political communities. As white women committed to antiracism, all three found themselves attempting the impossible: to resolve or contain racial inequality in the context of their relationships. And all three relationships, given the self-awareness of all *six* partners as racial actors, ultimately collapsed, apparently at least in part because of the burden of this task. (I cannot incorporate the perspectives of Lucinda, Stuart, and Miranda since I did not interview them.)

Having said that, though, it is important to reduce neither the relationships nor their demise to racial issues alone. Debby and her partner faced the unresolved issues of his mental illness and physical violence, for example. And the relationships all took place when the partners were young: at their start, Debby was fourteen, Cathy twenty-one, and Jeanine in her early twenties. While all three relationships ended, they all lasted for a substantial amount of time: Debby and Stuart were together eleven years, Cathy and Miranda four years, and Jeanine and Lucinda six years.

It is also important to note that while these particular interracial relationships ended, others did not. Thus, for example, Suzie Roberts's relationship with Vince, Frieda Kazen's relationship with her second husband (also African American), Louise Glebocki's relationship with her partner, and Sandy Alvarez's marriage continued to thrive. In fact, Frieda described her relationship as "the most comfortable I've ever had." And Louise said of her relationship:

> We've been together for seven years now. We're always constantly growing, together. We always love, a lot of times, the same thing, in terms of music, food, culture, entertainment, friends, everything. We're constantly growing, in that kind of way.

"Difference" Revisited

The refiguring of the significance of racism is but one of the ways in which, by looking at white women's actual experience of interracial relationships, one gains a sense of the discourse as having an impact on, but neither explaining nor containing, interracial couples' lives. Another piece of this discursive package in need of close examination is the image of interracial partners as always different from each other, specifically in terms of race or culture. In chapter 4, a number of women spoke of the difficulties that would be involved in surmounting cultural differences between two partners and their families. Implicit was the assumption that in any interracial relationship or marriage both partners emerge out of racially and culturally homogeneous families and networks, so that any crossracial peer connection would be a radically new departure. However, a more complicated picture of culture and class as axes of difference but also of similarities between partners emerged in talking to women in "mixed" relationships.

Just over half (six out of ten) of the women who had chosen biracial relationships had started life in families whose kin and social ties were racially homogeneous.[1] Helen Standish, Frieda Kazen, and Suzie Roberts came from monoracial families that were disturbed by their daughters' involvements with men of color. But there is more to the story. For one thing, each family and its individual members had different trajectories of acceptance and rejection of the relationships. For another, what emerges is *not* a picture of families meeting their daughters' partners and then being stymied by insurmountable cultural differences. Rather, families reacted to the *idea* of a racially different partner. Perhaps not surprisingly, the three women whose families were committed to antiracist politics (Jeanine Cohen, Sandy Alvarez, and Debby Rothman) had also grown up as part of more racially diverse social networks. These families were fully supportive of their daughters' primary relationships with people of color.

There was, then, a continuum of family connections outside their own ethnic and racial groups and of family acceptance of interracial relationships. Even further along this continuum was Louise Glebocki, from a family where relationships between white and Chicano men and women were not at all exceptional. Even analyzing them in terms of the out of the ordinary seemed to her to be inappropriate:

It's hard because I haven't thought about it in a long time, but now that I think about it . . . I come from a big family, they are either married to Chicano, Mexican, or a couple of my cousins are into Black guys. A couple lesbians. Another guy went the other way—homosexual. (Laughs) No one went the route of being—on my mom's side anyway—on Dad's side, back East, you'd see more of that white bread and mayonnaise kind of life.

Unlike Suzie Roberts's family, Louise's was not liable to be upset by the introduction of someone of color. Her long-standing involvement in Chicano culture also meant that, when I asked her about being in a "bicultural" relationship, she replied, "I never thought of it as that."

Louise's story thus calls into question the certainty that there will be cultural difference in an interracial relationship. In another instance, Frieda Kazen, who is Jewish, asserted that because both she and her partner came from New York, and because Jewish culture is prominent in New York, the two of them actually shared a degree of cultural similarity. Also, Frieda's ten years of involvement in teaching and community activism in Harlem and elsewhere in New York meant that she had had close Black friends before she met her husband.

Other women *did* experience a sense of cultural difference but did not necessarily view it as negative. Suzie Roberts and Donna Gonzaga, for example, both appreciatively described the Mexican, African American, and Portuguese families they had entered, contrasting the warmth of their spouses' extended families with their own smaller and emotionally colder nuclear ones. Women also talked of other axes of difference and similarity, naming class background and level of education as areas of commonality or divergence. The question of cultural difference, like that of family support, thus appears to be more complex, more dynamic, and more fluid here than it did in the voices we heard in chapter 4.

What about the Children?

In my discussion of the discourse against interracial relationships in chapter 4, it was clear that, if some of the women were critical of interracial couples, they were even more critical of the idea of those couples having children. They suggested that children whose parents are of different racial or ethnic heritages would be "mixed," not accepted by either of their parents' communities, and as a result would have a difficult time. I argued that these ideas depend on notions of belonging or identity as fundamentally based on biology, of racial difference as absolute, on the presumption that cultural communities exist entirely separately from one another, and on an exactly symmetrical distaste of all cultural communities for one another. Within this discourse, children emerge as "victims" punished for, in Ginny Rodd's words, "something their parents have done" (thereby, of course, construing interracial relationships as in themselves wrong or perhaps, more specifically, "sinful"). Given all of this, many of the women I quoted in chapter 4 felt that biracial couples should not have children. (As I noted in chapter 4, I am uncomfortable with the term "mixed" in relation to race, because it seems to found notions of racial identity on terms that are not only biological rather than social, political, or historical, but also *simplistically* biological. However, I am at a loss to think of an adequate alternative. "Biracial" and "bicultural," for example, seem to preclude the possibility of an individual's being linked by birth to three or more communities. I will continue to use the term "mixed"—but in quotation marks to remind the reader of its limitations.)

As with other dimensions of the discourse against interracial relationships, it is possible to assess this one in relation to the narratives of the women whose children are of bi- or multiracial heritage. Sandy Alvarez and her husband, who is Chicano, had a son in elementary school and a daughter in preschool at the time of the interview. Dot Humphrey's daughter, Frances, whom she adopted at birth in 1969, was the child of an African American father and a white mother. Frances was fifteeen at the time of the interview. Suzie Roberts's son and daughter, eleven and nine at the time of the interview, were of Mexican and white (Jewish) heritage. (Donna Gonzaga also had two daughters, adults by the time of the interview. They did not figure much in our conversations, so I will not be drawing on their stories here.)

Analyzing these children's experience is complicated, first, by the fact that I have access to it only through their mothers' accounts.[2] Their situations are also complex inasmuch as they concur with but also challenge different aspects of the discourse against interracial relationships. On the one hand, it was indeed difficult for these children's parents to provide them with an environment that fully reflected their parents' heritage. And, insofar as one can judge from parents' accounts of their children's experience, the children whose parents came from more than one racial-cultural community *did* at times struggle over questions of their own identity and sense of belonging. Moreover, for these children and their parents, discussions of needs and of identity were articulated in terms that sounded "biological." Thus, for example, a child with one Black parent might be considered either Black or at least partly Black, whether or not the child was raised in a family that included other African American people. Thus, part of the struggle of children of "mixed" heritage was how to bring their cultural, social, and biological identities into harmony. It should be stressed, though, that when these women raised issues of "biological" belonging, they were as much concerned with the political and social effects of ascribed racial categories as with an axiomatic linkage between natal heritage and appropriate cultural context.

As long as concern is framed entirely within the terms of the discourse against interracial relationships, however, it remains limited as an analysis and misguided in its conclusions. For an examination of the struggles faced by children of "mixed" heritage and their parents suggests the need to look to the social, economic, and political construction of race relations in the United States rather than to any simple or symmetrical tendency on the part of racial and cultural groups toward wholesale intolerance of other groups, of differentness, or of "mixedness." Moreover, the multifaceted impact of racism on *all* people of color shaped both the experience of these children (who in addition to being "mixed" are, of course, children of color) and their parents' concerns for their well-being. It is also critical to note that rather than being passive victims, children of "mixed" heritage emerged in their mothers' accounts as (depending on their ages) at times self-conscious about their situations and as active agents who made choices about how to negotiate their own identities.

Culture and identity were not, in practice, separable from other facets of individuals' situations. Issues such as the quality of ongoing relationships with parents and extended families affected the access bicultural children had to the different dimensions of their heritage. For example, Suzie Roberts's children were three and five years old when their parents' relationship ended. Their father kept in close touch with them at first, keeping them with him at weekends, but over time his involvement with them diminished. He began a relationship with a younger woman who resented the time and money he spent on the children. He also began to drink heavily, and the children witnessed physical fights between their father and his girlfriend. His contact with them finally stopped altogether, and at the time of the interview they had not seen him for two years. When I asked Suzie whether she had wanted to give the children a sense of their paternal heritage, she told me that there was no real context in which their Mexican heritage could be made meaningful. She explained:

> SUZIE: They know they are half Mexican, and I think they feel pretty good about that. [My son] keeps telling me now—now he's got this really strong Jewish identity—"I don't want to be half Mexican, I want to be all Jewish." But as they were growing up, yes I did. We kept it pretty strong. . . .

> RF: What do you think [your children's] relationship should be to [the Mexican] part of their identity, or their heritage?

> SUZIE: Well, I think it would be important for them to know the people in that part of their identity. Their grandmother died a few years ago. She was the person that *I* was linked with most, who I would like my kids to know the most, and, um, everybody else in that family, I don't know, they haven't really bothered to be supportive of us, or keep in contact, so it's pretty much split off. . . . I just don't feel any true cultural link with them, [for] my kids and myself. I always felt it was provided by their father. And I supported that, even after we split up. I supported them spending time with him and keeping that alive, but it just deteriorated. . . . They are at an age where they think they did something wrong. . . . So, and since they haven't seen him at all, I think that's when they, especially [my son] has really picked up the Jewish identity, and he really loves it. He feels strongly about being Jewish.

As Suzie's account makes clear, it is not possible to view culture or ethnic belonging as separable from other dimensions of experience. For one thing, in the context of their father's rejection of them, the children's rejection of his ethnic identity in favor of their mother's is understandable. Second, as Suzie indicates, it is difficult to engage in any significant way with a "culture" in the absence of daily, practical human connections with it. Culture and cultural belonging, in other words are concrete, not abstract, phenomena.

For both Sandy Alvarez and Dot Humphrey, the desire to provide contexts in which their children could identify with their fathers' Chicano and Black heritages clashed with issues of class. Quite simply, given a society in which racism is a key factor in the structuring of inequality, in which the vast majority of African

Americans and Chicanos are poor or working class, and in which there are, therefore, very few middle-class racially mixed communities or middle-class communities of color, both Sandy and Dot faced the choice of living either as class outsiders or else with limited access to the communities of color that were part of their children's heritage. The two families had made opposite choices: the Alvarez family lived in a middle-class, mainly white neighborhood, while Dot had lived almost entirely in working-class communities of color (or mixed communities) since Frances's birth in 1969. Neither of these decisions was fully satisfactory, either for the children or for their parents.

Sandy and her husband were both professionals. Sandy was a bilingual, Spanish-English teacher in a high school whose students were predominantly Chicano and Asian American. Her husband worked with teenagers in the juvenile justice system. I asked Sandy whether she and her husband made an effort to teach their children to appreciate both sides of their cultural identity. She laughed, so I continued:

RF: Or is that just something that is part of how they live their lives. I don't know, that might be an off-the-wall question. . . .

SANDY: No. Well, I mean we're not teaching them really about *either* culture, actually. My husband's the only one that goes into any long explanations of anything, with my son. I deal more on feeling levels, but I know he likes to teach about history, and things like that, which I guess would be balanced. But it's real important for my husband, for [my son]—he's older, so he's the one you can talk with on an intellectual level—for him to be proud to be Mexican, and to be proud to be—to tell you the truth, I think half of the reason he's really trying to instill this pride is because [my son] doesn't have any appearance of being Mexican, and he's not going to a Mexican school, and he's not going to really have a lot of cultural basis—part of me thinks he's trying to teach him not to be racist!

RF: Racist—?

SANDY: —against Mexicans, not thinking of himself that way. You know what I mean?

RF: Yes. Wait, no, I don't understand. Say that again.

SANDY: [My son] just looks like an Anglo, and he is half Anglo, and he doesn't want [my son] to be racist against Mexicans, not a Mexican being racist against Mexicans. Actually, you know, that's really an off-the-wall thought. And it's probably not—it's not even really the way I feel. I don't know why I even—he's trying to make him feel like he's Mexican. He's trying to make him feel like he's Mexican. When we

don't live where there are a lot of Mexicans, we haven't transferred him
to school where there are, which we wish—I mean, I would like to do
that, except that I want him to have neighborhood friends, too, and
don't want him to be on the bus an hour at either end. You know, if
there was a school here—But, see, there are Mexicans in his class. It's a
magnet school, so they bus some Mexicans out from [a different section
of town]. So it's not like he's totally isolated in an Anglo environment.
But by the time he goes to high school, I don't think we'll let him go to
[the local] high school, because it's all Anglo . . . and I don't think that's
good for anybody at all, but especially somebody that's Mexican, you
know, that you want him to identify more as being Mexican, my
husband does.

Ostensibly, the most startling aspect of Sandy's response to my
question was her suggestion of her husband's fear that as a light-
skinned Anglo-Mexican cut off from any Mexican community,
their son might actually take on the anti-Mexican racism that is
prevalent among whites in the United States. If this was indeed
her husband's fear, it suggests a conception of racial identity as
socially and contextually constructed and very different from the
"essentialist" or biology-based idea of identity implied in the discourse against interracial relationships. Also striking is the fact
that, having made this suggestion, Sandy took it back. It is unclear why—and it could well be that my being slow to understand
her point meant that she lost her self-confidence in making it. It
is also possible that she really changed her mind on this issue, or
that she suddenly felt disloyal, either to her son for implying he
might be racist or to her husband for implying he might distrust
his son.

   A crucial question emerges here: how is identity founded? On
the one hand, both parents are clear that, as the son of a Mexican
father and an Anglo mother, their son *is* as Mexican as he is
Anglo—that identity is hereditary regardless of social context. On
the other hand, the need to specifically *teach* him that he is Mexican, given that Mexican identity is not reinforced in his daily life
at school or in the local community, indicates that identity is not
guaranteed by heredity, but must also be *socially* produced, by
friends, community, and teachers. The household environment,
is of course, both Anglo and Mexican (in Sandy's terminology),
but since the rest of the environment reflects only one side of the
family's ethnicity, even the extra efforts of Sandy's husband appear to be a massive struggle against a current flowing in the
opposite direction. In this context, Mexican identity is in effect

sidelined into lessons about history, rather than being an organic dimension of daily practice.

It is also clear that Sandy, and perhaps her husband too, felt the need to weigh against other concerns (long hours of travel to reach school and friends) the benefits derived from contact with a Chicano community. This schism between Mexicanness and daily life takes us back to the notion of "social geography" explored in chapter 3. For while, in their working lives, both Sandy and her husband continued to move in racially mixed environments, the same was not true for their children.

In Sandy's view, a major factor limiting her children's contact with Chicano communities was, in fact, class. In the city where they currently lived, Sandy said, there was no middle-class or racially integrated Chicano community—as there was in Los Angeles, where she and her husband both grew up. (In fact, Sandy herself had grown up in *working*-class, racially mixed neighborhoods; see chapter 3.) Given their economic upward mobility and the stratification of U.S. society by race linked to class, the family's class and their racial or cultural identities were now in contradiction with each other: they could live among either their economic or their ethnic peers, but not both. Sandy was concerned about this, not only for her children, but for her husband too:

> SANDY: That's why I often think Santa Barbara would be *so* nice. The thing that would be nice about it for my husband would be that he would have Mexican peers. People that were college educated, that were working in the community, and, you know, wouldn't feel like such an isolated—
>
> RF: So you've thought of moving down south?
>
> SANDY: Yeah. Not because of the racist issue. Because for me, the warmth. (Laughs) That is a factor, though, that it would be nicer. But I wouldn't have a job, so— And it's more expensive to live. But it's warm there, and you can go to the beach. That's not relevant to you and your study, but it's relevant to me and my life!

In short, Sandy knew of few locations in the United States that would fully reflect the family's collective identity. And while she yearned to move to one of them, economic factors held them back. It is also significant that Sandy referred to the problem of context as "the racist issue," underscoring once again that the issue here is not that of all communities' inability to deal with outsiders, but asymmetrical hostility and the structuring of the economy and material environment by race and class hierarchy.

As the single mother of an adopted child whose heritage is both African American and white, Dot Humphrey, unlike Sandy, did not have a coparent who reflected the "other half" of her daughter's heritage. From the beginning, Dot had concerns about

> what I could provide her in terms of Black culture that, if she had been adopted by a Black family, she would have gotten. I felt that she would have gotten more of an ability to perhaps have someone who understood and had to deal with racism, knew how to deal with it better than I did. And that she might have more of a cultural identification.

One sees here, as elsewhere, the significance of racism as the critical but frequently unnamed term in discourses on race, culture, self and other, and interracial relationships. For "providing for Frances" culturally meant, in part, offering her tools to cope with racism. It is also important to note here the complexities embedded in Dot's words about cultural identity. First, identity is again linked to Frances's biological father's heritage, despite the fact that she had no contact with him. But here it becomes clear that belonging is indeed ascribed for, like it or not, precisely because her father was African American, Frances will be a target of racism. Second, it is unclear here whether Dot feels Frances should be "provided for" in terms of both African American and European American cultures or only in terms of African American culture. As Dot later pointed out to me, however, it was not necessary for her to make any extra effort to reinforce the white part of Frances's birth parents' heritage: it was readily available to her, from the dominant culture, from Dot herself, and from Dot's mainly white networks.

Given her concerns over both racism and Frances's right to be connected to African American culture, Dot felt it was crucial to live in neighborhoods and school districts where there would be Black adults and children in Frances's life. This was neither straightforward nor unproblematic, however. When Dot took Frances to play with other neighborhood children or to Black community events, she was frequently the only white person present. In such situations, Dot felt, both she *and* Frances's friends' mothers wondered what to talk to one another about! The issues here were not simply race or unwillingness to communicate across cultures, but the result of a clustering of factors, some linked to racism and class inequality and others not. As a lesbian, for example, Dot at times felt she had little in common with the

African American heterosexual women she met, as it were, through Frances. Moreover, unlike some of the other women I interviewed for this study, Dot had friendship networks that were, apparently, mostly white. Unfortunately, it was not only Dot who felt out of place or different in predominantly Black and poor neighborhoods, for her difference also affected her daughter. Dot said that for Frances:

> It's sort of a weird situation to be living in a neighborhood that's pretty much of a working-class and welfare neighborhood—in some ways it's almost the only mixed neighborhood that you can live in, in Oakland at least . . . and to have a mother who's sort of an intellectual. So that there's some ways in which I'm not really a part of the community. Although always in a neighborhood like that there will be one or two people that I really get along with. . . . But in general, I'm different from the other people in the neighborhood.

As Dot feared when she adopted Frances, there were ways in which Frances had to grapple with her racial identity that went beyond anything that her mother, as a white woman, had ever faced. For, through her growing-up years, Frances experienced a range of reactions to who she was from white people and from people of color, partly as a child of "mixed" heritage, but partly also as a Black child with a light complexion. As a small child in a Head Start preschool program in Baltimore, for example, she was favored by white and East Indian teachers because of her light skin and straight hair. By contrast, in elementary school in Oakland, she felt excluded as teachers praised the looks of children with darker skin and nappy hair. More recently, Frances's Black classmates had told her that she could not participate in the Martin Luther King Day celebration at school because she was a "honkie." These painful experiences seemed to have as much to do with the racism and "internalized racism" of those around Frances as her with bicultural heritage per se, again compromising and challenging the discourse against interracial relationships.

It is possible, once again, to complicate and recontextualize the discourse of anxiety over children of "mixed" heritage. As Dot continued to talk, it became clear that as Frances grew older she had also grown in self-confidence, making decisions about whom she wanted to associate with, given who *she* is in the world:

> It has been very hard for her—the feeling of never fitting into any place, and she talks a lot about other people being "like me." She will say, "I

need to be around other people who are *like me*." And that's a fairly
narrow group of people. I mean, she doesn't necessarily mean that you
have to be mixed, but if you aren't mixed, then you have to be in a
neighborhood in which your family has white friends. . . . By that she
means that kids who are in an all-Black social environment all the time
don't have the same sort of mixture that she does in her life.

I don't think she started feeling that until after she got to be eleven or
twelve. It seemed to take a big turn then. And I noticed that when she
went to . . . a school that was racially mixed, all of her new friends in
that school were Black. They were almost all light-skinned, and one was
mixed. And her boyfriend from that school was mixed. And all of her
boyfriends—I don't think she's had a white boyfriend that I know of.
They've all been either Puerto Rican or Chicano or Black.

Frances also, Dot said, exerted her authority at different times
in other ways, for a while refusing to discuss racism with her
mother. Dot explained that Frances has also handled her mother's
whiteness in varying ways, at times not wanting friends to meet
Dot because she is white and at other times using her mother's
whiteness to shock people. Frances was also, it seemed, very clear
about her own and her mother's racial and cultural heritage:

RF: I was thinking about one of these friends of mine [who is a white
woman with a daughter who is partly white and partly African
American]. I happened to go to a wedding that she also went to, and we
were sitting together. The name of the hall was Orion Hall, but
originally we had all thought it was Aryan Hall, which blew us all away,
because we couldn't imagine why anybody would have a wedding
reception in a place with a name like this. But she was joking with her
daughter about it and saying, "Oh, you and I would get thrown out of
this place if it was really Aryan," and was, like, joking around with the
whole issue. Is that something that has been part of it with you?

DOT: Right. But I couldn't say that to Frances, because if I said that
she'd say, "I'd get thrown out, you wouldn't!" She'd be quite blunt
about it. "Look, Mom, I'm Black, you're not!" She definitely does not
want me to pretend, which I think can be a tendency for white women
who are around Black people a lot, to pretend that you are part of this
culture, or whatever, but you really aren't. She doesn't like that. She
thinks that's false. . . . She herself never tries to sound Black. Her speech
is sort of halfway in between.

Frances's struggles are connected with but not limited to biracial-
ness, and her situation is different from that proposed by the discourse in several ways: Frances is not a victim, but a person acting
with thought and purpose in a difficult situation; not a person rejected by everyone, but a person who chooses connections with

people whose experiences are most similar to her own; not a person terminally torn between two cultures (although Dot described times when Frances has felt a great sadness about the limited extent of her connections to African American culture), but a person conscious of herself as specifically multi- or bicultural. Thus Frances is clear that she is different from her mother because she is not white, but also different from African Americans who do not have white people in their lives. Her identity, then, is both politically ascribed (with biology as the "alibi" for that ascription) and culturally crafted, not reducible either to whiteness or to Blackness, and also more than a simple addition of the two.

Conclusion

Racial identity and racism shape white women's lives: that is the repeated argument of this book. In this chapter I have explored that which is immanent in this book but for the most part not addressed head-on: the impact of racism on people of color in the United States. Looking at white women's primary relationships with people of color underscores how racial identities, race privilege, and racial subordination are constructed. I argued in chapter 3 that white women's position in a society that is racially hierarchical must be analyzed in relation to the subordinated positions of people of color, but that very frequently race privilege is a lived but not seen aspect of white experience, given socially segregated material environments and discursive environments that militate against conscious attention to racism.

By contrast, primary relationships with people of color are a context in which white women become much more conscious of the racial ordering of society. As the parents or partners of people of color, the women I talked with witnessed and experienced the effects of racism much more directly than most other white people. But, as chapter 6 will show, there are other routes to white awareness of racism. It is also true that, for many of the women, interracial primary relationships followed from, rather than precipitated, close connections with communities of color and knowledge about racism and race privilege.

White women in interracial primary relationships found themselves in changed positions in the racial order, albeit on contingent and provisional terms. The range of possible meanings of white femininity, for example, was transformed in interracial contexts.

Symbolically, these women's inclusion in their "rightful" places in the racial order seemed transformable too as, in their efforts to maintain race purity, white families questioned their daughters' membership in their natal families and communities.

As we have seen in chapters 4 and 5, these white women were "answerable to" the discourse against interracial relationships in multiple ways. As with other dimensions of the racial order, however, the discourses against interracial relationships and children of bi- or multiracial heritage neither adequately described their subjects nor fully constrained their lives.

6

Thinking Through Race

What does it mean to suggest that white women "think through race"? Given that in a sense this entire book is about how white women think through race, delimiting the scope of this chapter is a difficult task. In earlier chapters on childhood and on interracial relationships, I have explored the mutual constitution of material environments and conceptual frameworks, arguing that while they are in constant interplay, they are analytically distinguishable from one another.

The relationship between people and discourses that emerges from these narratives is complex and multifaceted. I have shown, for example, that white women's childhood experiences of the racial patterning of their environments did not simply entail direct apprehension of the material realm so much as a process in which material landscapes were experienced and given meaning through conceptual frameworks, through discourse. I have also pointed out that the women frequently reinterpreted their material landscapes over time, in effect remaking their experiences and seeing them, as it were, through new eyes.

In discussing interracial relationships (in chapters 4 and 5), I argued that racist discourses have a range of separable effects on white women's experience. Thus, for some women, a discourse against interracial relationships provided the framework by means of which they conceptualized and evaluated such relationships. Others found that same discourse inadequate and, in fact, wrong as an interpretive apparatus for understanding interracial couples' experience, operating instead as one of the "external" factors that affected their lives. For this latter group, the discourse (or, to be precise, the actions of others on the basis of their "belief" in the discourse) was in effect part of the material rather than the conceptual environment. And for still others, the discourse against interracial relationships was a conceptual apparatus with power to influence their feelings against their better judgment, as it were,

producing a mix of self-consciousness, self-criticism, and simultaneous complicity with elements of racist discourses.

These white women, then, were neither passive nor identical
to one another in the modes of their inscription into discourses on
race, but they were also limited within identifiable parameters.
Consciously and unconsciously, the women engaged with shifting
histories of race and racism as well as with shifting material relations patterned by race. In pointing to the historical roots of particular discursive elements (the aftereffects of pseudoscientific racism and antimiscegenation laws in shaping present-day responses
to interracial couples, the repetition of elements of colonial discourse in late twentieth century constructions of cultural authenticity), I have begun to suggest that conceptual transformation
does not take place randomly, but rather in response to what has
gone before and in the context of choosing among or challenging
preexisting discursive frameworks. In the present chapter I will
explore how white women think through race and pursue in more
detail questions about white women's inscription into discourses
on race difference.

The very use of the term "race" raises the idea of difference, for
"race" is above all a marker of difference, an axis of differentiation. What kind of difference race is and what difference race
makes in real terms are the questions that are contested in competing modes of thinking through race. Thus, for example, some
women said that race makes, or should make, no difference between people. Others discussed the significance of race in terms
of cultural differences or economic and sociopolitical differences.
The women also placed different kinds of value on "seeing difference": for some, seeing race differences at all made one a "racist,"
while for others, not seeing the differences race makes was a "racist" oversight.

The discourse that views race as a marker of ontological, essential, or biological difference—a discourse that dominated white
thinking on race for much of U.S. history and that I refer to here
as essentialist racism (see chapter 1)—is in many ways the absent
presence in these women's discussions of race and difference.
None of the women I interviewed described herself as consciously
or explicitly espousing the idea of race as an axis of ontological or
biological difference and inequality. However, I suggest that
much of what the women said about the kind of difference race
makes refers back to that mode of thinking through race.

Essentialist racism has left a legacy that continues to mark discourses on race difference in a range of ways. First, precisely because it proposed race as a significant axis of difference, essentialist racism remains the benchmark against which other discourses on race are articulated. In other words, the articulation and deployment of essentialist racism approximately five hundred years ago marks the moment when, so to speak, *race was made into a difference* and simultaneously into a rationale for racial inequality. It is in ongoing response to that moment that movements and individuals—for or against the empowerment of people of color—continue to articulate analyses of difference and sameness with respect to race. Thus, for example, when the women I interviewed insisted that "we are all the same under the skin," within what I have described as a color-evasive and power-evasive discursive repertoire, they did so partly in response to essentialist racism. Second, in significant ways the notion of ontological racial difference underlies other, ostensibly cultural, conceptualizations of race difference (see chapters 4, 5, and 7). Third, essentialist racism—particularly intentional, explicit racial discrimination—remains, for most white people, including many of the women I interviewed, paradigmatic of racism. This, as I have argued, renders structural and institutional dimensions of racism less easily conceptualized and apparently less noteworthy (chapter 3). Finally, although essentialist racism is not the dominant discursive repertoire on race difference in the United States, its corollary, racially structured political and economic inequity, continues to shape material reality. Given this, all of the women I interviewed were forced to grapple in one way or another with the material reality of racial inequality.

By pointing to an early and significant moment of essentialist racism in the United States, I do not intend to reduce all subsequent thinking to that moment. For while referring back implicitly to essentialist racism, these women also drew, for the most part much more consciously and explicitly, on later moments in the history of ideas about race and ethnicity in the United States. Centrally, I will argue that the majority of the women were in fact thinking through race within or against a second moment of race discourse. This moment, whose elements, I would argue, remain dominant in the United States today, is characterized by variations on color-evasive and power-evasive themes, which themselves built directly on the assimilationist theories that challenged essentialist racism in the first decades of the twentieth century. Some of the women also drew on elements of a third, race-cognizant, moment in U.S. race discourse that opposes both the first and second moments. For it articulates the new characterizations of race difference (including awareness of structural and instititional inequity and valorization of subordinated cultures) that emerged out of civil rights and later movements for the cultural and economic empowerment of people of color from the late 1950s to the present day.

These three moments—essentialist racism, color- and power-evasiveness, and race-cognizant reassertions and reorientations of race difference—can, as I suggested in chapter 1, be considered as the first, second, and third phases in U.S. race discourse in the sense that they originated in that order; however, past the point of their emergence they can no longer be conceptualized as unfolding chronologically in any simple sense. Rather, each, in different contexts, takes center stage as the organizing paradigm or retreats to the status of a repertoire that provides discursive elements but does not dictate overarching form or structure. From the point of view of white women thinking through race, these three moments together constituted the universe of discourse within which race was made meaningful, with elements combined and recombined, used in articulation with or against one another, and deployed with varying degrees of intentionality.

The challenge in talking about white women thinking through race is capturing the correct balance between their "entrapment" in discourse and their conscious engagement with it. The ways in which the women I interviewed combined or linked discursive elements were neither random nor necessarily original, but for the most part repetitive and linked to larger social trends and movements. At the same time, their process was frequently self-conscious and anything but naive. Some of the women had been active against racism either in political movements or in their workplaces, and for them conceptual frameworks were explicitly linked to social change. The notion of discursive repertoires seems to me to be an effective metaphor for this purpose, for it conveys something of the tension between agency and innovation on the one hand and the "givenness" of a universe of discourse on the other.[1]

The women frequently referred to the universe of discourse on race that framed the interview and their lives. At times they described the United States in terms of a changing scenario of race relations; some, for example, noted with approval the end of the Jim Crow era, and others expressed disappointment over what they perceived to be the separatism or "extremism" of autonomous movements of people of color. At other times they described *themselves* as changing, moving out of one mode of thinking through race and into another (for example, several southern-raised women described themselves as having moved from un-questioning acceptance of racial segregation to contact and friend-ships with people of color after moving to California). They also commented on their own shifting attitudes and worldviews: many white feminists described themselves as "waking up" from past unconsciousness of racism. Others very consciously set limits on their willingness to accept or participate in critique of racism.

The women's language and thought about race was idiosyn-cratic and individual. But again, idiosyncratic strategies were linked to the larger picture, whether consciously or not. Some of the women described (or enacted in our conversations) conscious decisions about how to talk about race in the context of their es-timation of the "racist status quo" in American society. For ex-ample, choices of how to name African American men and women indicated cognizance of how *girl* and *boy*, have been used as racist appellations for Black people. Thus, when Pat Bowen described her twelve-year-old African American schoolfriends as "women," she was, I believe, overcompensating for the possibly derogatory implications of calling them "girls." Sandy Alvarez, speaking of a Black "boy" who asked her out on a date in junior high school, was at pains to add that "of course he really was a boy then." In a similar vein, women named and renamed partic-ular groups in the course of speaking about them, vacillating, for example, among "Spanish," "Mexican," "Mexican American," and "Chicano." Each of these names evokes a particular moment in racial and colonial history, recalling the presence of the colo-nizer or the agency of the colonized in diverse ways.

Beyond the details of language, the struggle to deal personally with a particular dimension of the racial order seemed to run through some of the women's entire life stories. For example, as Debby Rothman spoke to me about racial tensions in her work-place, she repeatedly expressed her concern that, were I to write about her experience, I might discourage my white readers from participating in multiracial activity. This kind of concern over "damage control" given a racist society was a repeated theme in my interviews with Debby. She had hesitated to tell anyone about the physical violence in her eleven-year relationship with an African American man for fear of feeding whites' racist hostility, toward either Black men or interracial relationships (see chapter 5). She also described having once been mugged in Queens, New York: repeatedly questioned by white friends and relatives about the race of her assailant, she was relieved to have been able to report that although he was Black, so were the police officer who chased him down and the passers-by who stopped to help her.

"Thinking through race" has an intentional triple meaning in this chapter. First and most literally, it suggests a conscious process whereby the women I interviewed thought about race, race difference, and racism and about the impact of all three on themselves, on others, and on society at large. For some this process was already an ongoing part of their lives; for others it was occasioned by the interview itself. As this chapter will show, thinking about race at times led to self-questioning and had implications for political activism; at other times, thinking through race resulted in justifying the racial status quo and rationalizing the speaker's place in it. A second sense of "thinking through race" suggests that all present thinking about race must take place in an already constituted field of racialized relations, material and conceptual. In this regard, one task of this chapter will be to examine the ways in which modes of talking about race are articulated in relation to each other in a complex network of cross-referencing. Third, "thinking through race" implies thinking from within a racially identified body, thinking as a self that is racially positioned in society.

Color Evasion: Dodging "Difference"

Among the reasons to begin this exploration of discursive repertoires by examining color- and power-evasiveness is that it remains dominant in U.S. "public" race discourse. For many white people in the United States, including a good number of the women I interviewed, "color-blindness"—a mode of thinking about race organized around an effort to not "see," or at any rate not to acknowledge, race differences—continues to be the "polite" language of race.[2] Second, I want to suggest that color evasion actually involves a selective engagement with difference, rather than no engagement at all. Third, it is crucial to examine this discursive repertoire because of its contradictions: it has in its various guises been taken to be antiracist, but color evasion, with its corollary of power evasion, ultimately has had reactionary results through most of the twentieth century. It is useful, then, to follow the logic and pathways of color evasiveness through the women's narratives and to examine both the ways in which it has been deployed against essentialist racism and the ways it leads white women back into complicity with structural and institutional dimensions of inequality. In this regard, it seems to me that there are some salutary lessons to be learned about the new kinds of selectivity currently emerging in U.S. society—selectivities that apparently embrace cultural and other parameters of diversity, but do so in ways that leave hierarchies intact and, in this sense, remain as power evasive as their "color-blind" antecedents. (I will return to these points later.)

> To me, they are like me or anyone else—they're human—it's like I told my kids, they work for a living like we do. Just because they are Black is no saying their food is give to them [sic]. If you cut them, they bleed red blood, same as we do.

As I have argued, the women's strategies for talking about race difference often implicitly responded to *other* strategies. In her insistence here that African Americans are "human," Ginny Rodd referred to a recent past (both nationally and in her own life) in which people of African descent were, precisely, *not* viewed as human. But at the same time as it sought to undo essentialist racism, there was something chilling and distancing about the way Ginny voiced her opinion.

Ginny grew up and spent her early married life in rural Alabama, in the 1930s, 1940s, and 1950s. When she encountered Black people—infrequently, since she rarely left the farm—segregation was rigidly enforced in the ways that were common at that time and place. As Ginny said, euphemistically, the area was "strict on Blacks." "Strictness" in practice meant stringent controls on African American people: Black people sat in the back of the bus and whites in the front, white people refused to buy goods touched by Black people, and the town nearest to Ginny's family smallholding imposed a curfew on the Black population. In this context, Ginny's insistence on the common humanity of African American and white people was an explicit rejection of the essentialist racism with which she was raised. The blood metaphor Ginny used is crucial, for it located sameness in the body—precisely the location of *difference* in genetic or biological theories of white superiority. Further, of course, blood is under the skin, and skin has been and remains the foremost signifier of racial difference.

Ginny's statement that African Americans "work for a living, just like we do" was particularly significant, for throughout our discussions Ginny's articulation of her own identity focused on work and on her ability to work long hours and survive on poor wages. Thus, when I asked her to describe herself at the start of the interview, she began, "I've worked hard all of my life." Ginny several times critically measured others' prejudices against both African Americans and Latinos against her respect for them as workers who did jobs that white workers rejected. In this way, her description moved beyond cliché to an assertion of sameness based on what she held most dear about herself.

Ginny was not alone in emphasizing sameness as a way of rejecting the idea of white racial superiority. Irene Esterley, a native of Detroit ten or fifteen years Ginny's senior, told me that she wanted her grandchildren to meet people with a range of racial and cultural origins because "the more you do so, the more you realize there *is* no difference." A third example is seventy-three-year-old Joan Bracknell, raised in the Bay Area—as she put it, "an Okie from Oakland":

RF: So you think that's the best way to be—color-blind?

JOAN: Yes. Don't just look at them and immediately say, "Oh, I shouldn't like them."

Joan grew up in a working-class community in Oakland, the only child in an all-female household: herself, her divorced mother, and her widowed grandmother. The adults in Joan's family rented and ran a boardinghouse in a racially mixed (Black, Asian, and white) neighborhood; Joan helped out after school. It became clear through the interview that Joan did *not* claim not to see race differences so much as to take the position that either one should find something nice to say about every ethnic group or one should say nothing at all. She emphasized the importance in her adult life of "meeting people halfway" and described her reaction to the increasing presence of people of "other" ethnic groups in San Francisco with the words "So what?" She remembered being friends with a Black child at school who shared her first name:

> It was funny. There was the Black Joan and the white Joan.

Joan described her childhood sense of racial and cultural difference using an image drawn from the world of her favorite creatures—cats:

> I really don't think I even thought I was different from them. I just took it in stride—like a bunch of kittens—all of them are different colors.

There is, perhaps, a mixed message here: to "not notice" is different from "taking it in stride," which implies noting a potential obstacle but managing not to trip over it. The metaphor, on the one hand, clarifies the desire underlying Joan's position: an acknowledgment of differentiation that is innocent of hostility. But, on the other hand, the idea that noticing a person's "color" is not a good thing to do, even an offensive thing to do, suggests that "color," which here means nonwhiteness, is bad in and of itself.

White women who grew up before the 1960s came to adulthood well before the emergence and public visibility of the movements that emphasized cultural pride and renewal among people of color. During their formative years, there were only two ways of looking at race difference: either it connoted hierarchy or it did not (or should not) mean anything at all. Theirs was, then, a historically situated rejection of the salience of race difference. To expect women of Ginny's, Irene's, and Joan's ages to talk, particularly about their childhood years, in terms other than these is to risk the error of ahistoricity—to ask them to "preinvent" discourses on racial and cultural identity that did not emerge until much later.

However, it was striking that not only these older women continued to think about their lives in the 1980s in "color-blind" terms: much *younger* women did so also, underscoring the continued significance of color evasiveness as the dominant language of race in the United States. For many of the women, to be caught in the act of seeing race was to be caught being "prejudiced" ("racism" was not for the most part a term that this group of

women used). This automatic link came through in the words of
Marty Douglass, who was under thirty at the time of the
interview:

> RF: Do you remember the first time you noticed that somebody else was
> a different color from you?

> MARTY: I never paid that much attention. . . . I guess [my father] was
> prejudiced, in a sense, but we [kids] never became prejudiced. I'm still
> not prejudiced.

Given that within this discourse it was "bad" to see difference
and "good" not to, it is perhaps not surprising that more generalized images of innocence and guilt, purity and impurity also
came into play with respect to racism or "prejudice." Joan's image
of the youthful innocence of kittens was paralleled in this regard
by other women's linkage of innocence and guilt to youth and
age. Both Marty Douglass and Evelyn Steinman told anecdotes
that emphasized that their children were too young to be tainted
by racial prejudice. Evelyn described an encounter between her
son (then six) and an aunt that clearly captured this mental map:

> One day I came home [and] Aunty Jean had been taking care of him.
> And he, very, very serious, took me into the study, and he said,
> "Mother, Aunty Jean said something very bad today." And I said, "She
> did? Because she's such a sweet little person. What did she say?" He said,
> "She said 'nigger.' " . . . And he was so upset about this. And I said,
> "Well, honey, we have to forgive Aunty Jean, she doesn't really mean it
> the way it sounds," and I said, "We just must try to forgive her that.
> Because she's a very kind person, and she's very kind, to you and to
> me." All right, he would accept that. But that was very distressing
> to him.

The terms of Evelyn's analysis are as interesting as her conclusions. There are, in effect, two "innocents" involved. The "most
innocent" party is Evelyn's son, whose youthful virtue is established on two counts: first by his horror at Aunty Jean's language
and second by his willingness to forgive her transgression. The
second is Aunty Jean (not coincidentally also described as "a little
person"). Her use of racist language is "forgiven" or overridden
by her essential goodness in other spheres of life. A number of
possibilities are thus generated within the terms of the story, all
of which have both Christian and legalistic overtones. Children
are conceived as too young to be corrupt. Adults may be found
"not guilty" by reason of lack of intent, by recourse to a balance

sheet of good and bad acts, and by their honorary "littleness" (essential innocence). Finally, those who are "real racists" or, in the language of this discourse, "really prejudiced," who would by implication have to be adult and fully cognizant of their racism/ prejudice (essentially bad), are an absent presence in Evelyn's story.

Whereas earlier, seeing race meant being racist and being racist meant being "bad," causation here is reversed: a person who is good cannot by definition be racist, hence "little" Aunty Jean cannot really emerge as complicit with racism within the logic of Evelyn's analysis. This is an important moment in the color- and power-evasive repertoire, for this is the logic that undergirds legislative and judicial approaches to both workplace race discrimination and hate crime, placing the burden of proof on the intent of the perpetrator rather than on the effects of an event or situation on its victim(s). The issues of sin, guilt, and innocence resurfaced in some of the other women's attempts to think through the question of their own complicity with white power structures.

In a further permutation of the issue of innocence and guilt, Ginny Rodd told me the story of her father's horror at seeing a young Black boy beaten with a braided leather whip by white men in a small town in Florida after he inadvertently got off a Greyhound bus in "white territory." Ginny commented that "my father said it was the worst thing he ever saw. It would have been different if it had been a grown man." The burden of Ginny's story was that her father was a compassionate man, not given to the excesses of racism. But it has other, altogether more disturbing, implications. Suggesting that the child was innocent of being Black by virtue of his youth, it implies that Black adults are inherently guilty. This in turn implies that Blackness is "bad" in and of itself.[3]

The sharp cutting edge of color-blindness is revealed here: within this discursive repertoire, people of color are "good" only insofar as their "coloredness" can be bracketed and ignored, and this bracketing is contingent on the ability or the decision—in fact, the virtue—of a "noncolored"—or white—self. Color-blindness, despite the best intentions of its adherents, in this sense preserves the power structure inherent in essentialist racism.

This discursive repertoire intersects in several ways with liberal humanism as a philosophical discourse. First, it proposes an essential human sameness to which "race" is added as a secondary characteristic. This assertion of a distinction between selfhood and racialness makes it possible for white women to claim that they do not see the color, or race, of those with whom they interact, but rather see "under the skin" to the "real" person beneath. The notion of humans as composed of a core or essence to which other qualities are added later perhaps also helps explain the linkage of childhood with innocence or inherent purity, so that white children apparently cannot take on the role of racial oppressors and, at least by Ginny's reckoning, children of color cannot by definition be a racial threat.

The women's insistence that they did not see differences of race or color can be understood at least in part as an attempt to distance themselves from essentialist racism. I have noted too the antiracist roots of this mode of speech in the 1920s. In addition, civil rights leaders, including Martin Luther King, Jr., used elements of a "color-blind" discourse in demanding change in the the late 1950s and early 1960s. Dr. King dreamed of "the time when a man will be judged for the content of his character and not for the color of his skin."

The demands of the civil rights movement have yet to be met: character and merit are *not* the basis on which individuals take their places in a hierarchical social structure still organized by, among other things, race. As I have suggested in other chapters, race does shape meaning and experience, although for social, political, historical, and cultural reasons, rather than as a result of essential racial difference.

A generous interpretation of this color-blind discourse might see these women as confusing desire with reality, "ought" with "is." A more cynical view might see intentional evasion or denial. It is, as I have suggested, at times possible to sort out the former from the latter in these narratives. Perhaps more important, however, is to look at the results of thinking through race in these terms.

One concomitant of viewing people in terms of universal sameness overlaid with individual difference is the disinclination to think in terms of social or political aggregates. In these narratives, emphasis on the individual over the group either as cause or as target of racism had a leveling effect that made room for charges of discrimination against white people in institutional settings. Thus, Irene Esterley described her frustration at looking for a teaching job in a school district that was at that time primarily recruiting teachers of color:

> I resent it particularly because I feel that people should be considered for who they are as a human being and not as this, that, or the other—who you are, regardless of outside trappings—[there's an] inner person, shouting to get out.

Irene's commitment to respecting the individual in this context is more likely to work against greater racial equality than for it, leading her to overlook the *social* context for affirmative action programs that seek to remedy years of structured inequality and thereby promote expression of the talents and merit of individuals of color. Here we hit the limits of philosophical humanism, for it does not enable Irene to think in social or collective terms about the life chances of individuals.

Now You See It, Now You Don't: Difference and Power Evasion

These women's efforts to "not see" race difference despite its continued salience in society and in their own lives generated a fault line or contradiction in their consciousness. In this context, a number of strategies for talking about race and culture emerged, effectively dividing the discursive terrain into areas of "safe" and "dangerous" differences, "pleasant" and "nasty" differences, and generating modes of talking about difference that evaded questions of power. In this way, the women I interviewed grappled with and tried to pacify the contradiction between a society structured in dominance and the desire to see society only in terms of universal sameness and individual difference. The peace was an uneasy one, however, always on the brink of being disturbed.

A number of euphemisms used by these women appeared to serve the function of avoiding naming power. Evelyn Steinman, for example, consistently described Black people as "colorful," simultaneously acknowledging and dodging their Blackness. Some women used the familiar cliché "I don't care if he's Black, brown, yellow, or green," a phrase that camouflages socially significant differences of color in a welter of meaningless ones.

There were also at times hints at the possibility that, for some women, descriptions of people of color that evaded naming race (and therefore power) differences formed what one might describe as a "polite" or "public" language of race that contrasted with other, private languages. For instance, in talking to me, Ginny Rodd most often referred to her son-in-law, whose heritage was Mexican Filipino, as "Spanish," choosing an appellation that avoided drawing attention to his color and to the inequality between colonizer and colonized. At one point, however, she cheerfully described playful interactions between her "Spanish" son-in-law and his small son (Ginny's grandson) in which, as Ginny described it, they referred to one another affectionately as "Mexican."

As should by now be clear, difference was by no means a unitary category in these narratives, but was complexly subdivided. Irene Esterley provided me with an opportunity for close analysis of the naming of differences by reading a prepared introductory statement at the beginning of the interview and thereby setting, she felt, the parameters of relevance for our conversation. Irene's statement offered an inventory of constructions of difference marked by her age, class, and political viewpoint. Irene was probably in her early sixties. She had declined to give her exact age, describing herself instead as "mature." Her earliest memories were of the Depression years, when her family was poor. But by the time of World War II, her father had made enough money for the family to move to a wealthier neighborhood, and for Irene to attend an exclusive girls' school. Her statement ran as follows:

> IRENE: I was born and raised in the Detroit area, so there are very few cultures or races that I haven't been exposed to in my lifetime. During the years that I was growing up, the melting pot theory was . . . being used, so there was a lot of mixing up, and people didn't feel separate as much as they do today, with the different cultures and races feeling that they need to be completely separate to preserve their heritage.
>
> I went to the University of Michigan, which had the very first exchange program, so I also was exposed to people, maybe not personally, but of a foreign element. So I didn't think much about it. Then, since I've been in California I've done a lot of teaching . . . , so I was exposed to different races and cultures there also. So that just gives you a little smattering of why I feel I have been exposed to other races and cultures. And sometimes the two overlap.
>
> RF: Yeah. Well good. That gives me an idea—
>
> IRENE: —of what to ask me—
>
> RF: —of things to come back to.

IRENE: I have other notes and things. I did go through the Detroit race riot as well as the Watts race riot.

RF: Oh, OK. I'd definitely like to ask you about that.

IRENE: And I have had, you know, help, live-in, you know, had some Black ladies living in my home when I was a girl, so I—and other friends of mine—had Black servants. I went to the University of Mexico [on a student exchange program] where I lived with a Protestant minister who had Mexican maids in his home, so I've been exposed to that. But I don't consider that a different race, it's a different culture—

RF: Oh, I see.

IRENE: —and that's why I asked you how much you're talking about race and how much you are talking about culture or foreign people. . . . And then I have other notes here, of people I've met in the last few years that I felt were very interesting—some Chinese, one lady from Hong Kong that I learned some interesting facts from. So after you ask me questions, I can let you look at my notes and see if there's anything else you particularly want to . . .

RF: OK. Great. That's really helpful.

On the surface, the burden of Irene's message is proliferation and inclusiveness: much contact with many people, almost to the point of being blasé—"I didn't think too much about it." However, there is actually a highly variegated set of differentiations here.

The melting pot, race riots, and separatism are historical markers and also indicators of degrees of rapprochement and opposition between "different" people. Irene preferred the melting pot, with its connotations of intercultural communication, to the later moments. But later discussion clarified that she did not apply the melting pot and separatist images to the same groups. The melting pot involved her (German) family's connections with Scottish, Welsh, Jewish, and Anglo (in short, white) Americans, while separatism was a choice she associated with people of color.

There is a range of class and power relationships in the contacts she described: while the "melting pot," exchange programs, and friendships suggested peer status, the presence of live-in domestic workers and teacher-student relationships did not. The most obviously power-imbalanced relationship—that with domestic workers—was the cause, perhaps coincidentally, of the most hesitation and rephrasing. The choice of "ladies" is also a rephrasing of history, since white people probably referred to Black women as "girls" in the period of which Irene is speaking.

Irene assigns Others across a threefold classification of differentness, including racial others, cultural others, and foreigners, in a process marked by historical, political, and regional context. Thus, Irene named her recent Chinese acquaintances as cultural others or foreigners, but not as racial others. However, had Irene grown up on the West Coast of the United States, and had she encountered her Chinese friends not as tourists but as immigrants, she would more likely have named them in racial terms. The same is probably true of the Mexican people to whom she refers.

Her awareness of white ethnic identities was also a function of region and generation, of the incompleteness, in Detroit in the 1930s and 1940s, of the assimilationist project of the melting pot. As a child of German immigrants, Irene was also very conscious of her own cultural identity, which again marks her off from younger interviewees, for whom, as we will see in the next chapter, their cultural identities seemed more neutral than specifiable.

The only people Irene unambiguously views as an "Other race" are African Americans. This had to do in part with questions of power: not only were Irene's peers in a power-imbalanced and even oppositional relationship with Black people, but the relationship was an active one, ongoing in the community in which Irene grew up. By contrast, the power-imbalanced relationship between the United States and Mexico took place at a distance. But beyond the local, it is also true that "blackness" is historically a more consistently marked space of racial alterity than most others, from the standpoint of white selves. All of this underscores the historical, social, and political rather than "natural" content of racial classification.

It was striking that while Irene cheerfully discussed with me her interactions with "foreigners" and cultural Others, as well as her feelings about them, she approached talk about her relationships with African Americans much more cautiously. What becomes clearer about color evasiveness, then, is that more than evading questions of difference wholesale, this discursive repertoire selectively engages difference, evading questions of power. While certain kinds of difference or differentiation can be seen and discussed with abandon, others are evaded if at all possible. A comparison of the ways Irene constructs difference, beginning with her connection to Jewish culture, clarifies all of these points and makes them concrete.

Before high school, in the Depression years, Irene grew up in her grandmother's house, a member of the only non-Jewish family in a Jewish neighborhood. Irene spoke with pleasure of her childhood involvement with Jewish culture:

> The Jewish holiday [Hanukkah], they give you a present every day, and because my friends were getting a present every day, my mother and grandmother thought that they didn't want me to feel left out. So they followed the Jewish tradition, and I got a different present every day. And that was the best year I ever had!

Irene was familiar with Jewish food partly thanks to Miriam, a Jewish woman who was a boarder in the house. And Irene's grandmother, like their Jewish neighbors, bought bagels and matzos and made noodles:

> RF: So there were some similarities—
>
> IRENE: Well, it's European. But as far as that goes it could be that some of our family was Jewish before they became gentile. . . . After all, it's a religion, it's really not a race. . . . However, I feel very comfortable with the Jewish culture because of being exposed, I suppose.

What comes across first here is Irene's pleasurable connection with Jewish culture and her family's active role in enabling it. Similarities between Irene's own family and European (or Ashkenazi) Jews was perceived as possibly extending to kinship. Jewishness, for Irene, was thus a mutable category of belonging: Irene could travel into that culture and Jewish people could travel out. "Not a race" in this context seemed, then, to indicate impermanence and the absence of a biological basis. But Irene maintained a sense of difference from Jewish people, as her return to the "exposure" metaphor clarified. Further, Irene added, her parents definitely expected her to marry within her own religious and ethnic group.

Irene's descriptions of Black people were very different, as were her relationships with them. There was no sense, for example, of Irene or her family drawing on or sharing parts of African American culture. Her contact with African American people (not surprisingly, given the date and region) was distant, impersonal, class-imbalanced, and based at times on employment or patronage. The only African Americans who came into Irene's neighborhood did so as "help," that is, as domestic workers. Outside her own neighborhood, Irene had occasional contact with Black people when her grandmother's church held rummage sales, which always took place in the Black community.

In addition to a sense of social distance, Irene described her interaction with African Americans in more explicitly oppositional terms. She drew on the white "popular memory" of Detroit to tell an apocryphal story:

> When I was in high school we'd go downtown shopping. And I remember one day specifically I was going into the big department store, and they had the revolving door. And as I got in, this great big fat Black lady got in with me and I could hardly breathe, and I got through, and I thought, "Wow, that was crowded," and I found out afterwards that they had something called "push day," where, that day of the week, anybody who was white who was downtown, they would do something to harass them. And until then, that had never been a problem. And it wasn't too long after that that the Belle Isle race riot occurred.[4]

Irene's story seemed somehow to naturalize the Detroit race riot, to explain it in terms of Black "unruliness" rather than Black grievances. Irene spoke of inequality in a contradictory manner. She noted, for example, that in Detroit during her childhood years, African Americans did not have access to middle-class and upper middle class levels of income. Here, she was apparently recognizing injustice. But immediately afterward, she added that Black people "deservedly" had a reputation for destroying property, so that realtors were correct in keeping Blacks out of white neighborhoods.

It is perhaps not surprising in this context that Irene's description of the Detroit race riots of 1944 posed but immediately rejected the possibility that Black people had legitimate grievances. This ambivalence produced a description that was thoroughly self-contradictory:

> I really don't know what precipitated it. Because, as far as I know, I think that Black people had jobs, or work. I don't remember many Black people having the skilled labor jobs, however. They did mostly things like the gardening, domestic help, doormen, a lot of Black people working in the hotels downtown, and [as] doormen for the department stores. As far as in factory work, or skilled labor, I don't think there were many Black people involved in that, but then there were no Jewish people involved in it either. Jewish people would not do manual labor. Mostly the Jewish people were the doctors and the lawyers and the businesspeople.

Something other than a simple denial, a straightforward failure to take note of race and cultural difference, is clearly going on here.

For in fact Irene was quite willing and able—albeit apparently in-accurately, since she had grown up in a poor, Jewish neighbor-hood whose residents were presumably neither doctors nor law-yers, nor even business owners—to associate different sectors of the job market with different groups of people. Contradictions and nonsensical statements proliferated at the point of examining the variance in power and resources that those differences might have implied. Also striking here is the way in which the empiri-cal, daily evidence of Irene's life was overridden by anti-Jewish stereotypes, as she categorized Jewish people as wealthy profes-sionals despite the fact that she lived in a working-class Jewish neighborhood.

Because Irene could name differences only when they did not entail acknowledging differences of power, power evasion fre-quently led to a kind of flight from feelings. Irene's description of a Black neighborhood (in response to my question) was interest-ing in the way it seemed to repress potentially "bad" feelings about race difference:

> IRENE: There was one other Black area of Detroit . . . you had to drive through it to get to downtown, but nobody felt any fear.
>
> RF: Do you remember what you did feel?
>
> IRENE: Nothing! That was just the Black area.

Irene repeated this pattern at one point in talking about her re-lationship to the Jewish boarder in her grandmother's house:

> We knew she was Jewish and she knew we were Protestant, and that was as far as it went. There was no feeling of "I'm Jewish; you're gentile."

As we have seen, Irene's feelings went much further and deeper than a mere "knowing." Given what we already know about Irene's warm relationship with Miriam and others in the Jewish community, it is clearer in this instance that flight from feeling accompanies a desire to "not see" difference at moments when the act of noticing difference might involve noticing potential for mu-tual hostility or opposition.

This claim not to "feel" echoed Marty Douglass's axiomatic link between noticing color difference and being racist, described earlier in this chapter. As elsewhere, euphemism was an alterna-

tive to denial, so that Irene said there was no "strangeness" between her family and their Jewish neighbors.

Interestingly, in a society such as the United States in which
power and privilege are not organized in simple binary terms but
rather in more multifaceted ones, the same modes of speech by
means of which the women "evaded" cognizance of others'
oppression were sometimes turned back on the white women
themselves. Thus, some women, including Irene, talked of their
own experiences of marginalization or subordination by means of
a similar flight from feeling. Irene, for example, described it as
"interesting" that girls at the expensive high school she attended
shunned her as "nueva riche" [sic]. And in a dramatically self-
contradictory sequence, Dora Hauser, an eighty-three-year-old
Jewish New Yorker who had grown up in upper middle class,
mainly non-Jewish social networks, went out of her way to dis-
count the significance of any anti-Semitism she had experienced
during her childhood:

> RF: Some of the women I interviewed had experienced people making
> hostile remarks about their being Jewish.
>
> DORA: Well, people *always* make hostile remarks. But you didn't know
> these people, didn't pay any attention.
>
> RF: Do you remember hearing things, as a child?
>
> DORA:: No. If anyone said anything of that sort, my father would knock
> them down, frankly. He wouldn't tolerate it.
>
> RF: So it didn't come up in your school, for example?
>
> DORA: No. If it did, you took it as ignorance. Prejudice and ignorance.

Here, Dora contradicted herself several times, first denying, then
acknowledging, and finally minimizing or explaining away any
incidence of anti-Semitism. In another distancing move, she referred to herself in the second person.

If the sharp edge of color evasion resides in its repression or
denial of the differences that race makes in people's lives, power
evasion is a permutation of that repression: rather than complete
nonacknowledgment of any kind of difference, power evasion involves a selective attention to difference, allowing into conscious
scrutiny—even conscious embrace—those differences that make
the speaker feel good but continuing to evade by means of partial
description, euphemism, and self-contradiction those that make

the speaker feel bad. The latter, as I have shown, involved the naming of inequality, power imbalance, hatred, or fear. As with color evasion, one senses in some of these narratives a desire to overcome interracial hostility behind the impulse toward power-blindness. The outcome of this attempt, however, was frequently a lack of attention to the areas of power imbalance that in fact generate hostility, social distance, and "bad feelings" in general.

As we will see in the next section, other women articulated ideas about race difference that in many ways challenged and inverted the terms of this color- and power-evasive constellation, drawing in order to do so upon ways of thinking about race generated in what I have called the third moment in U.S. race discourse. However, I will suggest that some, though not all, of these women remained caught within the terms of power evasion. Further, as I will explore more fully in chapter 7, the process of selective engagement with difference continued to shape most women's exploration of questions about their own and others' cultural identity.

Race Cognizance: Rethinking Race, Rethinking Power

While the discursive repertoire of color evasion was organized around the desire to assert essential *sameness*, the discursive repertoire that I will here describe as race cognizant insisted on the importance of recognizing *difference*—but with difference understood in historical, political, social, or cultural terms rather than essentialist ones. As I will show, the race-cognizant women differed from one another in important ways. However, they shared two linked convictions: first, that race makes a difference in people's lives and second, that racism is a significant factor in shaping contemporary U.S. society.

While opposite in principle the color-/power-evasive and race-cognizant repertoires were by no means separable in practice. For one thing, these two repertoires in fact responded to one another's terms, so that, as we will see, some women described in explicit terms their own passage out of color-"blindness" and into race cognizance. Secondly, race-cognizant women, some more than others, continued to articulate their analyses of racism in dualistic and moralistic terms that deployed the structure of liberal humanism and elements of power evasiveness.

Perhaps the factor that most seriously compromises the possibility of couching a comparison of color and power evasion with race cognizance in terms of simple opposition is their very different political statuses and links to power. For while the former, as I have argued, is politically dominant, the positions that I am linking here under the heading of race cognizance are, largely speaking, marginal. The marginality or nonnormativeness of race cognizance, among white Americans and in public discourse, centrally shaped race-cognizant women's routes of access to this discursive repertoire, their modes of voicing it, and their degrees of self-consciousness about race.

Like color and power evasiveness, the race-cognizant discursive repertoire was traceable to particular historical moments and political movements: movements for decolonization in the Third World; post-World War II civil rights activism; the Black, Chicano, Asian, and Native American antiracist, nationalist, and cultural renewal movements of the 1960s and 1970s; and, finally, the articulation of distinctively feminist versions of antiracism initiated by women of color through the 1980s. Because of the non-hegemonic status of these strategies for thinking through race, their origins in specific moments were frequently more obvious to the white women who drew on them. Tamara Green, for example, explained that "I went to Guatemala and began to identify as an internationalist. That changed everything." In similar vein, Donna Gonzaga said, "I feel I got a really good grounding in the principles of solidarity from [the African American liberation organization to which she had belonged for many years]." Their relationships, close or distant, to specific movements affected the precise forms taken by these women's race cognizance. A few had participated in race-cognizant discourse in more than one context (for example, in both left groups and feminism). The latter group, perhaps not surprisingly, had the most multifaceted perspectives on racism.

Almost by definition, these race-cognizant women had to have stepped outside the mainstream in conscious, even if accidental, ways in order to have developed critical perspective on the discursive status quo. Many women attempted to explain to me how their experiences or perspectives had come to differ from those of the majority of white people in the United States, some telling me that they had been raised by parents who were politically active in antiracist work and others saying that life had taken them by chance into multiracial or predominantly nonwhite work-places. Clearly, however, many people have chance encounters with antiracist discourses; the difficult question to answer is why some individuals respond positively to them, while others do not. In this regard, two women were so struck by the unexpectedness of their commitment to antiracism, given the families in which they had grown up, that they resorted to metaphysical explana-tions for it, hinting at the possiblity of past lives in which their circumstances had been different from those into which they were born "this time around."

These race-cognizant women were mostly more conscious of their perspectives qua perspectives than were their color- and power-evasive counterparts. They were self-consciously politi-cally positioned in other ways, too, naming themselves as femi-nists, leftists, internationalists or as individuals who, while not identifying primarily with particular movements or tendencies, were concerned about issues of social justice, both in the United States and beyond. However, it is important to underscore that here I am pointing to differences of degree rather than of kind: as I argued earlier, women who drew on the color- and power-evasive repertoire did not do so without agency and self-consciousness; conversely, as I will suggest later, women who drew on race-cognizant discursive strategies frequently remained unconsciously, unintentionally, or unwillingly caught within modes of thinking through race that they would have preferred to eschew.

The overarching principles of race cognizance are, as I stated earlier, the ideas that race makes a difference in people's lives and that racism makes a difference in U.S. society. But in exploring the kinds of difference race makes, different women emphasized different factors. For example, I came to associate with white feminists a careful attention to the ways racism shaped white ex-periences, attitudes, and worldview, as well as to what one might call the "micropolitics" of race in shaping daily life. Others were more concerned with structural or institutional racial inequality and were less convinced of the value of examining the ways race and racism shaped white selves. These were not, however, always mutually exclusive foci, since some women had been involved in work in both of these areas.

Race-cognizant approaches were articulated against both essen-tialist racism and color and power evasiveness. Here differences of emphasis were in part dependent on generation. Marjorie Hoffman, for example, had been a political activist since the 1920s. Her antiracist work had taken place mostly in the southern United States, beginning at the end of World War II and continuing through the emergence of the Student Nonviolent Coordinating Committee in the late 1960s. Her critical race cognizance focused on challenging essentialist racism, segregation, and blatant political and economic inequity. But for others, and in particular younger women raised in the context of a color-evasive public language of race, the concern was to question their own previous perspectives: they argued that "before, I didn't see racism, but now I do" or that "before, I didn't see my *own* racism, my *own* race privilege, but now I do."

Race cognizance articulates explicitly the contradiction that racism represents: on the one hand, it acknowledges the existence of racial inequality and white privilege and, on the other, does not lean on ontological or essential difference in order to justify inequality or explain it away. (By contrast, the color- and power-evasive repertoire is organized around the effort to repress or evade this contradiction.) Race cognizance in this sense generated a range of political and existential questions about white complicity with racism, and these women sought to grapple with such questions in individual or collective ways. For some the possibility of resolution rested in political activism, while others seemed at the point of facing this contradiction actually to turn once again toward power-evasive formulations.

Race Cognizance: Transforming Silence into Language . . .

For some younger white women, raised in the context of a well-established color- and power-evasive hegemony, race cognizance was relatively new.[5] They arrived at it in a range of contexts, including feminist networks, college campuses, and church groups as well as more diffusely from the influence of friends or siblings. These women unanimously described themselves as being on trajectories from lesser to greater awareness of racism, using metaphors including "awakening," and "coming to" (as from unconsciousness or a coma) to describe their newfound perceptions about race and racism. Possibly because of the newness of the process, these women were able to describe with stark clarity the impact of both the "old" and "new" ways of perceiving themselves and their environments. Thus, for example, Chris Patterson bluntly stated:

> When I look back, I think of myself as such a naive white girl. Not even just naive—naive by isolation, by separation. Also coming from the white, privileged class . . . means you don't have to look at anything else. You are never forced to until you choose to, because your life is so unaffected by things like racism.

In fact, as I have argued (and as Chris herself also said), white women's lives are affected by racism, but frequently in ways that simultaneously conceal or normalize race privilege from the standpoint of its beneficiaries. Chris was not alone in linking her lack of awareness of racism with her own race and class privilege. Tamara Green made explicit both a childhood in which privilege was "normalized" and the process of reinterpretation after which she saw the effects of both class and race privilege on how she had previously perceived her environment. Describing her childhood as "very largely white" and "solidly middle class," Tamara argued that "tunnel vision" kept her from seeing class differences between herself and those of her friends who were much poorer:

> TAMARA: I came from a place of relative privilege, where it was not, it didn't make me feel bad to have differences. Whereas it probably made some of my other friends feel bad to see the differences between their situation and mine.
>
> RF: You've talked about how you had quite a few good friends who lived in small apartments [compared to your large house with a swimming pool] . . . ?
>
> TAMARA: See, I didn't realize it made a difference, . . . that that meant they were poor. That they couldn't afford to do things I could afford to do. I literally had no awareness of that fact. Which shocks me, but it's true.

Tamara spoke of other things she had not noticed: as we talked, for example, she struggled to remember whether school desegregation had brought students of color before or after she left high school. She also remembered midstream that for much of her adolescence her family had employed live-in Latin American women as housekeepers, mainly to take care of her younger sister.

As children, both Chris and Tamara had in fact occupied material landscapes that were in significant ways similar to those of their "color-blind" counterparts, characterized, for example, by residential segregation rather than integration and by class-

imbalanced relationships with people of color. As they applied
new conceptual frameworks to those landscapes, however, the
meaning of their experience shifted. This produced the multilay-
ered effect, by now familiar in this text, whereby white women
described and redescribed their material environments by means
of different discursive repertoires, self-critically comparing the effects of each. For both Tamara and Chris, this process of reinterpretation was a key element both of race cognizance and of developing antiracist practice.[6]

If these women's message about social geography was that
"racism was there all along, but we didn't see it," most made parallel points about themselves as subjects. An important dimension
of emergent race cognizance and antiracism for this group was
individuals' acknowledgment of their own racist attitudes or actions. In Patricia Bowen's words:

> I have certain learned automatic reactions or associations with people of
> other races, and I think in that process you're throwing those into
> turmoil, and dredging up a lot of stuff, and making changes, and finding
> out a lot about what they are.

As Beth Ellison put it:

> More [of my] friends than not tend to believe that they grew up with no
> racist attitudes whatsoever. Which may or may not be true. I'd like to
> believe that about myself, but I can't, because it's not true.

When these white feminists saw racism, they referred not only
to the external world and the experience of people of color, but
also to new senses of self: a sharpened awareness of how racism
had structured their own lives and of the extent to which their
own thinking had been, and continued to be, informed by racism.
These women also struggled with questions of how to proceed in
the context of a new sense of self as deeply embedded in racism.

Beth Ellison's description of the shifts in her understanding of
racism when she moved to the San Francisco Bay Area after a
childhood and young adulthood spent in Virginia and Alabama
(see chapter 3) exemplified this process. For one thing, Beth had
to come to terms with the persistence of the Ku Klux Klan, contrary, as she put it, to her "uninformed hopes" that the Klan, "like
a dinosaur, . . . was slowly becoming extinct":

> I think that generally when I was in the South, I had a, maybe kind of
> an optimistic feeling that schools had been integrated, that things were

only going to get better and that the Klan must surely be dying out. . . .
I missed what happened in Greensboro, North Carolina, I—things like
that I didn't read about, 'cause I didn't read the paper. . . . And then I
got out here and found that it was alive and well, and in California too.[7]

Having moved to the Bay Area from predominantly white residentially and socially segregated environments in the South, Beth
found that:

> The atmosphere here was different. . . . For the first time in my life I
> started having Black friends, and then I started realizing that I'd grown
> up thinking that I didn't have that much in common with Black people,
> that they weren't as well educated as I was. I started reexamining that,
> especially when I discovered some Black women writers like Toni
> Morrison and Alice Walker. I realized that it wasn't just because I was
> white that I loved to read, or had gone to school. . . .
>
> What came as a shock to me was that I could have grown up without
> thinking about it, believing that Black people were less educated than I
> was. . . . I found *that* more shocking than that there *were* intelligent
> Black people around.

New realizations called past perceptions into question, set old assumptions in a new frame. Her history made Beth self-conscious
in relating to Black people:

> I was real aware of not ever having had any Black friends before. . . . I
> also was aware of what a racist environment I'd grown up in, and how I
> had grown up with kind of an unexamined racist attitude myself. . . .
> For the first time in my life I felt kind of inferior to some of the Black
> people I ran into at first, because it seemed like politically aware and
> culturally aware Black people that I knew seemed to have a stronger
> sense of being Black than I had of being white. . . . There seemed to be
> more of a cohesive community. . . .
>
> After a while because I saw Black people around and hung out with
> them I felt more like—well, more that they were people that I knew.

Beth's words about race difference and racism are strikingly different from those of Irene Esterley that I quoted earlier. Where
Irene skirted around her discomfort and seemed to waver in her
consciousness of the social distance that shaped her relationships
with Black people, Beth's discourse was more explicit. She described her sense of superiority, its giving way to a feeling inferiority and the sense of a closing social distance, but continued
tension as a result of her own relationship to racism. She told the
following story to illustrate this tension:

The other night . . . I was in a coffeehouse, and I had left my table just for a minute. Without thinking, I'd left a pack of cigarettes there, and when I came back to the table with a friend, there was a Black guy that was sitting there. I guess he thought nobody was sitting there. So we let him know that it was our table, and he got up and left. And then I realized that my pack of cigarettes were gone. So I approached him and asked him if he'd seen a pack of cigarettes there, if he picked them up. He became very insulted and drew himself up and said that, contrary to the stereotype that white people have, not every Black person is a thief.

And if I hadn't felt so much like, "Uh-oh, am I thinking this guy stole these because he's Black?" or "How can I redress his wound now?" If I had felt like this was just a guy that had a problem—I thought a few minutes later that what I could have said is that contrary to stereotypes, not all *white* people think all Black people are thieves. I think I would have said that if I hadn't been so drawn aback. . . . I still have some sensitivity that would make me stop immediately and say, "Oh, gosh, I'm being racist, I'd better quit this," even though I knew full well that I wasn't: I was only saying that to him because he was sitting there.

As this story makes clear, Beth had a very elaborate sense of herself as mutually constructed into a dynamic of racial tension with Black people carried over from childhood (see chapter 3). It is striking, in fact, that Beth's primary focus remained on her relationships with *Black* Americans rather than with other people of color, even though the San Francisco area is more multiracial than biracial. What is going on here, I suggest, is Beth's struggle to reexamine the particulars of the biracial dynamic in which she had been involved since childhood.

Beth also had a complex and mobile relationship with, as the white feminists I interviewed would have put it, "her own racism." She knew herself to be, first, racist and, second, desirous of *not* being racist. Third, she was unsure how racist she might still be but, fourth, knew that she wasn't intending to be racist on that occasion. Finally, she was concerned and sensitive in response to this complicated state of mind. Compare Beth's response with Irene Esterley's account of her feelings toward the Black community: "Nothing! That was just the Black neighborhood!"

Not surprisingly, the implications of this complex awareness were not clear-cut for Beth. For one thing, she suggested, her sensitivity might mean treating the other person less as a human being and more as a representative of a certain group. The value of her hard-won sensitivity was in this sense called into question:

There has been so much racism, like there has been so much sexism, and ageism, and whatever else for a long time, but— And so I feel torn between thinking, well, this is something that's got to change and I want to think about it and I want to be part of changing it. And I get torn between being hypersensitive like that and thinking that I just want to be more natural, and that I would wish this had already changed, and that perhaps I can be more a part of changing by just wiping out racism altogether from my mind, but I guess you have to be hypersensitive maybe before you can—you have to know what you are purging . . . and why.

Beth also drew parallels with her own situation as a woman:

> Sometimes I feel that that's kind of patronizing. . . . It bothers me to hear a man, for instance, call himself a feminist, when I think, "How can he understand what it's like to be a woman?" and sometimes I think that my sensitivity is, is kind of displaced [sic], that I can't really understand what it's like to be Black.

There are two abrupt shifts in Beth's focus here. One is from the goal of developing awareness of her role in the drama (and thus, one could say, of her part in perpetuating racism), to a goal, which in fact she rejects as presumptuous, of complete empathy with people of color. The second is to a reduced notion of ending racism—from ending the circumstances that produced Beth's "racial tension" to a desire (however understandable) simply to end the tension itself. There is almost a move back into the desire that characterizes power evasiveness—the desire not to have to see racism any more.

Chris Patterson's childhood was one in which, as she described it, she had not needed to think about race or racism. This, she ruefully explained, carried over into her adult life, leaving her ill-equipped for any kind of multiracial work in what she described as her "politically active period," attempting to build a lesbian feminist community in the southern city to which she moved after college:

> It was a personal move towards taking control of my life and surroundings. Not being passive in my community, the city. But it was not a crossracial idea I had in mind. It was partly because [the city] is strongly segregated, but is close to overcoming that. But it was so difficult for me to even understand race, racism. . . . We'd talk. We'd have events and say, "God, there are no women of color here. They are all white women." I started doing a women's coffeehouse at the YWCA. It was a racially mixed workplace but the women of color were all in the

lower strata. We'd talk about how we could reach out, but didn't know how to reach out to the women of color in the city. . . .

Someone would say, "Well, I think there's a Black lesbian bar in such-and-such neighborhood." Everyone would go, "Really? You mean there are Black lesbians?" It was comical how cut off from it we were. Our goal was to create a space where every woman could come, and we weren't fulfilling that because we were only serving one community.

Chris's story contains elements that are by now familiar in these white women's narratives: social distance from people of color despite their physical presence—here, as often, in a class-imbalanced or "serving" role. As a result, the collective sense of community, womanhood, lesbianism was, by default, conceived in white terms. And although Chris began to recognize the whiteness of her frame of reference, she was nonetheless unable to see at that point how to widen the material framework for her community-building efforts.

Chris had moved to the San Francisco Bay Area less than a year before we talked. As she became conscious of the racial boundedness of her community and began to be articulate about its limitations, she found her network falling away: confronting racism meant pulling away from old friends in the South whose racism, she said, sounded "really loud" to her now. Challenging them seemed problematic, for several reasons:

Sometimes I feel there's a barrier there and they won't hear. And I think it's someone's own process to go through. It can't necessarily be taught. Also, there's a barrier because I've moved away. Each time I write a letter or come back, I'm off on another trip, so it's dismissed as "Chris's even weirder." Also, there's a fear of hurting our friendship even more, if I confront it. I make it clear that I don't want to hear. I say, "Don't say 'nigger' in front of me," because they sometimes do. It bothers me so much that I give an ultimatum: "Don't do it or don't come." They're becoming more aware of it for my sake. It may rub off on them, too. But they can be very prejudiced and think nothing of it. I must have been the same myself at one time. Although I don't like to think so.

Chris, like the other white feminists I have described, operates on the assumption—in the case of her friends borne out by their actions—that racism is within white people, waiting to be noticed.

Key to race cognizance for Chris, Beth, Tamara, Pat, and others was a commitment to close and careful analysis of racism's impact on themselves. In dramatic contrast with color- and power-evasive women, they insisted that racism was something in which *they* had a part: "my racism" was a phrase used as frequently by these white feminist women as the claim that "there is no difference" was made by color- and power-evasive women. This way of thinking about racism was shaped by several factors, not the least of which was their awareness of the very immediate critique of feminist racism coming from U.S. women of color, who have asserted that white feminists are often as racist as other white people. Moreover, their view of racism included awareness of institutional, social, and structural factors, rather than confining attention to individual "prejudice" and discrimination.

A more generalized feminist commitment to the idea that "the personal is political" gave shape and direction to these women's race cognizance. The claim that "the personal is political" has multiple meanings within feminism. Especially relevant here, feminists have called for the analysis in social and political terms of experiences and phenomena that might otherwise be construed as "individual," and much of feminist theory has analyzed "selves" and consciousness as constructed out of complex interactions with society and culture.[8] Drawing on both feminism and other social movements, women of color have, through the past decade, frequently situated their analyses of the intersection of racism and sexism within this personal-political matrix. By the same token, those white women who have written and spoken publicly about racism from within feminist contexts have for the most part adopted the same approach (see chapter 1).

Indicative of this linkage of the personal to the social realm, feminist women often answered my question "How would you describe yourself?" in terms of social aggregates, political identities, or roles. Chris Patterson, for example, said, "I would describe myself as a white woman from an upper middle class New York suburb," explaining that she had begun to name herself "white" after realizing that white people, because of race privilege, are not for the most part expected to name themselves in racial terms. Here, identity became part of a politicized, social-structural terrain. By contrast, women whose discussions about race drew primarily on the color- and power-evasive repertoire were more likely to describe themselves in terms of individual characteristics: "I'm a hard worker," "I'm a lonely person," for example. In this sense, these feminist women's race cognizance,

and their views of themselves in general, differed dramatically
from the view embedded in the "color-blind" repertoire of a human core only superficially touched by social relations.

But there were limits to these women's race cognizance. Chris,
for example, said that, having learned a great deal about anti-
Semitism and racism through conversations with Jewish and
white women friends (but not with women of color), she did not
know how to proceed:

> I've changed an incredible amount. Looking at my life, I suppose I
> haven't, it hasn't been important enough for me to change externally too
> yet. Because if it was, I would have. . . . I don't know what it involves.
> I suppose that's why I haven't. . . . I guess the popular phrase now is
> "practicing your antiracism."

The two alternative ways of "practicing antiracism" that Chris
suggested were in fact strikingly different from one another:
working with a Black nationalist party and making friends with
women of color. While the former presumably reflected Chris's
concern about structural racism, the latter seemed more amorphous as a goal, possibly linked to a desire to change the narrow
social context in which she had hitherto struggled toward cognizance of the meaning and effects of racism. Chris added:

> A lot of white women who get into discussion about racism, and go
> into the internal process of it, might get to a point of clarity about where
> their prejudices and racist thought are, feeling, "So that's great, now I'm
> not so racist anymore!" And then stop there. . . . You're cleansed of
> certain sins and now you can go home.

As Chris's comment suggests, elements of the color- and
power-evasive repertoire continued to shape these women's thinking. In her ironic description of women who feel "cleansed" after
analyzing their relationships with racism, Chris used the same images of sin and redemption that, I argued earlier, were implicit in
power-evasive discussions of racism. Both Chris and Beth valued
introspection as much as social change as antiracist practices, and
their self-analysis powerfully transformed their sense of themselves as white. As Chris described it, however, there was an ever-
present possibility of introspection becoming an end in itself or
turning into an individualism much like that underlying color-
and power-blindness. Each woman described the quest for race
cognizance as a private journey rather than a collective or social
one.

As a result of all this, the issue of white women's complicity with racism threatened to become an existential rather than a political question. The motivation for this turn toward individualism, as was the case when women drew on the the color- and power-evasive repertoire, was not always clear. For both Beth and Chris, it seemed at times to stem from lack of motivation to further pursue the task of challenging racism, but at other times to result from lack of ideas about *how* to do it. Whatever their motivation, however, the end result was the same: while not exactly power-*evasive*, neither were these women "power-strategic." In other words, they had found neither strategies nor a discursive repertoire that would enable them to build on a heightened awareness of racial structuring in their own lives in order to reach toward their stated desire, a society (or a world) that might somehow move beyond racism.

The absence of a language with which to analyze in sufficiently complex fashion the relationship between the white self and racism as a system of domination threatened at times to generate not just confusion, but also anger and backlash on the part of race-cognizant women. Chris, for example, described the positioning of white people by talking about U.S. imperialism:

> A parallel that comes to mind, I don't know why, is that white people—
> it's almost how the U.S. is to the rest of the world. It's big, it has a lot
> of fucked-up ways about it, but at the same time goes all over the world
> and sticks its nose in everywhere, as if it has the right to be there and
> can do whatever it feels like doing, just because it's the biggest, most
> powerful country. That's a parallel to whites like, uh, "I have some sort
> of right or privilege."

Chris was not alone in linking racism to colonization. Cathy Thomas, a lesbian feminist in her early twenties (see chapter 5), posed a rhetorical question that powerfully encapsulated the impact of imperial expansion on culture and material life:

> What is there to us? Besides the largest colonial legacy anyone has ever
> seen in history, and the complete rewriting of everything anyone else
> knows himself by?

In a third instance, Clare Traverso said, in response to a question from me about what "white" meant to her:

> I think of people like the Ku Klux Klanners when I think of "white."
> And *I'm* not Ku Klux Klan. But my subconscious says, "Yes, you are,"

because that's what we learn about what white is, "White did this, white did that, to this people, to that people"—that's not all that we are! You know, there's something good in us, what is it? And where is it, and can't we articulate that too?

And maybe people think it's already articulated—"We're wonderful, we have the right to take from you." But there's something else—isn't there?

In each of these formulations one sees elements of both power-evasive and race-cognizant repertoires. All of these ways of naming white people—by reference to U.S. imperialism, European colonialism, the Klan—present an explicit challenge to the refusal of the color- and power-evasive repertoire to describe complicity between individual white selves and white-dominated power structures. The choice of "big" systems and extremist groups to describe everyday racism and ordinary white people also powerfully asserts the idea that *no* white person is exempt from participation in racist discourse or practice. (Remember that within the color- and power-evasive discursive repertoire, systems of domination were for the most part not named at all, much less criticized, and that that repertoire strives to maintain a clear separation between "good" and "bad," "racist" and "nonracist" individuals.) In these ways, then, Chris, Cathy, and Clare perhaps sought to invert the terms of the discursive status quo as well as to articulate a form of race cognizance linked to the personal-political matrix I described earlier.

However, neither the Klan image nor that of colonialism as they were used by Cathy, Clare, and Chris provided the women with a sense of the everyday structuring of their lives by racism. Taking the Klan as paradigmatic places racism at the extreme edge of the category of individual, voluntaristic actions that, I suggested earlier, characterize "racism" or "prejudice" from within a color- and power-evasive repertoire. The models of colonialism and neoimperialism have, at least, the advantage that they view racism as structuring historical forces. However, they too can have connotations of the foreign, the far away, and the long past.

Invoking the Klan, neoimperialism, and colonialism interchangeably creates a picture that is even more confusing. It is true that colonial or neocolonial power and the political extreme right are not unconnected nor, for the most part, are they philosophically at odds with one another. In addition, a country like the United States, premised on colonial and neocolonial power, might be apt to tolerate the extreme right—and even to use it to police its race-class structure. From the standpoint of a white individual, however, being an inheritor of colonialism is a very different proposition from being an activist of the racist extreme right. The two involve very different kinds of agency, and challenging each requires different responses. For the former is a mode of agency achieved by default: one is implicated in one's racial positioning whether one chooses to be or not.

In short, although these women drew, in characterizing racism, on the terms of reference of a range of race-cognizant movements, both antiracist and anti-imperialist, they did so in ways that simply exposed but did not undo the dualism of the dominant discourse. As in the color- and power-evasive repertoire, these descriptions of complicity are constructed as dualisms: either an individual is fully complicit with racism and imperialism or not complicit at all. Where the former repertoire was organized around evading questions of power, privilege, or complicity, however, Cathy, Chris, and Clare risked falling into the opposite trap—asserting a complicity with racial domination that was totally encompassing, totally definitive of whiteness and of individual white selves.

Citing the Klan and colonialism as exemplars of white complicity with racism is a powerful rhetorical move if the goal is to disrupt the complacency of color and power evasiveness. Like most rhetorical strategies, however, both are simultaneously reductive and excessive if they are used literally as tools for analyzing the status of white (non–Klan-supporting) selves in relation to racial domination. (By contrast, more complex and materially based analyses of the Klan, colonialism, and neoimperialism are important elements of antiracist strategy.)

Thus, Chris, Cathy, and Clare spoke of an undifferentiated "we" of domination. Cathy suggested that there is nothing to "us" except active participation in colonialism, and Clare expressed her fear that, in fact she *is* like a Ku Klux Klan member, both because she is white and because as a white person she is linked to colonialism in a general sense. Some of the potential effects of these simple inversions of color and power evasion were evident in Clare's back-and-forth movement between two poles: "I am like the Klan/U.S. imperialism" and "I am *not* like the Klan/U.S. imperialism." Clare was clear, it seemed, that while neither statement was fully correct, neither was fully *incorrect*, either. But at the same time she was puzzled about how to escape this dualism.

Clare had raised linked concerns both in relation to her job as a teacher and her experience of discussions about racism in college. Working in a predominantly Mexican American high school, Clare had presented students with materials on the civil rights movement, hoping, she explained, to encourage students toward a politicized analysis of their own lives. But as she did so, she felt that they were likely to view her as their enemy:

> We're talking about all these things and it's almost like the whole thing could turn on me! . . .
>   Maybe it's like I was afraid of my students, afraid of those discussions at the university. I don't understand it and I feel I'm afraid to make a mistake. I want them to understand *me*, and be patient with *me*. I mean, it's not my fault if I got born in a white ghetto. I didn't have a choice. . . . I *do* want to learn about other people, don't want to be insensitive to them. And I want to feel proud about being who I am, too, . . . and not feel guilty about everything, like I do, a lot of times.

In Clare's statement, elements of both power-evasive and race-cognizant repertoires are interwoven. On one level, there is a desire to learn and to be sensitive, perhaps to move toward mutual communication. Yet Clare's plea, while it refers to the criticism of entrenched white ethnocentrism frequently articulated by students and activists of color in universities and other institutional settings through the 1970s and 1980s, took the form of inversion as she noted *her* desire to be understood, *her* wish for "pride" in herself and used "ghetto" to describe her childhood. The effect here is evasion, of both the realities of the racial order and of the priorities of antiracist struggle, for it appropriates to the racially dominant white self some of the demands and terminology of culturally and racially subordinated groups. There is also an either-or feel to this formulation—perhaps a fear that only whites *or* people of color can be "understood," but not both. All of this echoes the dualistic formulation so characteristic of the color- and power-evasive repertoire.

Interestingly enough, Clare's words also simplified her own childhood experience, which was, as she described it, not "all white" in any straightforward sense. Rather, Clare grew up working class, in a small California town. Her childhood entailed complex and unequal relationships with Native American and Chicano neighbors, as well as contact with communities on the other side of the Mexican border (see chapter 3). One might suggest here that, in the absence of a discursive repertoire adequate to capture the physical experience of her life, Clare resorted to discursive strategies that actually falsify the, so to speak, "real" conditions of her life.

If Clare had earlier placed herself entirely within the parameters of a "we" of authors of racism, in these latter statements she placed herself entirely outside them ("It's not my fault . . ."). And although these are opposite formulations, the latter is, I suggest, an effect of the former. For a simple identification of all white people with the far-right racism of the Klan or with U.S. imperialism (terms that themselves designate very different modes of deployment of power) does little to clarify the complex relationship between white individuals and a racially stratified social structure.

Clare was thus constrained by a contradictory equation from which there was no exit, able to argue only "I am entirely responsible for racism" or "I am not at all responsible for racism." Both sides of the equation are unrealistic: to disentangle oneself from racism by renouncing membership in a Klan to which one never belonged and to untie the connection by attempting *not* to have been born white are equally impractical. In both instances, racism came to stand for a static condition of being, possibly even an "original sin" that the white individual could never undo. Here, despite Clare's activist work both in and outside the classroom, the discursive repertoire on which she drew transformed the question of white complicity with racism from a political to an existential one.

Cathy Thomas, in the years before I interviewed her, had been a key mover in a lesbian feminist university-based community, committed to speaking out loudly and forcefully not only against sexism and heterosexism, but also against race and class oppression. For her, the process of "coming to" about racism had felt like a rude awakening by means of a pail of cold water. As we saw in chapter 5, Cathy had taken seriously a set of linked criticisms about white privilege, standpoint, and voice raised by men and women of color and given particular focus within the lesbian feminist networks to which she belonged. If it had ever existed, the possibility of white women being seen *only* as targets of oppression, or as a group opposed to oppression in any simple sense, was receding before the idea that, in Cathy's words,

> White women really do need to look at themselves as a group, because
> white women as a group are fucked up.

White women, in other words, were being encouraged to take
stock of their racial positions and become self-critical. However,
as Cathy described it, criticism and self-criticism rapidly became
totalizing. Cathy's account does not make clear the extent to
which women of color and white women participated in this process. However, its effect, for Cathy, was that:

> We got a definition that white women equals "power over" from the
> wrong source, from the source of history. And white women got
> reduced to that somehow.

Cathy added, speaking simultaneously to others and about herself:

> I took on the whole ridiculous, sordid murderous past of white
> people. . . . It's a dead end . . . that generates backlash, because people
> don't know why they have to hate themselves, they don't remember
> doing anything horrendous in their lives. They never lynched anybody,
> their ancestors may have, but they themselves—"When do you stop
> paying?" is a big question. It was for me.

Like Clare, Cathy expressed anger at what finally seemed to her
the falsity of totally identifying herself with a position of domination. Again like Clare's story, there are elements of inversion
here, so that Cathy saw herself as suffering as a result of racism.
Finally, Cathy's reduction of racism to lynching or, to put it the
other way around, her use of lynching to stand in for the totality
of racism, creates an equation without exit: it is not possible, she
contends correctly, for her to prove herself innocent of racism by
renouncing modes of racist violence in which she did not
participate.

In reaction to a total identification of whiteness with racism,
Cathy had over a period of years adopted a range of strategies.
Chief among them was her attempt to make an exception of herself, to separate from other white lesbian women and instead participate as fully as possible in her lover's Chicana culture, even to
the point of attempting to adopt a Chicana identity for herself (see
chapter 5). By the time I talked with her, she saw the inadequacy
and impossibility of that strategy. Perhaps as a result, she had also
begun to rethink the impossible dualism whereby she had felt that
only by being "not white" could she effect any transformation in
her relationship to racism:

CATHY: I'm not into watching myself at every turn anymore. I'm not into seeing myself from the outside as a stupid white girl who can't do anything but put her foot in it.

RF: Is that how you've been seeing yourself?

CATHY: Well, that's for when I was with Miranda. That's what white girls were about. . . . I mean, fuck it. I'm just going to live my life and trust myself to be a human being. . . . If you're involved in making sure you're heart's in the right place, and finding out what about it isn't right, and taking steps about that, it's the most you can do.

On the surface, Cathy's call for a return to the "heart" seemed like an invocation of the utopian desire of color-blindness, the idea that if we can get past all the differences and racism on the surface, we are good people underneath. As Cathy elaborated on the questions she had recently begun to ask herself, however, what emerged was an effort to step beyond a dualistic framework of innocence and guilt:

Instead of standing around and thrashing ourselves about shit, it's important to be able to just sit down and talk about it—"Well, yeah, our hearts are in the right place, but it's still not coming together." Or "What about my grief? What about the shit that I've had to go through because of the sins of the fathers?" I have an identity that doesn't have to do with my volition, but I've been profiting from it from birth. So what does that make me, and where does my responsibility lie? And where does my blame lie? And do I have a right to be angry because I did not create this society, but I am paying for it? And do I have a right to be pissed because my friendships are crippled because of something that I came into the world not knowing anything about, but benefiting by? . . . What does it mean to take angry space as a white woman? Usually we're so busy feeling guilty, we never get near it. But there has to be more than that.

It's been made a really loaded and difficult process that the timid among us won't go near. Because there's no space made to make mistakes. No space made to say, "This doesn't happen overnight, and furthermore [racism's] not a personality trait."

In contrast to the anxiety with which Clare almost seemed to be seeking "absolution" from her ex-classmates and students of color, Cathy's tone here was angry, even defiant. In addition, her questions sounded as though they had the potential to move her away from either-or, unidirectional views of white complicity with racism toward more complex analyses. Within them, for example, it might be contended that white women have responsibilities in relation to racism *even though* there are aspects of it that they did not create, or that white women both benefit from racism *and* experience its negative impact on their personal relationships. Moreover, she suggested, just as it is necessary to step away from a color- and power-evasive repertoire in order to recognize racism, it is necessary to step away from a dualistic framework in order to challenge racism. But clearly Cathy needed to keep grappling with questions about the white individual who, in Cathy's view, should be given space and encouragement in order to arrive at an understanding of her relationship with racism. In this sense, questions about the positioning of white individuals remained separate from issues of structural change.

Cathy, like others I quoted earlier, viewed the power and privilege associated with whiteness in strongly negative terms. But the kinds of analysis in which these women were caught up, and in particular the contest between, on the one hand, the dualism and individualism of the color- and power-evasive repertoire and, on the other, the recognition of power, privilege, and domination associated with the race-cognizant repertoire, created the possibility of short-circuiting and individuating antiracist impulses and, if nothing else, holding in check antiracist action outside the individual, introspective arena.

. . . and Language into Action

The final group of women on whom I will focus in this chapter is women whose commitment to antiracism was longer established. This group had in common a focus on questions of structural change with respect to racism; to differing degrees, these women were also concerned about white subjectivity and white people's personal responsibility for and complicity with racism. Perhaps in part because of their longer involvement with antiracism, these women were less preoccupied with existential questions about the meaning of whiteness. But, more importantly, this group saw political activism as the best way to resolve or at least address white complicity with racism. Their focus was, for the most part, more collective than individual, and their analyses of whites' relationship with racism more active than static.

It is not, I think, coincidental that these women were introduced to antiracism in movements led by people of color rather than in the numerically and conceptually white-dominated feminist movement. Although two of them, Jeanine Cohen and

Donna Gonzaga, identified themselves with the U.S. feminist movement, both had been introduced to antiracism and anti-imperialism elsewhere. Jeanine, a South African, had grown up in a family deeply involved in the antiapartheid struggle. She herself had participated in work brigades in Nicaragua and Cuba and in the feminist movements of the United States and the United Kingdom. Frieda Kazen, having completed college and lacking the money for an apprenticeship in textile design, had taken the only teaching job she was offered, in an elementary school in Harlem, in New York City. Entering the school—as she remembered it, "a little microcosm that worked"—at the height of the Black Power movement and the second Harlem Renaissance had catapulted her into a decade of participation in multiracial community arts projects in New York.

As I spoke to these women, it was clear that they considered it axiomatic that racism was a critical issue in society, a system of domination that needed to be changed. Questions about effective strategies for change were more interesting to them than questions about how they became race-cognizant. Although they often emphasized that they did not have adequate answers, they might at times have been responding directly to those women for whom race cognizance was a relatively new phenomenon, raising but addressing more strategically and less dualistically the same issues about guilt, responsibility, race privilege, complicity with racial domination, and the inadequacy of "totalizing" analyses of white privilege.

For the women relatively new to race cognizance, examination of white subjects' relationship to the social structure was a productive preoccupation, but one that was ultimately limited in both form and scope. Marjorie Hoffman, an activist on the left since the 1920s and now a Gray Panther in her seventies, was highly critical of what she viewed as "soul-searching" approaches to racism, calling them, not without sarcasm, "middle-class pastimes" and adding, "You can do it endlessly, and it makes you feel *so* good."

Marjorie's trenchant observations about white "soul searching" made sense given the kind of antiracist work in which she had been involved since the 1940s: work in a race relations institute focused on eradicating institutional discrimination; an action-research project in which she and a Black co-worker traveled the railroads in order to document the separate and unequal treatment

of passengers; and, finally, fund-raising for the Student Nonviolent Coordinating Committee during the civil rights movement.
As I pursued my questions further, however, it became clear that
Marjorie's position was also premised on a view of the relationship between selves and society different from that associated with
feminism:

> RF: I was asking you before, about the whole thing about different
> understandings of—different priorities, I guess, around antiracist work.
> So the institute would focus on institutional stuff, right? And then we
> were talking about that versus "soul searching," if you like. And what
> that partly speaks to could be class, but it could also be different
> understandings of what racism is. I guess one of the things about the
> women's movement that I think is real important is the relationship
> between personal and political life, and the whole notion that, if you live
> in a particular kind of social structure, you don't just inhabit it, but it
> also shapes who you are, and how you are. And that—
>
> MARJORIE: —so that we have to also try to shape that structure.
>
> RF: Mhm. We have to shape the structure, but we also have to recognize
> that as agents we are already shaped by the structure that we're trying to
> change.
>
> MARJORIE: Yeah, but if we're conscious of that, can't we turn around
> and reshape the structure that distorted us into a form we don't like?
>
> RF: Mhm. Definitely. I mean, that's the thing that we have to do.
>
> MARJORIE: I don't think we've come up with the formula on that yet,
> and I don't know that there is any.
>
> RF: So I suppose for me that's the reason for "soul searching," is to make
> us into better, more capable activists, in relation to the structure.
>
> MARJORIE: Yeah. The only reason I'm a little bit caustic about it is, it can
> develop into an endless pastime that leads to nothing. And yet you can
> wallow in your discoveries of your inner self. Without doing a damn
> thing about it. . . .
>   [But] the converse—of being politically active in any kind of a
> program and not recognizing the contradictions or the limitations of self
> in it, or the distorted ego satisfactions that we're indulging—is equally
> weak. It can be devastating.

The question being explored here, in short, was how to change
society *and* white people, given that both are distorted by racism.
Marjorie here took the position that, fundamentally, one needs to
change the structure in order to change the white subject, and that
by paying too much attention to the white subject, activists run
the risk of neglecting the structure they seek to change. Nonetheless, Marjorie, moving toward the complexity shared by

many of these long-term activists, qualified her argument by emphasizing the dangers inherent in acting politically without self-understanding.

Generation was certainly a factor that shaped Marjorie's dismissal of any attention to the construction of subjectivity by race, just as it created the younger women's need for it. Simply put, Marjorie had grown up and been active politically in the era of essentialist racism, while many young white feminists were born into that of color and power evasion. Thus, while Marjorie viewed race privilege as so obvious as not to require elaboration, younger, and especially middle class, white women had experienced race privilege as normalized to the point of invisibility. But whatever the reasons, Marjorie's focus as an activist was on the impact of racism on people of color, and not, as for the younger feminists, concerned with how racism shapes *white* people as well as people of color.

Jeanine Cohen's childhood in South Africa, in a Jewish family deeply involved in the antiapartheid struggle, provided her with important lessons, as she thought about racism and antiracism in the United States. Her family's political connections meant that Jeanine's earliest memories were of close, loving contacts with Black activists, both those who came illegally to her parents' home and those she was taken by her father to visit in Black townships. This early experience, Jeanine felt, was crucial to her sense of the common humanity of white and Black people (something that was *not* self-evident to most of the white people in her neighborhood and school in Johannesburg). In the context of apartheid, however, there was no way for Black and white people to interact freely. For example, Jeanine told me how, when she was three or four, she had run to hug a Black adult friend when she saw him in the street outside her house. He had pushed her sharply away, insistently whispering, "Get away from me!" Her distress and the explanations that followed this and similar incidents meant that Jeanine consciously felt the impact of racism early on. From a young age, Jeanine said, she had also felt guilty because:

JEANINE: I was aware of the privilege I had. I was aware that as a white person, I didn't have to tolerate living the way Black people did, that I could move freely in the world in a way they couldn't. And somehow, somewhere, I felt that I was responsible. . . . And I think it was true of my parents. . . . I think [guilt] somewhat motivated them. I mean, they were incensed by the injustice, but some of it was guilt about being white people, and having stuff. And that by being there, you participate in that. It's like by being in America you participate in imperialism, not by choice but because we reap the benefits. Whether we want to or not, we do, and it's the same thing in South Africa.

RF: I think guilt definitely is something that white women in the U.S. feel, and that I felt, certainly, when I first started comprehending my position in relation to racism. . . .

JEANINE: I guess I've begun to shift. I go back to my child[hood] experience and say that, in the end, what is essential is that we *be* human beings. I mean, that sounds so corny, on some level. (Laughs) But it's like, ultimately, those divisions are false. And I believe that it's in everyone's interests—
   It's true, I think, that on some level my parents [were] patronizing, even in their attempts to struggle against racism, that they played out some racist dynamics with Black people. That they organized as white people and somehow . . . didn't understand that Black people didn't necessarily organize in the way that they were organizing. They made a lot of errors on that level. But, you know, I think that that's a process that people have to go through, and it's a process that both sides, in a way, have to wage together. Or it'll never change. I guess that's my [disagreement with] separatism as a political strategy. Because I think people have got to accept that it's everyone's experience, one side or the other. And therefore it's everybody's responsibility. Together.

Jeanine, like the women who had come to race cognizance through the U.S. feminist movement, seemed well aware that being white meant having advantages inaccessible to Black South Africans—although unlike the others, she came to that realization early, as a result of childhood experience. As Jeanine suggested, she was neither "above" guilt nor beyond it in thinking about the meaning of her complicity with racism as a system in South Africa and in the United States (see also chapter 5). Guilt emerged here as an obvious, almost reasonable, reaction to awareness of the contradiction that privilege represented in her life, a contradiction that she still struggled with. However, Jeanine also named other emotions she felt in response to racism: anger and frustration over injustice, an ongoing sense of the common humanity of people and the constructedness of racial divisions and racial inequality, and a sense that both white and Black people had been caused pain by apartheid, however differently.
   Her belief in common humanity and varying kinds of pain was *not*, however, an occasion for evasion of the political consequences of "false" divisions or of the irreducibility of white priv-

ilege. Rather, common implication in racism necessitated, in Jeanine's view, a shared struggle against it: the differences between white and Black South Africans called for change rather than stasis. Thus, when white people are patronizing in their approach to antiracism, this calls for a change in strategy and tactics, *not* for an existential crisis or withdrawal from action on the part of whites.

Jeanine held to her analysis when we discussed the merits of autonomous discussions about racism among white women in the United States. Jeanine argued that it was neither practical nor desirable for white women to separately explore their racism and then present feminist women of color with a fait accompli:

> JEANINE: It isn't real. It never is like that. It's a process. The fact is that people have got to challenge each other. And have got to be compassionate with each other. . . .
>
> [E]ach person has their story to tell. It's like, each person has their relative experience, of oppression, of participating in oppressing other people, or whatever. We have a great deal to teach each other. People of color and white people have a great deal to teach each other, without it being the way it is now, a lot, where white people are definitely co-opting and oppressing people of color. And the response they then get is one of—a lot, a violent reaction. Quite understandably. But not, in the end, the answer.
>
> RF: I guess it requires white women to respond to the anger of women of color—to bring it into the feminist movement—in a way that says, "Yes, I know why you're angry, and I'm going to try and move from the original position that you are responding to with anger." That's kind of the next step that has to happen, I think.
>
> JEANINE: Yes. And for women of color who are angry to say, "I'm angry, I have a right to be angry, and now what do I do?" Because that leap has to be made as well.

Once more, Jeanine emphasized the possibility of change both on the part of white people and in the racial order more generally. Again her focus was on people working together across racial lines as a more effective option than white people working individually or collectively to analyze their implication in racism. The anger, compassion, challenge, and different, power–laden but not absolute, experiences of living with oppression of which she spoke contrast with the dualistic formulations with which Clare, Chris, and Cathy struggled. Finally, Jeanine added that, for white and middle-class women, practice is ultimately more significant than identity in determining one's relationship to systems of domination:

> I didn't have a choice to be born what I am. I didn't have a choice that I was brought up in a middle-class background. But I have a choice about how I use it now. I have a choice about what stands I make in my life. I have a choice about how I use the privilege I have. . . . It's what you do with it, is the issue.

Building Marjorie's contribution onto Jeanine's, one might suggest here that the subject/structure dilemma—the question of whether and how white people should focus on their own racism or turn immediately toward coalition—might best be approached by means of simultaneous rather than sequential attention. Thinking about white people not so much as authors but as inheritors of racism enabled Jeanine to turn her attention away from white guilt. It also helped her to see what her role as a white woman might be in the task of dismantling the edifice of racism.

It was significant that for Jeanine the words of anti-imperialist activists Steven Biko and Amilcar Cabral were inspirational. As she described them, Biko had emphasized that any solution to apartheid in South Africa would have to include whites, and Cabral that individuals' political positioning, not their racial identity, should determine how they are perceived. For Jeanine, a great deal was at stake in this kind of analysis: a path not only toward resolution of the contradictions of racism in terms of their impact on people of color, but also toward healing the scars wrought by apartheid in her own life, symbolically reuniting her in struggle with those men and women from whom she had been separated in her earlier years.

Donna Gonzaga's approach to activism revolved around three ideas: first, a belief in "solidarity" as the most appropriate mode of antiracist work for white people; second, focus on structural and institutional change, whether on a small or large scale; and third, distrust of what she called "subjective" politics based on individual assertions about what is or is not "correct" behavior, whether in the arena of race or of class politics.

Donna's thinking had been formed by lessons gained from contact with 1970s Black Power activism, her longtime (but now ended) membership in the white solidarity committee of a Black nationalist organization, and, more recently, participation in the movement for solidarity with Central America and "sister-to-sister" support work with women's organizations in Mexico City. All of this continued to shape her sense of the centrality of race and nation in understanding her place in U.S. society. Thus, Donna firmly stated that:

> I *agree* [with the Black nationalist organization] that this country's got to fundamentally change. I *agree* that it was founded on the genocide of Native people and the slavery and genocide of African people. I know that. And I know that our forefathers and mothers participated in that, whether apathetically so or actively so.

However, rather than framing a dualistic analysis that "forgot" gender and class in its emphasis on racism, Donna added that:

> But then, on the other hand, I didn't create it. And my mother didn't create it. We didn't have power, because we were working-class people. We don't have power. So I'm not going to take all the responsibility. And I don't hate myself as a white person. It's just an understanding that, you know, we have a responsibility. . . . We do have a role in this [struggle], we do have a place in it.

Donna's sense that racism and colonialism are central to U.S. history also translated into a belief that changing the life conditions of working-class women like herself was integrally linked to ending racial domination. Because of this, she felt that in order to bring about change, white activists need to recognize,

> and it's a deep blow, or comprehension, that we [white people] are not really the movers and shakers of history, and particularly now. And the more I travel, the more I go to other countries, the more I realize that. . . .
>
> Solidarity is a wonderful place to be. It's not like being beholden, it's like using your resources, acknowledging, "Yes, I have certain access to things because of my white skin privilege, and I want to take those things and share them with you. Because I feel an affinity with you." I feel like, these are my allies.
>
> A lot of people are afraid to experience that because they are afraid that it's going to take something away from them. And I think they also have a lot of guilt and fear that they are going to be treated the ways that white people have treated [people of color] and the ways that we have treated Third World people. They really are afraid, and I frankly don't think that would happen.

Solidarity, however, is not a simple process. For one thing, said Donna, it presupposes the existence of movements with which to be "in solidarity." Donna felt, for example, that in the absence of a mass movement of people of color comparable to the civil rights and Black Power movements of the 1960s and 1970s, it would be both impractical and inappropriate for her—or any other white person—to think that she could challenge U.S. racism in any large-scale way. If there were such a movement, she said,

> then I would know more what my role is going to be. But I feel like, as it is, none of us has a movement. The women's movement is what? It's not a movement, it's little enclaves. . . . There's nothing really holding us together.

Moreover, Donna suggested that solidarity should not mean negating either one's own identity or the reality of one's own relationships to subordination as well as privilege. Despite their rhetoric, leaders of the party to which she belonged for several years had, she felt, at times played on the guilt of white activists. In this sense, the Central America solidarity movement had in recent years felt like a practical place for Donna to work:

> The thing about Nicaragua is that they said, "We need your help, we want you to do this," but we could define for ourselves how we wanted to do that. And they have been open to gay and lesbian brigades, they've been open to new ideas.

In the meantime, Donna had not been passively waiting for a mass movement to arise in the United States. Rather, she explained, she felt most confident in analyzing and acting on issues of structural and institutional inequality in her immediate surroundings. Thus, for example, in her workplace (a feminist non-profit agency) she had worked with women of color to remedy a situation in which they had no influence over agency decisions and policy. But Donna was also frustrated with her white co-workers' approach to challenging racism, which she felt paralleled the situation among white feminists in general:

> I think it's true that [change] is happening in certain sectors, and at least the rhetoric of being antiracist happens. But I think it's still being done in a way that white women define the terms for how racism is being understood. And it's sort of, like, if you don't personalize it—they want it totally done in this personalized style, they don't want to deal with the whole other big picture. And they want it to be, "Oh, I won't say this any more," "Oh, was I being—?" And it keeps it on such a trivial level. And I feel like it's very superficial, and I feel like, we're not gonna get *down* and really deal (this is what I think Black women are saying) until

you're prepared to listen and understand what the real issue is. It's not just about this little interaction. . . .

And that's why, when that struggle came up at [my workplace]— where it was like, this white woman was being— Racism is going to happen. But the real issue was the structural racism occurring there. The whole trip was being defined by all white women, from a totally white perspective. And this woman was put into a higher position. They went right over the heads of these two women of color, who had been there longer. . . . The only way I could relate to the whole issue was to say, "We need to change things here structurally, so that the women of color who are in positions of responsibility should have input into the hiring and firing, promotion and training."

Donna in fact used the term "racism" in a range of different ways, for the most part reserving it for the phenomenon named elsewhere in this book as "race privilege." Thus, Donna had said at one point in the interview, "I wouldn't say I'm any less racist than I used to be, so much as more conscious of it." But in regard to her workplace, Donna distinguished between "racism" in the sense of interpersonal interactions and "racism" in the sense of differential access to power.

It was in relation to individual "little interactions" that Donna's abhorrence of what she called "the subjective" came into play. Focus on the "subjective," Donna felt, created room for individual whims to be elevated to political principles. As a working-class woman, Donna felt that in the past she had participated in "accusing" other women of middle-class behavior. However, she and other working-class women frequently disagreed, she said, about what was "middle class" and what was not: she and a working-class friend had even disagreed over whether eating raisins was an inescapably bourgeois practice! Donna felt that the same thing might happen in relation to racism, with an individual woman of color insisting on the inappropriateness of an action that for another woman of color might be perfectly acceptable. Moreover, Donna felt, to "charge" people with their class or racial identity is to incite and play on guilt, and is ultimately beside the point, the latter, for Donna, being to bring about institutional and structural changes. These, in turn, would in Donna's view create situations where decisions about racial or class empowerment might be made more democratically, rather than by individuals who, however well-intentioned they might be, still had structural privilege. (On the other hand, as I have argued, histories of structural and institutional racism are frequently embedded in apparently trivial actions, words, or gestures. If nothing else, attention to the "subjective" might thus be used as opportunities to make those histories more visible and to learn from them.)

Rejecting the "subjective" did not, however, lead Donna to any lack of interest in exploring how women's daily lives are shaped by race and class. Pragmatism rather than anxiety characterized Donna's explorations, as it did Jeanine's. When she emphatically agreed with a Black nationalist analysis of U.S. history, Donna translated her sense of the interplay of race and class not into a cause for anxiety but into further confirmation of her analysis and of her sense that "solidarity," not leadership, was the most useful position for her to adopt. While Donna was married, for example, she had worked as a secretary for an insurance company. There, for the first time, she became friends with a Black woman, a co-worker:

It was just after I had my first baby. Remember, [my husband] got in an accident and almost died? . . . Well, I was working with a woman, she was about seven or eight years older than me. They had her keeping files, and she had to keep files of some of the most atrocious pictures of [accidents], people with burns, the worst, that nobody else would look at, really, they had her doing. And she had been there for years, doing the same job. Well, I came in, and I got promoted, right away. And I noticed it. I noticed the difference right away. And she and I just became friends. I was really freaked out [by my husband's accident] and she helped me through that period, emotionally. And she and I traded a twenty dollar bill back and forth for years, you know, where she'd loan me twenty, I'd loan her twenty, she'd loan me twenty. . . . From her, I really saw that her life, her job situation, [were] a lot different than mine. Just by the way I came in, I was young and white, and I got promoted, a couple times. And she stayed in the same place, her money was the same, she always had bills. I went to her place, and she—just had to do all kinds of things, to cope. And I didn't have to do that. Even though I was in a similar situation. Even after [my husband] and I broke up. There was a way in which I had an easier time of getting jobs.

I got out of the city, and she was envious, she wanted to but she couldn't. And I'd try to encourage her to come. You know, she just saw me as moving up and moving out, getting away, being able to have mobility that she didn't have. And when I got political, later on, I came back, and I was like, "Wow, it's going on in San Francisco, people are really political. They're not accepting this shit." And I realized that I had accepted her situation because she did. I knew there was a big difference between us, but until I met, and got, and heard, and felt a movement that said, "We've had enough, we don't have to live this way anymore,

I'm Black and I'm proud" and all that, I just sort of accepted that situation, and those differences. And when I tried to tell her about it, I think she got a little scared. And that made me realize that, you know, it wasn't a white person's place to give a Black person—or anybody really—their freedom. That was just, kind of, a real naive experience, I think, that I had of saying, "Hey! You don't have to take this anymore." But her conditions, and the possibilities around her weren't that different, and she couldn't just suddenly become a militant.

What links the voices of Marjorie, Jeanine, and Donna is their pragmatism: their determination neither to evade the specter of racism nor to become mesmerized by it and thereby frozen into inactivity, but rather to engage systematically in the process of making change. Their pragmatism also made them humble in their approach to social change—Donna specifically used that word in describing solidarity, and Marjorie commented that throughout her antiracist activism she had always learned and gained more than she gave. However, their humility did not seem to lead toward the guilt and self-hate that in Cathy's and Clare's accounts threatened to turn back on themselves in anger or frustration with the antiracist project.

Both the longevity and the contexts of these women's activism shaped their race cognizance. Concrete experience of antiracist or anti-imperialist work meant that they had had opportunities to see, feel, and evaluate the effects of diverse strategies. In addition, they had read about, thought about, and participated in some of the movements whose theory provided the reference markers for the younger race-cognizant women. This made their analyses more complex and more nuanced than those of women who used the Klan, lynching, or U.S. imperialism as points from which to begin naming racism and white domination, but couched them in dualistic terms that owed as much to power evasiveness as to the logic of the movements from which those reference points sprang.

These women demanded a great deal of themselves and of other white people, and at times they made some of the same demands on people of color. Here, their views once again contrasted with those of younger women, newer to antiracism (remember, for example, Cathy Thomas's saying that the "truth" lay with the perspectives of women of color). Jeanine and Donna argued for both white people and people of color to practice compassion, patience, and dialogue and to reject "guilt-tripping." At times it was hard to evaluate the extent to which their demands and strategies only made sense given the kinds of work these particular individuals (and other white people like them) had already done: how far, for example, would it be legitimate to ask activists of color to be patient with white women or men as yet unwilling or unable to become race cognizant in any meaningful way? However, I do not mean to suggest that these women's words are relevant only to themselves: they offer crucial models for women like Chris, Beth, Cathy, and Clare, newer to the process of thinking about racism and race privilege and working hard to disengage themselves from dualistic, no-exit analyses.

Conclusion

In examining white women's modes of thinking through race, I have argued that three discursive repertoires—essentialist racism, color and power evasion, and race cognizance—together constituted a universe of discourse on race difference and racism in these narratives. At stake in each of these repertoires is a set of questions about the kind of difference race makes in the formation both of subjects and of social structures.

The status of the white subject was at stake in these repertoires as much as, if not more than, that of the subject of color. Thus, for example, one key element of color and power evasion is the production of a white self innocent of racism. The power of that particular element of the color- and power-evasive repertoire is, moreover, evidenced in the fact that it, more than any other element, was carried over into the race cognizance of all but a few of the women I interviewed. The evasion of or engagement with white guilt and complicity with respect to racism are, in other words, perhaps what is at the heart of each of these discursive repertoires on the meaning of race difference—or at least at the heart of white appropriations of them. Lest this reading appear too cynical, let me qualify it, first by suggesting that anxiety about white complicity with racism is perhaps less central to a fully fledged race cognizance than to the other discursive repertoires examined here. Second, even evasion of color and power is, as I have suggested, ambivalent rather than unilateral in its focus on white noncomplicity. As such, it is structured so as to assert the idea of crossracial common humanity, albeit on white-

centered terms, at the same time as it averts the white gaze from the harsh realities of power imbalance.

White women's relationships to discursive repertoires are by no means simple. By the same token, these repertoires' locations in time and space are also complex. Thus, the chronological order of emergence of the repertoires dictated neither their power nor the terms of white women's engagements with them. I have shown that, rather than any smooth or unilinear progression of emergence, preeminence, and fading away of a succession of repertoires having taken place, in fact, color and power evasion and race cognizance responded to one another's terms, and that both of these repertoires referred back, implicitly and explicitly, to the terms of essentialist racism. I have argued that, while essentialist racism—the notion that race makes a difference at the level of biology and being—continues to furnish elements of these white women's thinking about race, it was color and power evasion that dominated these narratives and in fact dominates public languages of race in the United States of today. The third repertoire, that of race cognizance, is, I have argued, a more recent and comparatively subordinate mode of thinking through race.

Because essentialist racism marked the inauguration of race as a meaningful difference, it continues to be the framework in and against which later discursive repertoires are elaborated. In other words, *because* race has been made into a difference, later discursive repertoires cannot simply abolish it, but must engage it. And because race difference was produced in *essentialist* rather than any other terms, it is to those essentialist terms that later critique remains accountable.

However, the extent to which the culture continues to be discursively caught in the terms of race has as much to do with the continued *material* salience of race as with discursive history per se. The integral relationships between material inequality and discursive repertoires was evident, for example, in the structuring of the color- and power-evasive repertoire. For that repertoire attempts to abolish race difference by means of evading the naming of differences of power organized by racial category and simultaneously evading acknowledgment of individual complicity with those very same differences of power or privilege ("It doesn't happen, and when it does, it's not my fault"). Again, as some of women moved toward race-cognizant strategies for thinking through race, the point at which appropriations of that reper

emerge out of internal contradiction, toward more coherent articulations of the meanings of race difference, is the point when
women began to link discursive reformulations of race to material
transformations of the racial order. In other words, the contradiction that discursive repertoires on race address—that between an
ontological human equality and the political context of racial inequality—can be exposed or obscured linguistically, but not resolved. Thus, one reaches here, as elsewhere in this text, the limit
point of the value of a focus on discourse, and attention is drawn
once again to the crucial interplay of discourse and material life.

7

Questions of Culture and Belonging

To be a Heinz 57 American, a white, class-confused American, land of the Kleenex type American, is so formless in and of itself. It only takes shape in relation to other people.

—*Cathy Thomas*

We had a traditional dinner at Thanksgiving and at Christmastime. But the only thing that would be celebrated for any nationality would be St. Paddy's Day.

—*Marty Douglass*

When we would take off for Yom Kippur or Rosh Hashanah, [the school] would say that we had to have the homework done that following day, and make up the work. And I remember my parents saying, "But there's no writing [on High Holidays]," and there was a big fuss.

—*Frieda Kazen*

In this chapter I focus on white women's descriptions of their cultural identities and in this context critically analyze dominant conceptions of culture. In the first section I explore the intersecting meanings of whiteness and Americanness as cultural constructs, analyzing their simultaneous conceptualization in many of the women's narratives as cultural norm and cultural residue. In the second section I ask how else white women name themselves in terms of cultural belonging within or alongside whiteness. In the third section, I look in detail at Ashkenazi Jewish women's narratives, for it was in these that a sense of cultural belonging was most fully articulated and, moreover, articulated as dynamic, transformable, lived experience. I conclude the chapter by proposing directions for a new analysis of white cultural practice and identity.

The chapter will meditate on the deployment and effects of two modes of conceptualizing culture. First, a dominant conception of culture—one that, I will argue, is part of the legacy of European colonial expansion—was key to the ways in which these white women spoke of cultural spaces and identities, their own and others'. Here, cultures were conceived as discrete, bounded spaces, culture was viewed as separate from material life, and some groups of people were considered more "cultural" than others. Hence, many of the women said that they "did not have a culture." Second, I will be arguing for a more dynamic conception of culture—or, better, "cultural practice"—whereby culture is no longer viewed as a separate sphere of life. I will show that, in fact, the cultural practices represented in these interviews were continually transformed through their interactions with other systems, institutions, and logics. I will also argue that, rather than viewing white culture as "no culture," we need to analyze the social and political contexts in which, like race privilege, white cultural practices mark out a normative space and set of identities, which those who inhabit them, however, frequently cannot see or name.

As elsewhere in the narratives, the women's discussions of whiteness and their sense of identity and belonging were shaped by several interwoven discursive repertoires, each with an identifiable moment of emergence. To begin with, elements of the race cognizance examined in chapter 6, in particular some women's critique of whiteness and Americanness as complicit with racism and imperialism, were in play, so that the women at times named both whiteness and Americanness as distinctively "bad" cultures and undesirable identities because of their links to systems of domination. Second, the legacy of liberal humanism that led the women to construct race difference both dualistically and asymmetrically (chapter 6) was again in operation here, so that some of the women constructed whiteness simultaneously as generic or normative and as an apparently empty cultural space.

But in addition to these by now familiar repertoires, elements of a discourse that was distinctively colonial (which is to say, associated with West European colonial expansion into the Americas, Africa, and Asia) were crucial in giving form to white women's conceptions of culture. It will thus be useful at the outset to elaborate briefly on some of the relevant elements of colonial discourse.

First, as West European travelers and, later, colonizing forces encountered the native people of Africa, Asia, and the Americas, they for the most part viewed them as irremediably different from, and inferior to, themselves. The situation is complicated, though. For at times, colonial discourse took the form, straightforwardly, of "essentialist racism."[1] At other times, travelers, explorers, and, later, colonial administrators valorized aspects of the histories and cultures of those they colonized. However, they did so in ways that, for the most part, viewed colonized people as fundamentally different from and "Other" than Europeans.[2]

Two feminist critics of colonial discourse whose work is especially relevant here are Trinh T. Minh-ha and Chandra Talpade Mohanty. Trinh has analyzed the legacy of colonialism in United States discourses on culture, including feminist discourses. Provocatively linking the status of such apparently diverse locations as the Chinatowns and American Indian reservations of the United States and the Bantustans of South Africa, Trinh points out that the status of some cultures as nameable and "bounded" goes alongside their marginalization from the dominant culture. As she argues, "bounded" cultures, while apparently valorized, are in fact relegated to "reservations" (or Chinatowns) in the name of "preservation," a process that has the effect of reinforcing rather than dislodging the normativeness of the dominant culture.[3]

Mohanty has analyzed the colonial legacy in feminist texts on women and development policy. Placing recent feminist writing in historical context, she proposes that, in fact, the Western subject discursively constructs a sense of self through producing, naming, and (to paraphrase Trinh's terms) "bounding" a range of Others.[4] It seems to me that discourses of whiteness are very much like those of Westernness in that both "white" and "Western" subjects are distinguished in part by being "not Other." (In addition, of course, "white" and "Western" status are conferred on the same physical bodies, in the context of closely tied historical processes; however, these do not produce entirely coterminous discourses.)

Historians and cultural critics have argued that colonial discourse generated a distinctive view of "culture," at times viewing colonized peoples as representatives or remnants of once great, but now deteriorated, cultural forms. Another element of colonial discourse viewed "culture" as a realm separate from material life, and a third made a sharp distinction between modernity and tradition in which "traditional" societies were deemed repositories of culture, and modern societies not so.[5] New critical scholarship analyzing the colonial legacy in anthropology has challenged the view of culture as static rather than dynamic, and as most authentic when untouched by capitalism or industrialization.[6] Approaches emerging from this critique have sought to document much more carefully the interweaving of culture, economics, and politics, both local and global, and to analyze cultures as dynamic and mobile rather than stable.[7]

In a parallel and sometimes intersecting process, theorists in the interdisciplinary field of cultural studies also conceive the terrain of culture in these broadened terms. Thus, for example, for Stuart Hall, culture refers to "the actual, grounded terrain of practices, representations, languages and customs of any specific historical society," as well as "the contradictory forms of 'common sense' which have taken root in and helped to shape popular life."[8] It is to conceptions of culture as practical, dynamic, and interwoven with other spheres of life activity that I will turn in attempting to critically reexamine whiteness as unmarked cultural space. In speaking of culture in the expanded, "cultural studies" sense of the term, I have found a useful starting point in the words of British race theorist Paul Gilroy, who characterizes culture as "a field articulating the life world of subjects (albeit decentred) and the structures created by human activity."[9] Finally, I want to point out that when in this chapter I explore conceptions of culture and in that regard speak of "cultural practice," the term "practice" in the singular designates not a thing but a process or activity. (By analogy, if one were to say that "most women in the United States go out to work," the use of *work* in the singular would not imply that most U.S. women do the same work, but rather that, in general, they engage in the activity of working. I use *practice* in this active sense of the term.) Thus, "white cultural practice" does not suggest uniformity of belief system or worldview, but rather the idea that activity is taking place.

Whiteness As an "Unmarked" Cultural Category

America's supposed to be the melting pot. I know that I've got a huge number of nationalities in my blood, but how do I—what do I call myself? And hating this country as I do, I don't like to say I'm an American. Even though it is what I am. I hate identifying myself as only an American, because I have so much objections to Americans' place in the world. I don't know how I felt about that when I was growing up, but I never—I didn't like to pledge allegiance to the flag. . . . Still, at this point in my life, I wonder what it is that somebody with all this melting pot blood can call their own. . . .

Especially growing up in the sixties, when people *did* say "I'm proud to be Black," "I'm proud to be Hispanic," you know, and it became very popular to be proud of your ethnicity. And even feminists, you know, you could say, "I'm a woman," and be proud of it. But there's still a majority of the country that can't say they are proud of anything!

Suzie Roberts's words powerfully illustrate the key themes of this section and the linked, yet analytically separable, questions that stirred the women I interviewed as they examined their own identities: what had formed them, what they counted as (their own or others') cultural practice(s), and what constituted identities of which they could be proud. This section explores perceptions of whiteness as a location of culture and identity, focusing mainly on white feminist (that is, ostensibly "race-cognizant") women's views and contrasting their voices with those of more politically conservative women.

A set of historical and political processes helped to explain the status of white culture in these women's narratives. For those who drew on a race-cognizant repertoire, the collective sense of whiteness was marked by the post-1960s period, the emergence of new social movements against racism, and the persistence of racial inequality. In a parallel way, they saw the United States, and the world at large, in terms of an extended period of decolonization in which for many U.S. interventionism has lost its legitimacy. However, this is clearly by no means a postcolonial world. The question of "white right" or white and U.S. domination has thus been begged but not answered. In this context many of the women I interviewed, including even some of the conservative ones, appeared to be self-conscious about white power and racial inequality. In part because of their sense of the links and parallels between white racial dominance in the United States and U.S. domination on a global scale, there was a complex interweaving of questions about race and nation—whiteness and Americanness—in these women's thoughts about white culture. Similarly, conceptions of racial, national, and cultural belonging frequently leaked into one another.

On the one hand, then, these women's views of white culture seemed to be distinctively modern. But at the same time, their words drew on much earlier historical moments and participated in long-established modes of cultural description. In the broadest sense, Western colonial discourses on the white self, the non-white Other, and the white Other too, were very much in evidence. These discourses produced dualistic conceptualizations of whiteness versus other cultural forms. The women thus often spoke about culture in ways that reworked, and yet remained tied to, "older" forms of racism.

For a significant number of young white women, being white felt like being cultureless. Cathy Thomas, in the following description of whiteness, raised many of the themes alluded to by other feminist and race-cognizant women. She described what she saw as a lack of form and substance:

> . . . the formlessness of being white. Now if I was a middle western girl, or a New Yorker, if I had a fixed regional identity that was something palpable, then I'd be a white New Yorker, no doubt, but I'd still be a New Yorker. . . . Being a Californian, I'm sure it has its hallmarks, but to me they were invisible. . . . If I had an ethnic base to identify from, if I was even Irish American, that would have been something formed, if I was a working-class woman, that would have been something formed. But to be a Heinz 57 American, a white, class-confused American, land of the Kleenex type American, is so formless in and of itself. It only takes shape in relation to other people.

Whiteness as a cultural space is represented here as amorphous and indescribable, in contrast with a range of other identities marked by race, ethnicity, region, and class. Further, white culture is viewed here as "bad" culture. In fact, the extent to which identities can be named seems to show an inverse relationship to power in the U.S. social structure. The elisions, parallels, and differences between characterizations of white people, Americans, people of color, and so-called white ethnic groups will be explored through the chapter.

Cathy's own cultural positioning seemed to her impossible to grasp, shapeless and unnameable. It was easier to know others and to know, with certainty, what one was *not*. Providing a clue to one of the mechanisms operating here is the fact that, while Cathy viewed New Yorkers and midwesterners as having a cultural shape or identity, women from the East Coast and the Midwest also described or mourned their own seeming lack of culture. The self, where it is part of a dominant cultural group, does not have to name itself. In this regard, Chris Patterson hit the nail on the head, linking the power of white culture with the privilege not to be named:

> I'm probably at the stage where I'm beginning to see that you can come up with a definition of white. Before, I didn't know that you could turn it around and say, "Well what *does* white mean?" One thing is, it's taken for granted. . . . [To be white means to] have some sort of advantage or privilege, even if it's something as simple as not having a definition.

The notion of "turning it around" indicates Chris's realization that, most often, whites are the nondefined definers of other people. Or, to put it another way, whiteness comes to be an unmarked or neutral category, whereas other cultures are specifically marked "cultural."

Many of the women shared the habit of turning to elements of white culture as the unspoken norm. This assumption of a white norm was so prevalent that even Sandy Alvarez and Louise Glebocki, who were acutely aware of racial inequality as well as being members of racially mixed families, referred to "Mexican" music versus "regular" music, and regular meant "white."

Similarly, discussions of race difference and cultural diversity at times revealed a view in which people of color actually embodied difference and whites stood for sameness. Hence, Margaret Phillips said of her Jamaican daughter-in-law that: "She *really* comes with diversity." In spite of its brevity, and because of its curious structure, this short statement says a great deal. It implicitly designates whiteness as norm, and Jamaicans as having or bearing with them "differentness." At the risk of being crass, one might say that in this view, diversity is to the daughter-in-law as "the works" is to a hamburger—added on, adding color and flavor, but not exactly essential. Whiteness, seen by many of these women as boring, but nonetheless definitive, could also follow this analogy. This mode of thinking about "difference" expresses clearly the double-edged sword of what I have referred to as a color- and power-evasive repertoire, apparently valorizing cultural difference but doing so in a way that leaves racial and cultural hierarchies intact.

For a seemingly formless entity, then, white culture had a great deal of power, difficult to dislodge from its place in white consciousness as a point of reference for the measuring of others. Whiteness served simultaneously to eclipse and marginalize others (two modes of making the other inessential). Helen Standish's description of her growing-up years in a small New England town captured these processes well. Since the community was all white, the differences at issue were differences between whites. (This also enables an assessment of the links between white and nonwhite "marked" cultures.) Asked about her own cultural identity, Helen explained that "it didn't seem like a culture because everyone else was the same." She had, however, previously mentioned Italian Americans in the town, so I asked about their status. She responded as follows, adopting at first the voice of childhood:

> They are different, but I'm the same as everybody else. They speak Italian, but everybody else in the U.S. speaks English. They eat strange, different food, but I eat the same kind of food as everybody else in the U.S. . . . The way I was brought up was to think that everybody who was the same as me were "Americans," and the other people were of "such and such descent."

Viewing the Italian Americans as different and oneself as "same" serves, first, to marginalize, to push from the center, the former group. At the same time, claiming to be the same as *everyone* else makes other cultural groups invisible or eclipses them. Finally, there is a marginalizing of all those who are not like Helen's own family, leaving a residual, core or normative group who are the true Americans. The category of "American" represents simultaneously the normative and the residual, the dominant culture and a nonculture.

Although Helen talked here about whites, it is safe to guess that people of color would not have counted among the "same" group but among the communities of "such and such descent" (Mexican American, for example). Whites, within this discursive repertoire, became conceptually the real Americans, and only certain kinds of whites actually qualified. Whiteness and Americanness both stood as normative and exclusive categories in relation to which other cultures were identified and marginalized. And this clarifies that there are two kinds of whites, just as there are two kinds of Americans: those who are truly or only white, and those who are white but also something more—or is it something less?

In sum, whiteness often stood as an unmarked marker of others' differentness—whiteness not so much void or formlessness as norm. I associate this construction with colonialism and with the more recent assymetrical dualisms of liberal humanist views of culture, race, and identity. For the most part, this construction views nonwhite cultures as lesser, deviant, or pathological. However, another trajectory has been the inverse: conceptualizations of the cultures of peoples of color as somehow better than the dominant culture, perhaps more natural or more spiritual. These are positive evaluations of a sort, but they are equally dualistic. Many of the women I interviewed saw white culture as less appealing and found the cultures of the "different" people more interesting. As Helen Standish put it:

> [We had] Wonder bread, white bread. I'm more interested in, you know, "What's a bagel?" in other people's cultures rather than my own.

The claim that whiteness lacks form and content says more about the definitions of culture being used than it does about the content of whiteness. I will return to this point later. However, I would suggest that in describing themselves as cultureless these women are in fact identifying specific kinds of unwanted absences or presences in their own culture(s) as a generalized lack or non-existence. It thus becomes important to look at what they *did* say about the cultural content of whiteness.

Descriptions of the content of white culture were thin, to say the least. But despite the paucity of signifiers, there was a great deal of consistency across the narratives. First, there was naming based on color, the linking of white culture with white objects— the clichéd white bread and mayonnaise, for example. Freida Kazen's identification of whiteness as "bland," together with Helen Standish's "blah," also signified paleness or neutrality. The images connote several things—color itself (although exaggerated, and besides, bagels are usually white inside, too), lack of vitality (Wonder bread is highly processed), and homogeneity. However, these images are perched on a slippery slope, at once suggesting "white" identified as a color (though an unappealing one) and as an absence of color, that is, white as the unmarked marker.

Whiteness was often signified in these narratives by commodities and brands: Wonder bread, Kleenex, Heinz 57. In this identification whiteness came to be seen as spoiled by capitalism, and as being linked with capitalism in a way that other cultures supposedly are not. Another set of signifiers that constructed whiteness as uniquely tainted by capitalism had to do with the "modern condition": Dot Humphrey described white neighborhoods as

"more privatized," and Cathy Thomas used "alienated" to describe her cultural condition. Clare Traverso added to this theme,
mourning her own feeling of lack of identity, in contrast with images of her husband's Italian American background (and here,
Clare is again talking about perceived differences between whites):

> Food, old country, mama. Stories about a grandmother who can't speak
> English. . . . Candles, adobe houses, arts, music. [It] has emotion,
> feeling, belongingness that to me is unique.

In linking whiteness to capitalism and viewing nonwhite cultures as untainted by it, these women were again drawing on a
colonial discourse in which progress and industrialization were
seen as synonymous with Westernization, while the rest of the
world is seen as caught up in tradition and "culture." In addition,
one can identify, in white women's mourning over whiteness, elements of what Raymond Williams has called "pastoralism," or
nostalgia for a golden era now gone by (but in fact, says Williams,
one that never existed).[10]

The image of whiteness as corrupted and impoverished by capitalism is but one of a series of ways in which white culture was
seen as impure or tainted. White culture was also seen as tainted
by its relationship to power. For example, Clare Traverso clearly
counterposed white culture and white power, finding it difficult
to value the former because of the overwhelming weight of the
latter:

> The good things about whites are to do with folk arts, music. Because
> other things have power associated with them.

For many race-cognizant white women, white culture was also
made impure by its very efforts to maintain race purity. Dot
Humphrey, for example, characterized white neighborhoods as
places in which people were segregated by choice. For her, this
was a good reason to avoid living in them.

The link between whiteness and domination, however, was
frequently made in ways that both artificially isolated culture
from other factors and obscured economics. For at times, the
traits the women envied in Other cultures were in fact at least in
part the product of poverty or other dimensions of oppression.
Lack of money, for example, often means lack of privacy or
space, and it can be valorized as "more street life, less alienation."

Cathy Thomas's notion of Chicanas' relationship to the kitchen ("the hearth of the home") as a cultural "good" might be an idealized one that disregards the reality of intensive labor.

Another link between class and culture emerged in Louise Glebocki's reference to the working-class Chicanos she met as a child as less pretentious, "closer to the truth," more "down to earth." And Marjorie Hoffman spoke of the "earthy humor" of Black people, which she interpreted as, in the words of Langston Hughes, a means of "laughing to keep from crying." On the one hand, as has been pointed out especially by Black scholars and activists, the positions of people of color at the bottom of a social and economic hierarchy create the potential for a critique of the system as a whole and consciousness of the need to resist.[11] Indeed, I argue in this book that from the standpoint of race privilege, the system of racism is made structurally invisible. On the other hand, descriptions of this kind leave in place a troubling dichotomy that can be appropriated as easily by the right as by the left. For example, there is an inadvertent affinity between the image of Black people as "earthy" and the conservative racist view that African American culture leaves African American people ill equipped for advancement in the modern age. Here, echoing essentialist racism, both Chicanos and African Americans are placed on the borders of "nature" and "culture."

By the same token, often what was criticized as "white" was as much the product of middle-class status as of whiteness as such. Louise Glebocki's image of her fate had she married a white man was an image of a white-collar, nuclear family:

> Him saying, 'I'm home, dear,' and me with an apron on—ugh!

The intersections of class, race, and culture were obscured in other ways. Patricia Bowen was angry with some of her white feminist friends who, she felt, embraced as "cultural" certain aspects of African American, Chicano, and Native American cultures (including, for example, artwork or dance performances) but would reject as "tacky" (her term) those aspects of daily life that communities of color shared with working-class whites, such as the stores and supermarkets of poor neighborhoods. This, she felt, was tantamount to a selective expansion of middle-class aesthetic horizons, but not to true antiracism or to comprehension of the cultures of people of color. Having herself grown up in a white working-class family (see chapter 3), Pat also felt that middle-class white feminists were able to use selective engagement to avoid addressing their class privilege.

I have already indicated some of the problems inherent in this kind of conceptualization, suggesting that it tends to keep in place dichotomous constructions of "white" versus Other cultures, to separate "culture" from other dimensions of daily life, and to reify or strip of history *all* cultural forms. There are, then, a range of issues that need to be disentangled if we are to understand the location of "whiteness" in the terrain of culture. It is, I believe, useful to approach this question by means of a reconceptualization of the concept of culture itself. A culture, in the sense of the set of rules and practices by means of which a group organizes itself and its values, manners, and worldview—in other words, culture as "a field articulating the life-world of subjects . . . and the structures created by human activity"[12]—is an indispensable precondition to any individual's existence in the world. It is nonsensical in terms of this kind of definition to suggest that anyone could actually have "no culture." But this is not, as I have suggested, the mode of thinking about culture that these women are employing.

Whiteness emerges here as inextricably tied to domination partly as an effect of a discursive "draining process" applied to both whiteness and Americanness. In this process, any cultural practice engaged in by a white person that is not identical to the dominant culture is automatically counted as either "not really white"—and, for that matter, not really American, either—(but rather of such and such descent), or as "not really cultural" (but rather "economic"). There is a slipperiness to whiteness here: it shifts from "no culture" to "normal culture" to "bad culture" and back again. Simultaneously, a range of marginal or, in Trinh T. Minh-ha's terminology, "bounded" cultures are generated. These are viewed as enviable spaces, separate and untainted by relations of dominance or by linkage to other structures or systems. By contrast, whiteness is conceived as axiomatically tied to dominance, to economics, to political structures. In this process, both whiteness and nonwhiteness are reified, made into objects rather than processes, and robbed of historical context and human agency. (I will explore that historical context later.) As long as the discussion remains couched in these terms, a critique of whiteness remains a double-edged sword: for one thing, whiteness remains normative because there is no way to name the cultural practices associated with it *as* cultural. Moreover, as I have suggested, whether whiteness is viewed as artificial and dominating (and therefore "bad") or civilized (and therefore "good"), whiteness and all varieties of nonwhiteness continue to be viewed as ontologically different from one another.

A genuine sadness and frustration about the meaning of whiteness at this moment in history motivated these women to decry white culture. It becomes important, then, to recognize the grains of truth in their views of white culture. It is important to acknowledge their anger and frustration about the meaning of whiteness as we reach toward a politicized analysis of culture that is freer of colonial and pastoral legacies.

The terms "white" and "American" as these women used them signified domination in international and domestic terms. This link is both accurate and inaccurate. While it is true that, by and large, those in power in the United States are white, it is also true that not all those who are white are in power. Nor is the axiomatic linkage between Americanness and power accurate, because not all Americans have the same access to power. At the same time, the link between whiteness, Americanness, and power *are* accurate because, as we have seen, the terms "white" and "American" both function discursively to exclude people from normativity—including white people "of such and such descent." But here we need to distinguish between the fates of people of color and those of white people. Notwithstanding a complicated history, the boundaries of Americanness and whiteness have been much more fluid for "white ethnic" groups than for people of color.

There have been border skirmishes over the meaning of whiteness and Americanness since the inception of those terms. For white people, however, those skirmishes have been resolved through processes of assimilation, not exclusion. The late nineteenth and early twentieth centuries in the United States saw a systematic push toward the cultural homogenization of whites carried out through social reform movements and the schools. This push took place alongside the expansion of industrial capitalism, giving rise to the sense that whiteness signifies the production and consumption of commodities under capitalism.[13] But

recognition of this history should not be translated into an assertion that whites were stripped of culture (for to do that would be
to continue to adhere to a colonial view of "culture"). Instead one
must argue that certain cultural practices replaced others. Were
one to undertake a history of this "generic" white culture, it
would fragment into a thousand tributary elements, culturally
specific religious observances, and class survival mechanisms as
well as mass-produced commodities and mass media.

There are a number of dangers inherent in continuing to view
white culture as no culture. Whiteness appeared in the narratives
to function as both norm or core, that against which everything
else is measured, and as residue, that which is left after everything
else has been named. A far-reaching danger of whiteness coded as
"no culture" is that it leaves in place whiteness as defining a set of
normative cultural practices against which all are measured and
into which all are expected to fit. This normativity has under-
written oppression from the beginning of colonial expansion and
has had impact in multiple ways: from the American pioneers'
assumption of a norm of private property used to justify appropriation of land that within their worldview did not have an
owner, and the ideological construction of nations like Britain as
white,[14] to Western feminism's Eurocentric shaping of its movements and institutions. It is important for white feminists not to
continue to participate in these processes.

And if whiteness has a history, so do the cultures of people of
color, which are worked on, crafted, and created, rather than just
"there." For peoples of color in the United States, this work has
gone on as much in the context of relationships to imperialism
and capitalism as has the production of whiteness, though it has
been premised on exclusion and resistance to exclusion more than
on assimilation. Although not always or only forged in resistance,
the visibility and recognition of the cultures of U.S. peoples of
color in recent times *is* the product of individual and collective
struggle. Only a short time has elapsed since those struggles made
possible the introduction into public discourse of celebration and
valorization of their cultural forms. In short, it is important not
to reify any culture by failing to acknowledge its createdness, and
not to view it as always having been there in unchanging form.

Rather than feeling "cultureless," white women need to become
conscious of the histories and specificities of our cultural positions, and of the political, economic, and creative fusions that

form all cultures. The purpose of such an exercise is not, of course, to reinvert the dualisms and valorize whiteness so much as to develop a clearer sense of where and who we are.

Whiteness Inflected: Other Modes of Belonging

But where and who *are* we? While none of the women I interviewed felt that they were *not* white, whiteness seemed to be neither a clearly definable cultural terrain nor, for many of them, a desirable one. I have argued that a mix of awareness of white racial domination and colonial discourses on "culture" gives rise to a discourse on the meaning of "white" and Other cultures that, while it inverts the hierarchy that views nonwhite cultures as "bad" and white cultures as "good," remains dualistic. It is also, of course, the continuance of white racial domination that holds in place the status of whiteness as normative masquerading as "generic"—unadorned, basic, essential.

This section asks what, if not whiteness per se, these women identified with or named themselves by. The women at times named modes of belonging based on the regions in which they had grown up, their ancestors' countries of origin, religion, ethnicity, and class. Although apparently disparate, these were all categories around which different women articulated a sense of belonging or identity. Each of them provided, if nothing else, a name ("I am Irish," for example). Some women had been given, along with such names, a sense of the nonbelonging of others, a sense of superiority ("*Our* ancestors came over on the *Mayflower*") or a sense that others felt superior to *them*. At times, a woman's sense of belonging was reinforced by a perceived gulf of understanding or experience between her own group and other people, together with, conversely, a camaraderie or feeling of shared experience with others from the same class, regional, ethnic, or religious community.

On one level it is possible to comprehend all of these modes of identification in terms of the persistence of a dualistic discourse on culture. Underpinning their effectiveness as "belonging names" was, precisely, the fact that unlike the name "white" they were not ostensibly generic, which is to say, not normative to the point of invisibility. This, in turn, as I will argue, also had to do with cultural practices' differential relationships to power. However, through reading these women's accounts of belonging, it is possible to move from entrapment in the dualistic toward analysis of it. From there, one can move toward another, broader definition of culture: culture as a mode of organizing daily life and world-view; culture as inseparable from material life; and "bounded" cultures as, in fact, continually functioning "in and against" the dominant culture itself.

The narratives could be placed on a continuum of sorts, from "thin" descriptions of belonging to more detailed accounts. The descriptions were linked to particular groups' past and present re-lationships to power, past and present degrees of inclusion or ex-clusion from the dominant cultural space of whiteness. It is pos-sible, by looking at what the women said about their *own* cultural identities within and beyond whiteness, to ask the narratives to speak to one another: to compare one against another in order to deconstruct the dualistic view that regards "culture" as something that some people have while others do not and sees "cultures" as bounded, static, and enviable spaces of belonging. In concluding this section, I will use the idea of social and political salience to help analyze the meaning of different kinds of belonging.

In contrast with the small number of women who identified themselves as "white" without being asked to do so, it was strik-ing that, in the course of the interviews, all but one woman named at least one group with a geographical or religious referent with which she or her family identified. Moreover, the majority volunteered, rather than having to be asked for, the "belonging names" with which they identified, as in, for example, "I'd have to call myself a southerner" (Ginny Rodd) and "I was born in South Africa to Jewish progressives" (Jeanine Cohen).

Some of the women answered questions about childhood neighborhoods in terms of ethnicity:

> I grew up in a small town in New Jersey. It was mostly Italian, probably some Irish Catholic, pretty much a Christian town. We may have been the first Jewish family to move in.

Some women could offer details of the geographical origins of the last two to three generations of their families. But at the same time, in its most minimal form, cultural belonging seemed like an heirloom, a genealogy, perhaps an annual celebration, rather than a way of life. In response to a question from me, for example, Marty Douglass explained that she was a fifth-generation Califor-nian on her mother's side and that her mother's family had been in the town she lived in now by the time of the 1906 earthquake. She also thought there was some Italian blood in her maternal grandmother, because of her grandmother's dark hair, complexion, and surname. Marty said that her father was three-quarters Irish, his mother having emigrated from Ireland and his father having been part Irish too:

> RF: You were saying something [earlier] about St. Patrick's Day, and you were saying that was the only thing that you did that was typically Irish.
>
> MARTY: Yeah, it was about the food we ate. That was the only thing we ever ate that had to do with—we were raised that way, St. Paddy's Day, you know, that was Irish day. The day St. Patrick took all the slaves out of Ireland or something like that, you know, that's what they celebrated. So you were supposed to have corned beef and cabbage. A lot of people still do, you know, have corned beef and cabbage on St. Patrick's Day. But that was the only one. We had a traditional dinner at Thanksgiving and at Christmastime. But the only thing that would be celebrated for any nationality would be St. Paddy's Day.
>
> RF: And you did that with the feeling that you were Irish?
>
> MARTY: We *knew* we were Irish! But, no, we were told, "This is an Irish dish." Corned beef and cabbage. 'Course, my dad would have liked it every other day! So does my husband. He says, "Why only fix it on St. Patrick's Day?"
>
> RF: So you do it too?
>
> MARTY: Yes, he loves it. He's three-quarters Irish. That's where his mother's from.

We may note in passing that Thanksgiving is in fact also a holiday with specifically national and in fact racial origins, celebrating white colonizers' survival on the North American continent. It is probably because of its normativity in the context of the United States that Marty does not count it as a "national" holiday.

Many women's accounts fell into this pattern of "thin description," naming an ethnic heritage marked, basically, by simple knowledge of their genealogy in terms of their states or countries of origin, together with one or two signifiers—the celebration of a day, a relative's coloring or surname, a traditional food. For some, the feeling of identification was actually quite strong, as in Marty's emphatic statement, while for the most part having little or no impact on daily practice.

Interestingly, with the exception of Jewish women, this pattern of "thin description" was common to all the women raised in the 1950s and later on the West Coast: Louise Glebocki, Cathy

Thomas, Sandy Alvarez, Clare Traverso, Donna Gonzaga. Some of this "young Californian" group in fact knew much less than Marty about their families' ethnic origins. Cathy Thomas, for example, described her irritation with her father's dismissal of her questions about the family:

> He would say, "You're English, you're Irish, and you're Scottish"—in other words, he didn't know.

For the women under forty raised on the East Coast (and again, non-Jews), distinctions among different kinds of white folk were slightly more salient to daily practices, but mainly in terms of their parents constructing hierarchies of perceived status. For example, I have described Helen Standish's experience of inscription, as a child in Massachusetts, into a landscape of white ethnic groups distinguished by language, food, and status. But Helen's mother's insistence on her *Mayflower* ancestry did not correlate with any specific ways of acting in the world, aside from establishing a sense of herself as superior and shaping her behavior toward her Italian American neighbors.

Chris Patterson told a similar story, of being taught an attitude of scorn and hostility toward other white ethnic groups—people who were Jews, Poles, Germans—in the all-white neighborhood where she grew up. But although her parents commented freely on the food, child rearing, and morality of ethnic others, this did not go along with any strong sense on the part of Chris's own family of an ethnic identity of its own:

> RF: Did your family see themselves as part of a particular group—like there were German, Jewish, Polish—
>
> CHRIS: No—
>
> RF: —Irish?
>
> CHRIS: We were part Irish. There was always—especially in New England, you know your family heritage, so mine was Irish and English. But we never categorized ourselves. No.

In effect, then, for women like Chris and Helen, ethnicity was more meaningful as a descriptor of others than of self. Thus far, we have not seen much linkage between culture as name and culture in the fuller sense of "a field articulating the life-world of subjects . . . and the structures created by human activity." In other words, cultural and ethnic belonging in these women's conceptualization occupied a narrow sphere, remaining rather abstract as signifiers of identity.

Irene Esterley, a generation older, offered a richer description of the meaning of ethnicity. Irene grew up during the late 1920s and 1930s in Detroit, in an almost all Jewish neighborhood, but as the daughter of German gentile immigrant parents (see chapter 6). Irene had a strong sense of belonging to a German ethnic group and could talk in detail about its meaning in practical, daily terms. In fact, some of my questions about cultural belonging actually sounded rather foolish to Irene:

> RF: Were you always aware that you were German?
>
> IRENE: Well, with the fact that my grandparents and my mother were speaking German, yes. . . .
>   But as far as talking to me about being German, no. I had a sense—I mean, how could I not, with Germans on both sides of the family? My father's family was German too. You know, we have [she lists all the German surnames in the family]. I mean, how could I not know I'm German? (Laughs)

Language, then, was one obvious marker of ethnic identity. Irene's mother and paternal grandmother spoke German to one another, especially when they did not want Irene to understand them. Sadly for her, Irene's hopes of learning the language were thwarted by the onset of World War II, which prompted her high school to stop teaching German. Irene also spoke of the problems her grandfather had faced because of his inability to write in English, despite having been educated in Europe to read and write no fewer than six other languages. In contrast with those younger women who knew from which countries their forbears had come, but not when or why, Irene had spent summers with her extended family, hearing stories of the political disputes that had forced her grandparents to emigrate from Berlin to the United States. She also met family friends from Germany who commented with surprise and dismay on the family's downward mobility:

> I remember [the guests] saying "Your father would have been shocked to see all his sons working on the farm doing manual labor." They had been raised with servants.

Thus, when Irene said that her parents had not spoken to her about being German, this was, I think, an indicator of the centrality of Germanness in Irene's memories of childhood, rather than of its insignificance. Being German was, in other words, a fact of life rather than a feature of self that had to be brought into play by naming it.

When I explained to Irene why I was pursuing this line of questioning, her response was interesting:

IRENE: How could I not know I'm German?

RF: Yeah, it's true. I'm just thinking about it because I think a lot of people, whatever their background is, or their heritage is, they are very far away from that now, they are much more, "Well, I'm American, and—"

IRENE: Well then, I could remember my grandmother saying [that] during World War I the FBI agents came out and questioned them and everything, and watched them. And then during World War II they did also. But they were never arrested or harassed. It was just rather unsettling that they were watched.

RF: I was going to ask you how it was being German during World War II, whether you experienced prejudice from people.

IRENE: Oh, very much. Not me personally, because my father owned defense plants, and after all, my father, mother, and myself, we were all born in this country. But the man that took my high school graduation pictures, . . . right after he took our pictures he was arrested and put into like a concentration camp. They were rounding up all the—

RF: Wow!

IRENE: Well, it was the same thing they did with the Japanese, it was exactly the same time. And they say the Japanese were the only ones put in internment camps. Well, this man was put into the internment camp in Detroit. They actually put them in the fairgrounds, because it was already fenced in. By the time he got out, he had lost his home. Well, we did get our pictures, he was finally released as not being a subversive agent. However, it was rather distressing. . . . I went through a lot of things like that.

Here I suggested to Irene that many people regard themselves as simply "American." In response, Irene shifted the ground dramatically away from the relatively benign terrain of heritage and daily habits. In part she seemed to be saying, "How could I not know I'm German, when the American government has at times refused to treat us as Americans, viewing us instead as potentially hostile to state interests?"

It should be noted, however, that one gets a sense of all of this as part of childhood rather than a way of life with significance in the present. Indeed, this was so for all of the women whose thoughts on ethnicity I have explored thus far. Irene, while talking with a great deal of warmth about the cultural milieu in which she grew up, and with a continued sense of the injustice of the lack of any widespread awareness of German Americans' internment, did not, so far as I could tell, participate in any specifically German American community activities at the time of the interview nor structure her life in ways that felt "German" to her.

Ginny Rodd also grew up in a cultural context with distinctive hallmarks very different from the ones that shaped her life at the time that we talked. Ginny, who was born in 1930 and raised in rural Alabama, still considered herself a southerner, despite having left the southern United States thirty years earlier. Her life on the farm was one of unremitting hard work; even as a child she was responsible for a good many of the indoor and outdoor tasks on the farm, in addition to going to school. Ginny married at fifteen and, because of her husband's asthma, did all the farm work while he took care of the house.

In the 1950s the Rodds' smallholding was bankrupted by a hailstorm, and the family moved to California. From then on Ginny worked at a variety of jobs, first in factories and later as the housekeeper in a children's residential home. Ginny remembered the ways she found Californians different and even rude when she first came west. She described many ways in which life and customs were different in the rural community where she was a smallholder, from the appropriate age for children to be allowed to draw water from a well to the appropriate age to marry. But Ginny expressed little regret or nostalgia for the past:

RF: Did you notice a lot of differences between where you came from and where you came to?

GINNY: Oh, yeah. But you know, we—it's like I said, we both worked and we didn't really—what we were after was to make a living for our kids. And so I guess we didn't—we fished on weekends. We didn't go to town. Like me, I don't even hardly know my neighbors, and I've been living in this house for thirty years. . . .

RF: It's interesting, though, you do such different work now, and [have] such a different life and such a different community from the one you grew up in.

GINNY: Uh-huh. Yeah.

RF: Do you ever miss the old ways and the old days?

GINNY: Not really. . . . The other has passed, you know, and it couldn't ever be the same because my mother and father's gone, and then my oldest brother's gone, and then my brother and sisters are scattered, [to] Florida, here and there. And they've all got public works [jobs]. It would never be the same, you know, to go back to that. And the saddest fact there now, I think, uh, the government pays them so much to let their crops lay out, let their land lay out. . . . The government almost made it impossible for you to make a living by farming.

Ginny did not use the word "culture" or the vocabulary of "cultural difference" or "cultural specificity" in describing these two phases of her life. I am using that language to underscore the contrast between her telling of her story and the desire expressed by others for a simpler, more "traditional" life, for "cultural belonging." For one thing, the closer women are to the experience of inhabiting and living by a culture different from the one that surrounds them today, the richer are their descriptions of it. Ginny described in detail her daily routine on the farm, the equipment used for plowing, the rent her family paid to the landowner, and her diet, including recipes that fed the family when times were hard. In these ways, cultural practices were not reified or idealized but tied to types of work, to class, or to poverty. For example, it was as someone who, as she put it, "never had much of a kid's life," that Ginny considered herself to have been mature enough to marry at fifteen—early marriage, like the foods eaten by the family, was not simply a cultural practice without a material anchor. As was the case for Irene, Ginny's sense of the coherence of the ways she lived then and now—that which I am calling her "culture"—was tied to specific relationships with family members. Thus, one of the reasons she felt it would be impossible to return to the old life is the scattering of her family. Further, and again linking culture to material life, Ginny's clear feeling that "past is past" stems partly from the dismantling of the agricultural system that shaped rural southern life. Her desire in life was less to preserve her heritage than to "make a living for our kids." Finally, however, there is at least one cultural value or practice that Ginny *did* carry with her from Alabama to California: the structuring of life around hard, single-minded labor.

Similar lessons can be learned from Dot Humphrey's story. In fact, while Ginny was merely resigned to her changed life circumstances, Dot expressed mostly negative feelings about her own rural upbringing. As she described growing up in a Kansas farming community organized entirely around the Mennonite Church and another similar sect, Dot spoke of the repressiveness of the culture, the exclusion of her own family from most social networks (because the church was pacifist and her father had enlisted in the army during World War II), and also of the constraints on women's work customary in the community:

> DOT: My mother went to work when I was ten. So from then on I was expected to do all the work a woman does in the house. So I made meals, washed the dishes, cleaned the house, and did the laundry, did the ironing, watched my brother. . . .
>
> RF: You were saying your family was viewed as "white trash"—was that a class thing?
>
> DOT: Partially it was class. Partially it was that, because we weren't in the church, we sort of lost a certain air of respectability. . . . Even if you were poor, if you were in the church, somehow that made it easier and better. And my father was pretty outspoken and opinionated. He swore a lot, he smoked cigarettes. This was a fairly rigid community, so what people do nowadays, people didn't do then. Like you weren't allowed to play cards, so nobody played cards. And there was lots of junk piled all around his garage. The whole corner where we lived was sort of an eyesore, junk and jeeps and cars, etcetera. [Dot's father repaired farm machinery for a living.] And women did not work, it was definitely not appropriate for women to work, and my mother went to work when I was ten and that was also considered a bit scandalous. And then my father's sister was the first woman in the county that I know of who got a divorce and that was considered also quite scandalous.
>
> RF: Sort of put the clincher on things.
>
> DOT: Right. (Laughs heartily)

Thus Dot strove to escape, through education and later through marriage, the kind of tightknit community for which some of the other women yearned. (It is worth noting in passing that the women who yearned for membership in a traditional, tightly knit community, did not seem to conceive of those communities as internally conflictual, nor picture themselves as marginalized or excluded within them. This further underscores the romanticism of their desire.) As in Ginny's description, what we see in Dot's is a description of "culture" as intersecting with class and the struggle for material survival, as well as being marked by what Dot considered to be an oppressive, even "obsessive" (her term) workload for women. Dot as an adult had no desire at all to take on the kinds of "women's work" that marked her childhood or to go "back to the land."

In contrast to the ways in which some of the women relegated "culture" to a separate sphere of its own, for Dot the tie between economics and culture was more obvious. However, for some of the women the very materiality of specific habits or practices seemed to place them outside the domain of culture. For example, Clare Traverso remarked that her natal family's emphasis on "traditional" values such as not eating in restaurants and making, mending, or handing down clothes rather than buying them had to do with poverty, thus rejecting the possibility that they might be part of a distinctive cultural heritage. What we see here is the enactment of an element of the "dualistic" discourse on culture, which, as I have argued, reifies and artificially isolates the concept.

A number of women articulated identity based on class. For example, the part of her childhood that Dot carried with her into adulthood as a source of kinship or belonging with other women was not primarily ruralness, region of origin, past involvement in Christianity, or indeed anything specific to that realm usually designated "cultural." Rather, it was the sense of a shared working-class background that formed the basis for a connection with others:

> Most of my friends all along have been working-class white
> women. . . . I feel fairly aware of class among white women, and feel
> more comfortable among women who come from working-class
> backgrounds. . . .
>   Part of it is how people see themselves and the world. I think that
> women who have been brought up middle class without a consciousness
> of their being different, sort of, their being the norm, have that attitude
> towards life in general—taking things for granted, having a certain
> expectation that they deserve something, attitudes that are not natural to
> me, and I sometimes find hard to deal with. Even somebody like [she
> names a friend], who was raised working class in Massachusetts in a real
> different environment than I was in, there's still a certain kind of humor
> and way of talking to each other—things that you can take for granted.

The Politics of Belonging: A Note on "Salience"

I suggested in beginning this chapter that women's descriptions of cultural belonging can be placed along a continuum, and can be comprehended in part in terms of communities' past and present relationships to the dominant culture. The concepts of social and political salience are helpful in analyzing and accounting for the thickness or thinness of descriptions of a group or identity, the density of meanings associated with a cultural name. I understand the production of social and political salience to be a collective, not an individual, process, and I use the terms to refer to the extent to which a group is identified *as* a group, by its own members or by the dominant culture. Some examples may help illuminate the terms. Irene Esterley could give a rich description of the meaning of Germanness in her childhood partly because there was a *social* context for it: her family was still generationally close to immigration and her residential community was ethnically marked. At the same time, German identity had *political* significance at key moments during her childhood. One can speculate that, if Germanness had more political meaning in the USA today, Irene's ethnicity might be less a thing of the past and more a category with meaning in the present. By the same token, Irishness had little political or social salience in Marty's life in California in the 1960s and 1970s, and therefore Marty's description was "thin." However, it is possible to imagine circumstances in which Irishness might have greater salience: as with other dimensions of racial identity, white ethnicities and their meanings are historically, politically, and socially constructed.[15] Further, both Dot and Ginny continued to draw on those aspects of their rural heritage that remained relevant or useful while dropping others. For Dot this meant an identification with the class in which she grew up, for Ginny, a particular orientation to work. I will return to the notion of salience at the end of this chapter.

Ashkenazi Jewish Women's Narratives

Analyzing Jewish women's life narratives is not only interesting in its own right: it is also instructive about cultural belonging in general. If the density of descriptions of cultural belonging depends on the social and political salience of the group being described, it is not surprising that, by and large, the women who had most to say about their ethnic and cultural identities were the Jewish women—not surprising, given that Jewishness has more political salience in the present-day United States than any other white ethnicity. For these women, Jewish identity was articulated not only in terms of engagement with (or disinterest in) a cultural form, but also as a recognition of belonging to a group that had faced, and continues to face, discrimination and violence. It is in looking at Jewish women's life narratives that one can see most clearly the links between cultural belonging, cultural "bounded-ness," and cultural subordination or marginality. At the same time, one also sees clearly the nonboundedness of cultural belonging: its flexibility and intersection with other aspects of daily life.

Several points must be made here about the intersections of Jewishness and whiteness. The Jewish women I interviewed, and whom I take to be "white," are all Ashkenazi Jewish women: their families emigrated to the United States from northern, eastern, and western Europe. However, as I have argued throughout this book, racial naming and boundary marking are historically shifting and highly politicized. Ashkenazi Jews have frequently been viewed by non-Jews as racial Others, and continue to be viewed as such by some, notably the neo-Nazi movement. In this context, and given the persistence of anti-Semitism, some Ashkenazi Jewish men and women have argued that they are not white. However, none of the women I interviewed took this position. All considered themselves "white."

In rather the same way that Irene Esterley asked, "How could I not know I'm German?" being Jewish was for the great majority of this group axiomatic—a defining feature of their identity. Thus, for example, the first thing Jeanine Cohen said was, "I was born in South Africa to Jewish progressives." Similarly, Eve Schraeger said, "My identity is as a Jewish lesbian. For me, that assumes that I'm female and feminist. . . . I identify with my generation—I grew up in the 1950s—and with my class, which is upper middle class." Frieda Kazen, asked if she had been aware of being Jewish as a child, replied, "Definitely."

In addition to knowing that they were Jewish because they had been told they were, these women pointed to a range of cultural markers when I asked about their sense of self as Jewish. Some of the markers were the same as those of non-Jewish women with a strong sense of belonging to a "bounded" cultural group, including close connections with an extended family or community of the same cultural group and knowledge of their grandparents' immigration from Europe (or in the case of Hilda Perlman, who was in her eighties when I interviewed her, her own flight from Russia in 1922). Another factor was speaking a nondominant language: Hilda herself spoke Yiddish as her first language, Russian as her second, and English only as a third, learned after she came to the United States; others' parents had spoken Yiddish at home, especially while their own parents were alive. The Jewish women, unlike the other women I interviewed, also mentioned religious markers of identity: parents' desire to keep a kosher house or to send their children for religious instruction; the women's own interest as adults in learning Hebrew, attending synagogue, and celebrating Jewish holidays as well as, or instead of, the dominant culture's Christian ones. For, again unlike most of the other women, the Jewish women had a cultural identity that was for most a dimension of the present as well as the past. Finally, and again unlike the other women (with the partial exception of Irene Esterley), the Jewish women experienced the possibility or reality of hostility from outside the group.

These women's lives were, however, by no means identical to one another: there was no one way to be Jewish. One gets from these women a sense of cultural belonging as flexible—but flexible within a determinate range of options or meaningful expressions of Jewish identity. One might, for example, go to synagogue or not, be expected to "marry in" (that is, inside the Jewish community) or not, and still consider oneself Jewish. However, it was clear to all the women what the range of markers involved—no one, for example, imagined that eating corned beef and cabbage on St. Patrick's Day had anything to do with Jewish identity!

Their narratives also show clearly the ways in which cultural belonging intersected with other dimensions of social life. Keeping a kosher house (adhering to a diet prescribed by religious teaching, as well as buying meats and other foods prepared under rabbinical supervision) was a case in point. When Marjorie Hoffman was a small child in the second decade of this century, her family, from New York City, lived in rural Maine. There, her father made a living as a tailor, traveling to the lumber camps and taking orders for clothes. Marjorie's mother chose to buy kosher meat, although this meant having it specially delivered by train from two hundred miles away. This, Marjorie felt, was in part a means by which her mother could maintain a sense of her identity, since she was the only Jewish woman for miles around. But it also provided an excuse not to buy from the local butcher, whose products, she felt, were of poor quality. On the other hand, Joan Van Buren's mother, living in predominantly gentile Queens, New York, in the 1930s and running a hardware store as well as a family, found that keeping to a kosher diet was too difficult to manage and gave up the attempt. Dora Hauser (in her nineties when I interviewed her) told me as she described her family's lack of connection with its Jewish origins, "We ate ham, if that's any indication." (Ham, like other products from pigs, is definitely not kosher.)

Frieda Kazen's narrative illustrated some of the processes of adaptation and accommodation these women's families went through in order to maintain a Jewish identity in predominantly gentile environments. Frieda grew up in New Jersey, in a small town about fifteen minutes' drive from New York City. When I asked her about the ways in which she was aware of being Jewish, she said:

> We didn't have a temple in town, or anything like that, and we didn't belong to [one]—we did for a while in a neighboring town. Maybe for a year we went to Sunday school—I have a sister—but we didn't really like it, and I don't think my parents really were into that. My father's a pretty religious man. What he ended up doing was, on the High Holidays, they would get space in, like, the firehouse or one of the other public buildings, and have services. Hire a rabbi and a cantor and have services with other people in town who do not drive—who maybe even belonged to other temples but would not drive on High Holidays.

Frieda remembered feeling more conscious of being Jewish after beginning school:

> FRIEDA: I don't remember being conscious of it until I started school, and knowing that on certain days we didn't go to school, and that we didn't say the Lord's Prayer totally, in the morning. Or there was some portion of it that we didn't say? I don't remember.
>
> RF: Was that something that your parents taught you, in terms of when to say, and when not to say, or—?
>
> FRIEDA: Well, no, it's when we were going to the Sunday school they told us. But I remember our principal of our elementary school, during Christmas, asked me to get up and explain Hanukkah, and light candles, in front of the assembly. Which was quite devastating to me, because I didn't like to get up in front of people at *all*. . . .
>
> I think one of the [reasons why] my mother got angry at this rabbi [at Sunday school, was that] he said we should not participate in any of the Christmas things going on at the school. And she thought that was ridiculous. The idea that we shouldn't sing Christmas carols was ridiculous. So I think that's when we stopped going to that synagogue.

One sees here the ways in which the expectations of the school on the one hand and Jewish identity on the other were not identical and had to be negotiated, not without disagreements and some discomfort. Thus, for example, school assembly was structured around Christianity, and Frieda's rabbi asked her to negotiate that reality by avoiding participation in some of its rituals. Meanwhile, the school marked Frieda's Jewishness and thereby her differentness, albeit not in a hostile way, by asking her to enact a version of the Hanukkah ceremony of lighting candles. (It should be noted that, while in some sense this is a gesture of respect toward Jewish culture, it by no means "integrates" Judaism into the religious culture of the school.) Frieda's mother and the rabbi disagreed over how best to be Jewish in a Christian school. The issue was resolved by the family's leaving the synagogue— to which, in any case, neither the children nor their parents were very attached.

As Frieda grew older and had to do homework, however, things became more complicated:

FRIEDA: When we would take off for Yom Kippur or Rosh Hashanah, [the school] would say that we had to have the homework done that following day, and make up the work. And I remember my parents saying, "But there's no writing [on High Holidays]," and there was a big fuss.

RF: How did you feel about that one?

FRIEDA: I think we just were glad to be out of school for a couple of days, but we didn't want any privileges behind it. But it was a neat time. Because it was a very small group of us and we'd hang out outside the firehouse or wherever the services were going to be, and fast, and do all that. It kind of felt special.

RF: So was that your primary friendship group? Other Jewish kids?

FRIEDA: Actually, of my closest friends, two were. But people just get into groups, and there were the mature groups, and the younger groups, and kids who studied, and kids who didn't and, you know, you form your own little groups.

RF: What age are we talking about here?

FRIEDA: Probably fourth grade, fifth grade and on.

Again we see a clash of logics here. It is almost as though following religious teaching by not writing on the Jewish New Year or the Day of Atonement may be tantamount to expecting "special treatment." This concern follows the logic of the school and the dominant culture. The irony, of course, is that special arrangements are only necessary given the dominance of Christianity and the year round special treatment the Christian calendar received in the structuring of school life. The resolution here is less easy. Clearly the family was less willing to give up the High Holiday than they were to take their children out of Sunday school. Meanwhile, outside the logic of the school, for Frieda the holidays were a context in which to experience the specialness of Jewish identity in a more positive way, fasting and spending time with the other Jewish children in town. Finally, we are reminded that Jewishness is not the only salient feature of Frieda's sense of self: degrees of maturity and commitment to studying are as important as Jewish identity in building friendship groups.

Looking at these women's lives, we see cultural identity as something consciously built rather than just "there." In a town with no temple, the firehouse became a temporary synagogue. In it, both those who were *very* observant of religious law (people who would not drive on holy days and therefore could not go to their own temples) and those less observant (those who only "needed" a temple twice or three times a year) came together. We also see the ways cultural practice is of necessity negotiated and renegotiated in relation to other systems and logics.

For Frieda, the demands of school conflicted at times with the logic of Jewish belonging. By contrast, Tamara Green's description of parts of her childhood in Los Angeles in the 1960s and 1970s indicated the ways her ethnic group membership was expressed and reinforced as much in the context of public, supposedly culturally neutral (or if not that, culturally dominant) spaces like her school as through specifically cultural or religious practices:

> I grew up in a very white environment. And also, I've realized how much I sort of had . . . constructed my environment to the point where I thought I grew up in a mostly Jewish environment. When in fact, objectively, that was not the case. . . .
> [In elementary school] my best friend was not Jewish, but half Indian. Native American. And my other best friends were Jewish. And what I remember most was going to junior high school and going to everybody's bar mitzvah. In junior high school, they started tracking us, and putting us into honors classes. And as I recall, the honors classes were largely Jewish. But the rest of the school was not largely Jewish. It was, in fact, racially mixed and class mixed. . . . So I had a very stilted view of what our school was actually made up of.

Unlike Frieda, Tamara did not have to part company with the mainstream of school culture in order to "be Jewish." Adding to this effect, Tamara said that she and her schoolmates had spent time outside classes involved in a socialist Zionist youth group. What we are seeing here is *not* the school administration going out of its way to provide an environment sensitive to Jewish students. Rather, what accounts for the situation is the intersection of a marginalized ethnicity with class privilege, for the honors students were middle class as well as primarily Jewish. And we see the mechanisms of dominant class and racial identity discussed in earlier chapters coming together with Jewishness, discouraging Tamara and her classmates from being conscious of the students in less advantaged positions both in the school itself and in the larger society.

I have noted that in looking at these narratives one gets a sense of individuals consciously creating and recreating Jewish identity and their relationships to it. This process continued into the adult lives of these women. Tamara, for example, had not been raised to be religious:

> My parents tried but they were unsuccessful. We went to one year of Hebrew school, when I was probably in junior high school. The teacher's name was Mrs. Bernhart and we always called her "heartburn," and you know, we never really got through it. . . . Since then, through my younger sister, my parents have had a kind of Jewish revival—not necessarily religious, but cultural. And my sister *did* get bat mitzvahed, at her own insistence. But me and my brother never [did]—and we celebrated Christmas growing up, and now it's Hanukkah and the whole thing, but we grew up with Christmas trees.

While Tamara talked of changes in cultural practices taking place thanks to her sister, Eve Schraeger of her own volition moved from an upbringing that was, in her words, "assimilated" to much more active participation in and exploration of Jewish culture. Born in 1944 in suburban Chicago, Eve said that, although she had known she was Jewish, it had not been an important part of her sense of self. She had known perhaps half a dozen words of Yiddish, and the family had celebrated Christmas:

> We never even knew there was a disharmony between the fact that we were Jewish and the fact that we did Christmas. It just was a synthesis of the two cultures, and that was how we lived.

At the same time, Eve felt that, although they did not actually talk to her about marrying within the Jewish community, her parents would always discreetly find out, once she started dating, whether Eve's boyfriends were Jewish.

Eve spoke of "finding my Jewishness" after moving to Berkeley and becoming part of a lesbian feminist community:

EVE: I became lovers with someone who is very strongly Jewish identified, and I learned a lot and affirmed a lot in that time with her, and with our friends.

RF: Do you know what that meant—"finding your Jewishness"? How did that feel different from the Jewishness that you had grown up with?

EVE: Well, I had spent many years saying, "I'm not Jewish, but my parents are." I mean, I was in a lot of denial. And I believe I learned a lot of it from my mother and that she learned a lot of it from her father. "Yeah, we're Jewish but we know it's better to be something else, so we're not going to have much to do with this business of being Jewish." . . .

People would often assume that I was not Jewish, and I liked that at the time. I don't like it now. I mean, I never lied and said, "I am Episcopalian" or Catholic or anything else, I just said, "It may appear that I'm Jewish, but in fact I don't choose to be Jewish, so I'm not." And I guess that started changing somewhere in there, ten years ago, and I went through a lot of reading and a lot of groups and a lot of events about being Jewish. It's just become a very natural part of my life now. If people know me, they know I'm gay, they know I'm Jewish, because that's what I want them to know. . . .

RF: So what does being Jewish mean to you now? I guess that's a difficult question, since it's so much part of your life.

EVE: I'm not ready for that today! I can deal with the past—

RF: I mean, do you celebrate Jewish holidays, and so on?

EVE: Mhm. I do. And I still do some Jewish reading. And if there are people making comments that indicate that they don't have an understanding or a respect for being Jewish, I get on their case. I feel proud to be Jewish, I feel proud to be gay. I feel in both cases it's been a struggle, and we still have our lives and our culture. . . .

Being Jewish also means I have a community. There's a big, active gay Jewish community, lesbian Jewish community, but I also do a certain number of activities in the straight Jewish community.

RF: Like what?

EVE: Oh, I once took a class in local Jewish history over at the Jewish museum. Me and eight middle-aged matrons.

Eve also spoke of doing volunteer work at a Jewish elders' home. She did not at that time belong to a synagogue or to a women's religious group, but said she felt glad that they are there should she need them.

Eve spoke of "finding [her] Jewishness": in fact what she was doing was finding a new way of relating to the fact of being Jewish, and finding a *positive value* in her Jewishness. What we see in Eve's story is a process of consciously choosing or crafting a way of belonging, a mode of relating to Jewish cultural and religious practices and communities. For Eve, this involved rejecting many of her parents' choices about Jewish identity, especially those that looked like assimilation or responding to anti-Semitism by hiding. By contrast, Eve took pride in the fact that both gay and Jewish communities have flourished in the face of oppression.

In fact, this process is not so different from those that other Jewish women described going through in childhood. The major difference is that for them it was their parents rather than the women themselves who made many of the decisions. The parameters of cultural belonging are the same as those other Jewish women described, including choices over participation in Jewish community activities and knowledge of history. And also like those of other Jewish women and their families, Eve's mode of "being Jewish" intersected with other dimensions of her daily life and sense of self: for Eve, this meant, among other things, a conscious articulation of the links between Jewish and lesbian identity.

If Jewish cultures and communities continue to be socially salient, this is in part because they continue to be *politically* salient, through the persistence of anti-Semitism both in the memories and in the present-day experience of Jewish people. All of the Jewish women I interviewed had something to say about anti-Semitism, whether they addressed it as an issue in itself or related it to other forms of domination.

Several women identified themselves as Jewish in the context of other discussions, in ways that showed simultaneously the extent to which Jewishness was a taken-for-granted dimension of their lives and the extent to which anti-Semitism was also a consistent feature. Thus, for example, Evelyn Steinman told me that she had been shocked, on moving to Los Angeles from Chicago in the 1950s, to find that Mexican Americans as well as Black Americans faced housing discrimination. Then she added, "I *knew* there was prejudice against the Jews. Because we're Jewish. So that was known."

A sense of Jewish identity as ascribed rather than chosen came across in the words of Joan Van Buren. Joan grew up in the late

1920s and the 1930s in Queens, New York, with a clear sense of Jewish identity. She had a strong sense of minority status in her neighborhood, which was predominantly Italian American and German American, and in which organizations supporting Hitler and Mussolini sprang up during World War II. She remembers begging her parents to move to a Jewish neighborhood. Since they ran a hardware store and lived on the premises, however, moving was not practical. At the same time, partly because they were busy and partly because of their distaste for the goyim (non-Jews), Joan's parents kept to themselves, which, Joan felt, meant that she had fewer opportunities to make friends with the local children. At the time of the interview, Joan continued to be interested in her family history, and in fact showed me photographs of her grandparents and great-grandparents. However, she had found Judaism unsatisfying spiritually and had in later years become an ecumenical Christian. She had no involvement in any Jewish community, although:

> I have to live with having a Jewish background—of course, you know, I try to hide the scars and everything else like that—you know, I don't go around flaunting it, but I also don't deny it. Because I do regard myself as part of the Jewish cultural group. My husband said that, when he was talking with his father about marrying me, his father said, "Do you realize you are marrying someone of a different race?"

The "scars" here are, I think, a reference, simultaneously bitter and humorous, to her childhood in Queens—and perhaps also to the scars that are part of the legacy of anyone who is a potential target of anti-Semitism. Also referred to here is the way in which Ashkenazi Jews for much of this century in the United States and Europe have been placed on the borders of whiteness, at times viewed by the dominant white culture as cultural outsiders, and at times as *racial* outsiders—but in any case never as constitutive of the cultural norm.

At times the cultural markers of Jewishness became the focus of or context for anti-Semitism, and this in turn affected cultural practice. For example, Joan's life was made more uncomfortable because her parents always kept her out of school for the religious holidays, and therefore all the other children knew she was Jewish. It was partly in the context of fear of anti-Semitism that Eve's family tried hard *not* to show their Jewishness; and out of the same fear, Joan remembered her family warning her to be very careful of gentiles when she went away to college.

As Joan's story suggests, Jewish women mostly viewed their cultural identity as linked inextricably to being a target, or potential target, for oppression based on ethnicity. Evelyn Steinman described an interaction with her son that must have taken place in the early 1970s in which she emphasized to him, in stark and almost brutal terms, the inevitability of his Jewishness, and the link to anti-Jewish hostility that it implied:

EVELYN: I recall living in [a suburb of San Jose], and the family living across the street from us—our son at that time was probably seven or eight—the husband was a physician, and his wife was a very lovely woman. They had four or five kids. And the one son, Paul, who was about three or four years older than our son, always played with our son. In any event, my son came in one day and he said, "Are we Jews?" and I said, "Why are you asking that?" He said, "Well, I want to know if we're Jewish." And I said, "Well, in some social cases we would be considered a Jewish family, but we don't follow the religion, so other people might not consider us that at all. It's a question of whether you want to decide whether being a Jew is a religious aspect or if it's a cultural aspect." Well, he screamed and he ran down the hall, and he said, "I don't want to be a goddamn dirty Jew!" Where did he hear this? From his friend, Paul. I was so shocked, I couldn't believe it. So I just took that young man and I shook him. And I said, "Listen, goddammit. You *are* a goddamn dirty Jew and you are going to be a goddamn dirty Jew all your life, and you'd better be proud of it." That was the end of it. He never discussed it again.

RF: Did you bring it up to the other family?

EVELYN: What's the point? What's the point? They know. It's not going to change them.

As she told the story, it seemed clear that Evelyn began to respond to her son's question as though it were about culture. She explained to him that there is a degree of indeterminacy or flexibility in cultural belonging. Being Jewish, she wanted him to know, can be understood in different ways, none of which is necessarily more correct than another. However, it quickly became evident that his question was not about culture at all. Rather, it was about Otherness, about one's being or essence, understood reductively and hierarchically. Here, Evelyn felt, there was no flexibility: one *is* Jewish. The lesson Evelyn wanted her son to learn was that his Jewishness was ascribed, that it was not possible for him to wish it away, and that his only option was to embrace it. The anger with which she responded to her son was perhaps anger at the other family, displaced and directed at her child because she felt that changing the dominant culture's anti-Semitism was impossible—as expressed in her final, apparently despairing words: "What's the point? What's the point? They know. It's not going to change them."

The women's experience of anti-Semitism varied somewhat by generation and also by country of origin. One of the two women who were not born in the United States, Hilda Perlman, had lived from 1903 until 1922 in a Jewish ghetto in the Ukraine. In Russia, she told me, Jews tended to be poorer than the gentile Russians. In addition, the education system discriminated against them— for example, by setting school entrance examinations on the sabbath, when Jews were forbidden by religious law to write. The only "privilege" Jews were accorded, she said, was conscription into the czar's army. Women younger than Hilda, raised in the United States, remembered discrimination in jobs, housing, and university admission at least up to the 1950s. A friend of Joan's, for example, had pretended to be Unitarian in order to beat the anti-Jewish quota system operating in medical schools.

In more recent years, these women had experienced more verbal than institutional anti-Semitism. But Debby Rothman also spoke of pro-Christian biases in the labor union where she worked:

> There are times when I've been in [union] gatherings, and there's usually an invocation of some sort, a benediction or whatever. At most of the conventions that I've gone to that have gone on for several days [there will be an effort to respect all denominations]. But there have been one or two gatherings that I've been at where the blessings were heavily Christian, heavily fundamentalist Christian. And people would say things like, "We're all Christians here." . . . I know Black people are not exactly crazy about it when someone says, "That's very white of you" [meaning "That's very decent of you"]. [By analogy, I don't like it when] Christian values, Christian this and Christian that are thought of as the definition of goodness.

While the women did not feel that they were experiencing institutional discrimination, the memory of discrimination, and of course of the Holocaust, were too recent to be ignored. Debby Rothman described the impact on her own sense of well-being in comparison with her parents' outlook:

RF: You never experienced any hostility [as a child] because of being Jewish?

DEBBY: No. I did, a small amount, here in California. There was one boy who called me a dirty Jew. This was in high school. There was a guy that I was dating at the time and—I didn't even know it at the time because he didn't tell me, but other people told me—he went and beat up the kid who was calling me a dirty Jew. And he never called me that name again. It worked.

But for the most part, I really did not have any direct hostility. I certainly, from my own experience, did not grow up with the sense that "it's a hostile world out there." My parents suffered that more as kids growing up in New York and, as is the case with any, almost any Jews that I know of that are old enough to remember the Holocaust, it's an inescapable feeling. They know, just from knowing about the Holocaust, and knowing that all of my relatives who didn't get out were killed. My uncle went back to find any trace, and there was none. It is impossible for me to feel, as people I know who *aren't* Jewish may feel, that it's impossible for terrible social upheavals to take place in society like that. Because I know they can.

It is striking here that although Debby began by saying that she did not have the same outlook as her parents, she ended by showing that she was, in fact, conscious of the potential for a sudden upsurge of oppression. Other Jewish women articulated the same points, expressing the view that while violent anti-Semitism is *not* widespread now, it has been in the past and easily could be again.

It is thus clear that anti-Semitism experienced in the recent past as well in the present shapes Jewish identity. In exploring the meaning of Jewishness as a location of belonging, I have suggested that it is structured by different kinds of determinacy and flexibility. The first aspect of determinacy is provided by a shared set of cultural markers, and the first element of flexibility refers to the ways women and their families made and altered decisions about how to practice their Jewish identities, frequently in response to other dimensions of their environments. Being Jewish at this historical moment also means being viewed as a cultural or racial Other and potentially being a target of anti-Semitism. This creates a different kind of inflexibility or determinacy associated with belonging, one that is in most ways beyond the control of Jewish people themselves. However, Jews' status as a target of anti-Jewish hostility is not inevitable but historically contingent and alterable through political struggle, as well as being mediated through other axes of privilege and subordination—as are all systems of domination. And, like all oppressed groups, Jewish people continue to challenge their oppression.

Conclusion

How do white women name themselves in terms of culture, identity, and belonging, and why does it matter? As elsewhere in this book, we can see white women's words, worldviews, and "common sense" as embedded in a discursive history. Looking at these women's words about their own and others' racial, ethnic, religious, and class-based identities brings into the foreground a complex discursive terrain surrounding the term "culture." Analyzing it is particularly important given its linkage to white racial dominance. It is to a reexamination of discourses on culture that I will now turn.

I began this chapter by distinguishing between two ways of thinking about culture: one dominant discourse, in which "culture" indicates that which can be named, bounded, and separated from material life, and another construction of culture, potentially more useful to the development of antiracist perspectives, in which culture is viewed more broadly as *constructing daily practices and worldviews in complex relations with material life*. I have argued that the former construction of culture has worked powerfully to delimit, on the one hand, a set of "bounded" cultures and, on the other, a residual, normative space that, as far as most of its inhabitants are concerned, has no name and few distinguishing marks and thus is not, apparently, a cultural space. The name given that space in this book is "white culture."

White women are, by definition, practitioners of white culture. And although "whiteness" is apparently difficult for white people to name, previous chapters have shown that it nonetheless continuously shapes white women's experiences, practices, and views of self and other. A fundamental point, almost too obvious to make, is that given the dominant discourse on culture, it is easier for people to recognize their bounded cultural names than their dominant cultural ones. Thus, Marty Douglass described the St. Patrick's Day meal as a national celebration, but ruled out Thanksgiving— itself entirely bound up with a racially and culturally specific view of U.S. history—as a distinctively national practice.

Whiteness, as a set of normative cultural practices, is visible most clearly to those it definitively excludes and those to whom it does violence. Those who are securely housed within its borders usually do not examine it. The same is true of "Americanness" in relation to those whom it marginalizes or excludes, and of privileged class attitudes in relation to those who are not privileged. In addition, white American individuals are most able to name those parts of themselves and their daily practices that are least close to the center of power, least included in that which is normative.

In the context of these women's narratives, it seems to me that the ways in which specific cultures or identities could be named and described is linked to the extent to which those cultures are viewed as separate or different from normativeness. This in turn is for the most part linked to their nondominance or relative lack of power. Thus, when white women gave themselves "belonging names" in additon to "white," they were in effect drawing on past or present moments when particular white communities were excluded from normativity. In the same way that the cultural practices and identities of men and women of color are "marked" both culturally and racially because of their nondominant status, some white cultural groups also become "bounded" because of their past and present relationships to power.

Often, however, the *memory* of marginalization outlasts the marginalization itself, and the inhabiting of a name that indicates boundedness and marginality may long outlive both the moment of marginalization and the memory of subordination. There is, then, often a trace, a memory, of subordination in a name. But there were differences in the content and modes of description attached to names, and these differences too were linked to issues of power. For a woman whose belonging elsewhere bespoke subordination already long past, Irishness was a pleasant addition to the everyday. For a woman who remembered her parents' immigration and her own humiliation by the government, but remembered them as events of the past, "Americanness" was something that had been, but was no longer, withheld. By contrast, for the Ashkenazi Jewish women I interviewed, negotiating modes of whiteness continued into the present, as did the awareness that some kinds of differences are more powerful in the world than others. I have argued that it is political salience that sets apart Jewishness from other white ethnic identities in the present historical moment.[16]

I have used the concepts of political and social salience to analyze this continuum of meaning. In speaking of political salience,

I am referring to the ways racial and cultural differences operate in the United States: some differences of group membership *do* objectively signify differences in terms of life chances, while others do not. I have suggested that the more politically salient a group is, the more content there is to belonging to that group in terms of daily life and practice. The less politically salient a culture is, the more it has meaning only as an "heirloom" or an "ethnicity by choice."[17] In other words, political salience produces, or at least encourages the maintenance of, social salience. The feeling of belonging to something "formed" is, at least in part, ascribed through relations of domination and subordination.

Continuing to think about culture in dualistic terms has, I suggest, a range of negative consequences for white feminists and others. First, white women who yearn for belonging to a bounded, nameable culture, or who emphasize the parts of their heritage that are bounded over the parts that are dominant, run the risk of romanticizing the experience of being oppressed. Second, focusing on one's membership in a bounded group may mean failing to fully examine what it means to be part of a cultural and racial group that is dominant and normative.

The third risk in holding onto a dualistic view of culture is retaining an either-or analysis of cultural marginalization in which groups and individuals can only see themselves as either privileged or oppressed, failing, for example, to distinguish between past and present subordination, or between forced cultural assimilation and economic exclusion. In the context of thinking about their own ethnic identities, feminist women, including Italian Americans and Ashkenazi Jewish Americans, have at times through the second half of the 1980s argued that they are not white and should therefore be allowed to participate in caucuses of people of color in workplaces or political organizations, or that, conversely, they should not be asked to participate as white women in discussions about "white women against racism." The concept of political salience helps to disentangle the meaning of different kinds of ethnic belonging: for example, it becomes possible to conceptually separate the meanings of being, for example, African American, Jewish American, and Italian American at different moments in history, and to analyze in more complex ways the relationships of all three groups to power. This kind of conceptual separation is, it seems to me, a necessary prerequisite to analyzing the *connections* between different forms of oppression.[18]

Finally, within a dualistic framework for thinking about race and cultural difference, demands for racial and cultural parity, whether in a curriculum or a local government, frequently degenerate into efforts to "appreciate diversity," where this means appreciating those who are designated "diverse" or "different" rather than questioning the very system that constructs margins and a center. All of this happens, in short, when individuals or movements jump from side to side of received dualisms rather than engaging critically with the dualistic system itself.

I have argued that the more a culture is politically salient, the more it is visible and nameable. But what about that cultural space with the most political significance of all, the dominant space called whiteness? Again, thinking about definitions of culture helps clarify its status. Within the dualistic discourse on culture, whiteness can by definition have no meaning: as a normative space it is constructed precisely by the way in which it positions others at its borders. To put it another way, within that discourse, "whiteness" is indeed a space defined only by reference to those named cultures it has flung out to its perimeter.[19] Whiteness is in this sense fundamentally a relational category.

However, whiteness *does* have content inasmuch as it generates norms, ways of understanding history, ways of thinking about self and other, and even ways of thinking about the notion of culture itself. Thus whiteness needs to be examined and historicized. We need to look more closely at the content of the normative and attempt to analyze both its history and its consequences. Whiteness needs to be delimited and "localized." One step in this direction is antiracist writers' increasing use of the terms Euro-American or European American alongside African American, Asian American, Native American, Latino, and Chicano.[20] Using "European American" to describe white Americans has the advantage that it parallels and in a sense semantically equates communities of a range of geographical origins in relation to the United States. By the same token, however, this gesture "deracializes" and thus falsely equalizes communities who are, in terms of current reality, unequally positioned in the racial order. There is a sense, in other words, in which "European American," when it replaces "white," rather than being used alongside it, evades the racial dominance of European Americans at the present historical moment.

If the cultural dominance of whiteness were complete and unquestioned, it would perhaps go entirely unnamed. However, there are constantly struggles over the inclusion and exclusion of specific groups of people as well as over white domination, whether it is structural, institutional, or cultural. In times of perceived threat, the normative group may well attempt to reassert its normativity by asserting elements of its cultural practice more explicitly and exclusively. For example, although the social movements for racial equality that have continued from the 1960s to the present have generated only relatively modest steps toward social change, there have been various forms of backlash in response to them by individuals and groups seeking to assert earlier forms of cultural and racial normativity. These have included campaigns for "English only" laws in states where public institutions *already* conduct business only in English, controversies over educational curricula, and the resurgence of white supremacist political movements.

At this time in U.S. history, whiteness as a marked identity is explicitly articulated mainly in terms of the "white pride" of the far right.[21] In a sense, this produces a discursive bind for that small subgroup of white women and men concerned to engage in antiracist work: if whiteness is emptied of any content other than that which is associated with racism or capitalism, this leaves progressive whites apparently without a genealogy. This is partly a further effect of racist classification that notes or "marks" the race of nonwhite people but not whites.

To my mind, there is no immediate solution to this problem. Purely linguistic solutions cannot be effected in a political vacuum. To call Americans of European descent "white" in any celebratory fashion is almost inevitably, in the present political moment, a white supremacist act, an act of backlash. In fact, only when white activists and cultural workers name themselves racially in the context of antiracist work does naming oneself as "white" begin to have a different kind of meaning.

Much work remains to be done in actually making visible and undermining white culture's ties to domination. This is perhaps a more urgent priority than looking for the "good" aspects of white people's heritage. Satisfying our desire for a "nonugly" white tradition requires, as much as anything, the creation of a different political reality, a different balance of power, or, at the very least, the context of an active white antiracist movement that could generate a countercultural trajectory and identity.

In contrast with the white supremacisms of the far right, my continuing to use "white culture" and "white cultural practice" in this text as descriptors of the things white people do or the ways white people understand themselves should not, of course, be taken as suggesting that any practice or activity engaged in by white people is "white" in an inherent or timeless sense. Rather, as with all human activity, the cultural practices of white people in the United States in the late twentieth century must be viewed as contingent, historically produced, and transformable through collective and individual human endeavor. Nor can we view "white culture" or "white cultural practice" as a uniform terrain, such that one might expect all white people to identify in similar ways with the same set of core beliefs, practices, and symbols. Rather, as suggested in Paul Gilroy's definition, quoted earlier, we need to view cultural fields as decentered and, I would add, permeable. As I have suggested already, the borders of white *identity* have proven to be malleable over time. The same is, I suggest, true of white culture: through processes of syncretism and appropriation, a range of practices, symbols, and icons have been drawn from elsewhere into the cultural practice of white people.

Nor is white culture (in fact, culture in general) a material and discursive space produced and reproduced in a vacuum. Whiteness is inflected by nationhood, such that whiteness and Americanness, though by no means coterminous, are profoundly shaped by one another. Thus there are ways, for example, in which British "whiteness" and U.S. "whiteness" are similar to and different from one another, and those differences and similarities are traceable to historical, social, and political process. Similarly, whiteness, masculinity, and femininity are coproducers of one another, in ways that are, in their turn, crosscut by class and by the histories of racism and colonialism.[22]

Given the complexity and fragmented character of white cultural practice, one might ask why, then, it is necessary or productive to continue to use the term "white cultural practice" at all. There are several reasons. First, if the alternative is to continue to view whiteness and white people as "noncultural" or "cultureless," one result, as I have argued, is continuing to view dominant practices within a dualistic framework, such that practices *not* identifiable as originating from a "bounded" group might be variously viewed as normative, correct, modern, or universal, rather than as (in my view, more correctly) local and specifiable, but

dominant. Second, as this chapter has illustrated, "culture" designates a subjective sense of identity and belonging as much as it
designates activity or practice. Viewing whiteness as "no culture"
has the same double-edged effect on the question of identity as it
has on that of practice: white individuals at times view themselves
as "empty," yet at other times as the center or norm (the *real*
Americans). Naming whiteness and white people in this sense
helps dislodge the claims of both to rightful dominance.

Third, however, whiteness is indeed linked to dominance.
Given culture as a "field articulating the life-world of subjects . . .
and the structures created by human activity," it is by and large
the cultural practices of *white* people (though not all white people,
and certainly to varying degrees) by means of which individuals
in societies structured in racial dominance are asked to engage
with the institutions of those societies. Thus, to cite two examples, corporate culture and the culture of academia are culturally marked in ways that are (contingently) white as well as (also
contingently) gendered and, so to speak, "classed." The work-
shops offered to train non-U.S.-born engineers in the sporting
metaphors that oil the wheels of many U.S. workplaces and the
support groups for students of color and "reentry women"
throughout academia testify to the negative effects that unmarked
(white, American, male) cultural practices have on those who do
not, automatically, paticipate in them. Here again, naming whiteness as a cultural terrain, albeit a complex one that interacts with
a range of other constructs, is a vital aspect of questioning and
delimiting its authority.

From the standpoints of those it marginalizes or places in
"boundage," the dualistic discourse on culture is exposed as
simultaneously unreal and violent. From the standpoint of the
normative-residual space, however, "boundage" at times appears
fascinating or enticing, a desirable space in which to live. Besides
the work of critically analyzing that normative-residual space that
I am calling "white cultural practice," white American women
may also want to learn more about the histories that lie behind
that normativity, the multiple currents that came together to
make the normative space that white Americans now inhabit, and
the processes of assimilation, loss, and forgetting that took place
along the way. In doing this, care must be taken not to confuse
the traces of *past* subordination with the *present* subordination of
other communities and their cultural practices. Engagements with

"white ethnic" heritage that either romanticize the past or evade race privilege in the present continue to "deculturalize" and therefore "normalize" dominant cultural practice. Explorations both of dominant practices and of the incorporations and exclusions that produce the dominant may, I believe, enable us to engage in anti-racist work from a more complex standpoint and to enter into more radical, transformative relationships with white racial and cultural identities.

Epilogue: Racism, Antiracism, and the Meaning of Whiteness

It should by now be abundantly clear that race shapes white women's lives. The majority of the women I interviewed for this study did not consider themselves particularly interested in the racial order, or especially implicated in racism. All of them, however, said a great deal that was relevant to both. Successive chapters of this book have traveled the terrain of whiteness as material, cultural, and subjective location, exploring childhood, interracial relationships, discursive repertoires on race, and constructions of culture and identity. This process has, I hope, rendered more explicit and complex the meaning—or better, meanings—of whiteness in the contemporary United States. I have attempted to mark out the historical and contemporary conditions, material and discursive, that define and limit it. Through reading white women's life histories, I have examined the ways in which region, class, generation, and ethnicity further subdivide the terrain of lived experiences of whiteness. I have also indicated in preliminary ways how gender and sexuality may intersect with whiteness. In addition to marking out the limits and the "givenness" of whiteness, I have argued that the women I interviewed actively negotiated it. I have explored in detail the forms and content of that negotiation process.

Whiteness changes over time and space and is in no way a transhistorical essence. Rather, as I have argued, it is a complexly constructed product of local, regional, national, and global relations, past and present. Thus, the range of possible ways of living whiteness, for an individual white woman in a particular time and place, is delimited by the relations of racism *at that moment and in that place*. And if whiteness varies spatially and temporally, it is also a relational category, one that is coconstructed with a range of other racial and cultural categories, with class and with gender. This coconstruction is, however, fundamentally asymmetrical, for the term "whiteness" signals the production and reproduction of dominance rather than subordination, normativity rather than marginality, and privilege rather than disadvantage.[1] *WHETHER ACKNOWLEDGED OR NOT!*

In this text, the coconstruction of gender and whiteness were most visible in the arena of interracial sexuality and relationships (chapters 4 and 5). There, I argued, first, that the discourse against interracial relationships entails specifically racialized constructions of white femininity in relation to racialized masculinities. Second, I suggested that white women and men were placed, respectively, as victim and rescuer in the discourse against interracial sexuality, vis-à-vis the supposed sexual threat posed by men of color toward white women. Third, and in a sense exceeding the terms of the discourse against interracial sexuality, I suggested that white heterosexual women's choices of primary partners at times involved negotiations over preferred modes of living out femininity and living with men. Fourth, I argued that both heterosexual and lesbian white women's strategies for coping with the burdens that racism placed on interracial couples seemed at times to be distinctively "female" ones.

To speak about the intersections of femininity or femaleness and whiteness in the context of sexuality and partnerships is, however, only the beginning of the story. A range of further questions, most of which are beyond the scope of this study, present themselves. One set of questions concerns childhood. Here one might ask, for example, whether white boys and white girls use their environments in different ways. Were this so, boys might have different contexts from girls in which to interact with boys and girls, or men and women, of color. In relation to the fearful response of many white girls to peers of color, one can also ask whether white boys and white girls are socialized differently with regard to racial Others and hence whether white boys might be more hostile than fearful in interracial situations. (In fact, this difference, if it did exist, would be partly explicable in the context of the discourse on interracial sexuality just discussed.) Here I am, of course, speculating, for questions of this kind would have to be addressed in the context of a study that included both women and men.

How does the interweaving of material and discursive limitation, "local" variation, ascription, agency, and self-consciousness translate into individual trajectories through and within whiteness? On one level, it is impractical to unravel these strands, since they are lived, second by second, as interwoven. However, it is

But THE impact is there + Now!

also possible analytically—if artificially—to separate these strands
and place them on a continuum of fixity and mutability. And it is
also, I suggest, necessary to do so, for such an exercise might expose more clearly the points of pressure, of potential challenge to
racial domination. It is to this task, then, that I will now turn.

That which is most "given" about whiteness (and indeed about
the relations of race in general) is the materiality of its history—
the impossibility of undoing what has already taken place. For
example, at the risk of stating—and even oversimplifying—the
obvious, I would say that the Mexican-American War and the
Treaty of Guadalupe Hidalgo of 1848 created the border that Clare
Traverso and her classmates crossed in the early 1960s in order to
give clothes away to the poor. Ongoing neocolonial relations between the United States and Mexico contributed significantly to
the different fates of Clare's working-class family and the much
poorer families she encountered in Tijuana (see chapter 3). Similarly, a history of dramatically unequal Black-white relations, a
U.S. economy structured by race, and resistance to racism during
the civil rights movement underlay the existence of Beth Ellison's
all-white residential neighborhood, the possibility of a Black family moving into it in the late 1960s, and white neighbors' hostility
when they did so (see chapter 3). It would, in fact, be possible to
recover the histories embedded in every incident recounted in
each narrative.

The material structuring of daily life by race in the present
is *almost* as "given" as that of the past (almost, in the sense that
present-day material relations of racism are, at any moment, potentially transformable by collective, if not individual, action). As
some of the women ruefully pointed out, history was "not their
fault"—they merely inherited it, as its willing or unwilling beneficiaries. However, as I—and some of them—also pointed out,
history shaped the present(s) in which they lived their lives, placing them in a range of relationships with people of color that included relative privilege, social distance, explicitly articulated segregation, and local, fragile, and situationally specific forms of
quasi-integration. In the same way as one might historically situate each of these narratives, one could equally well map them in
a detailed way onto the racial order in the present.

White women also inhabited as given a universe of discourses
on race, on whiteness, on racial Others, and on racism, each of
which could be identified temporally and spatially in terms of

their emergence, but that coexisted in the present in uneven and complex ways. The key discursive repertoires in question here were, first, modes of naming culture and difference associated with west European colonial expansion; second, elements of "essentialist" racism again linked to European colonialism but also critical as rationale for Anglo settler colonialism and segregationism in what is now the USA; third, "assimilationist" or later "color- and power-evasive" strategies for thinking through race first articulated in the early decades of this century; and, fourth, what I have called "race-cognizant" repertoires that emerged in the latter half of the twentieth century and were linked both to U.S. liberation movements and to broader global struggles for decolonization. For the most part, I have argued, a color- and power-evasive repertoire was dominant, at least as a public language of race, in the times and places at which these interviews took place. Nonetheless, elements of the other repertoires were also in play.

This discursive environment was given, then, according to a complex logic and temporality. For I have argued that these white women lived, negotiated, appropriated, and rejected, at some times more consciously and intentionally than at others, the entire array of discursive repertoires. It was possible to identify individual trajectories of change with respect to discursive repertoires, which themselves mapped onto much broader social processes, both national and regional. Individual women at times self-consciously deployed one discursive repertoire against another (color evasiveness against essentialist racism, race cognizance against color evasiveness), and at other times appeared simultaneously caught within and critical of specific elements of one or another. In these ways, discourse was "given" and yet more fluid than the material relations of race. In ways that defied dualistic analysis, the women were apparently both self-conscious about the discursive history of race and not conscious of it; apparently both capable and not capable of changing their discursive repertoires.

In arguing that race shapes white women's lives, then, I am making a claim with two linked dimensions. First, white women's lives are marked by their diverse locations in the materiality of the racial order. But, second, white women's senses of self, other, identity, and worldview are also racialized, for they emerged here as repositories of the key elements of the history of the idea of race, in the United States and beyond. The white subject and the white imaginary thus by no means confine themselves to the present in their construction, but rather draw, consciously and unconsciously, on moments in the racial order long past in material terms. One is reminded of Antonio Gramsci's often-quoted comment on human subjectivity in general: "the consciousness of what one really is [entails] 'knowing thyself' as a product of the historical process to date which has deposited in you an infinity of traces, without leaving an inventory."[2] And, clearly, part of my task in this book has been, precisely, beginning an inventory of whiteness as a subjective terrain.

It was at the places of intersection and interconnection between materiality and discourse that contradiction, struggle, and the potential for change were in evidence. At times, to be sure, discursive repertoires and material relations apparently contained and reinforced one another—as, for example, when color- and power-evasive repertoires sat comfortably with middle-class and de facto racially segregated neighborhoods, generating accounts of apparently (but not actually) all-white lives. But at other times in these women's lives, material relations and discursive repertoires jostled against one another, exceeded and overruled one another. Here I am thinking, for example, of the ways in which the materiality of white women's involvements in interracial relationships problematized the discourse against them (chapter 5); and of the way in which the equivocations of the repertoire of color and power evasion were starkly foregrounded in attempts to account for a race riot (chapter 6) or in discussions of interracial couples' bearing children (chapter 4).

It would be a mistake to ask which comes first in the process of conceptual transformation—the "excess" of daily life, or the introduction of a different discursive repertoire—for in the context of these narratives, it was possible to observe the line of causality moving in both directions. Thus, for example, Louise Glebocki's childhood friendships with Chicanos and Mexicans and her sense of the similarity between their families and her own made it relatively easy for her to dismiss as racist the hostility to Chicanos expressed by her father and some of her white schoolmates. Similarly, Jeanine Cohen felt that her early, intimate connections with Black South Africans had made the logic of apartheid patently unbelievable as a mode of explaining the racial order. Conversely, for some of the women, exposure to new discursive repertoires actually generated reinterpretation of environments that had previously not seemed to them to need it. Examples here would be Chris Patterson and Ginny Rodd, both of whom had by their own accounts accepted as unproblematic environments and modes of description that they later called into question. Moreover, since in practice, discursive repertoires do not exist outside of material contexts, individuals' exposure to varying interpretive frameworks always took place in the context of broader social processes, whether "local" (as when an individual moved from one place to another) or more "global" (as when a broad social movement generated greater public visibility for particular modes of thinking through race).

The materiality of race and the discursive repertoires available to account for it thus frequently problematized one another. Just as this book has visited and revisited the narratives of white daily life, the women I interviewed did the same, reinterpreting childhood and adult landscapes through changing discursive repertoires. In this process, both past and present became less "given," in the sense that they were open to reinterpretation. The spatiality and temporality of experience were also altered in this process: for if the word *experience* describes the production of meaning at the intersection of material life and interpretive frameworks, these women experienced and reexperienced the same terrain, in ways that altered their landscapes, at least on the subjective level.

As the women applied new frameworks to old landscapes, the meanings that they gave to whiteness, implicitly or explicitly, were also conceptually transformed. However, reinterpretation per se guaranteed nothing about the content or outcome of that process. For while some discursive strategies were oriented toward critique of the racial order, others effectively reinforced (or at least did not call into question) past or present relations of racial domination. Moreover, some women whose reconceptualization *did* make racial injustice more visible nonetheless could not see how to take action in relation to it. In fact, only a few women I interviewed had taken what would seem to be the next step toward altering the meaning of whiteness in a significant way—using a critique of the racial order and their own positions within it as the basis for participation in changing that which is more "given" than either subjecthood or discourse: the material relations of racism.

If it would be presumptuous to attempt to generate a theory of social change here, it would be equally presumptuous to imagine

Subs can enforce a status that does at work

that all white women have an interest in helping to change the present racial order and meaning of whiteness, or see the need to do so. However, inasmuch as some do, this book can, perhaps, be used to generate some of the directions in which we might want to move.

Attention to the construction of white "experience" is important, both to transforming the meaning of whiteness and to transforming the relations of race in general. This is crucial in a social context in which the racial order is normalized and rationalized rather than upheld by coercion alone. Analyzing the connections between white daily lives and discursive orders may help make visible the processes by which the stability of whiteness—as location of privilege, as culturally normative space, and as standpoint—is secured and reproduced. In this context, reconceptualizing histories and refiguring racialized landscapes are political acts in themselves.

Analyzing the construction of whiteness is important as a means of reconceptualizing the grounds on which white activists participate in antiracist work. In that regard, this book may help generate a checklist of existing conceptualizations of both whiteness and racism and the potential strengths and weaknesses of each. I have, for example, criticized the "power-evasive" view that reduces racism to individual, intentional acts. Not only does that view distract white people's attention from the results of individual actions, it also evades a much broader range of historical and contemporary processes through which the racial order is maintained. Again, I have criticized conceptions of white complicity with racism that deploy as metaphor colonialism or neo-colonialism but do not trace in practical terms the real and varying relationships of white people to either project. Operating as, in a sense, secularized metaphors for "sin" and "evil," such conceptions are in fact simultaneously reductive and excessive, and actually have the potential to disempower and short-circuit white antiracism. By contrast, I have argued here that white complicity with racism should be understood—and challenged—in the complex, multifaceted terms in which it operates.

Examining the coconstruction of whiteness and other racial identities is useful because it may help lead white activists (and also, for that matter, activists of color) away from the incorporation of "old" discursive elements into "new" strategies. I have, for example, argued that we need to displace the colonial construction of whiteness as an "empty" cultural space, in part by refiguring it as constructed and dominant rather than as norm. Without reconceptualizing culture, we run the risk of reifying and dehistoricizing *all* cultural practices, valorizing or romanticizing some while discounting others as not cultural at all. But a dualistic framework is retained, for example, in new curricular programs that include attention to nondominant cultures but do not simultaneously reconceptualize or reexamine the status, content, and formation of whiteness. Similarly, references to women of color, but not white women, as "racial-ethnic women," implicitly suggest that race does *not* shape white identities or experience.

Beyond a point, however, the reinterpretation of white women's experience and the historicizing of whiteness are simply retellings of the same tale. Analysis of the place of whiteness in the racial order can and should be, rather than an end in itself, only one part of a much broader process of social change leveled both at the material relations of race and at discursive repertoires. It is not, in any case, realistic or meaningful to reconceptualize whiteness outside of racial domination when, in practical terms, whiteness still confers race privilege. It would be similarly naive to imagine that political will alone might bring about the kinds of shifts necessary to challenge those discourses that most effectively stabilize the racial order.

Ultimately, the process of altering present and future meanings of whiteness is inextricably connected to that of altering the meanings of other, coconstructed racial and cultural identities. That process is in turn linked to the effort to transform the racial order in both material and discursive terms and to alter, perhaps, more than anything, the distribution of power. Clearly, that project is not individual but collective. Nor does it rest with white activists alone, so much as with collective actions by people from a range of locations in the racial order.

Appendix

The Women Who Were Interviewed

The interviews took place between October 1984 and February 1987. The names used here are pseudonyms. Where appropriate to preserving confidentiality, names of towns have been omitted and personal details have been changed. The names of large cities, however, have been retained. In addition to background information, I note how I met each woman and what I knew about her at the start of the interview.

As I stated in chapter 2, I adopted a "purposive" rather than a random strategy for gathering interviews. The diversity of the whole group in terms of age, class, and region was monitored consciously through the two-year period of the research. Further, I divided the interviews into three subgroups: white women who, I imagined, might be more than usually conscious of gender as a system of domination; white women whom I knew to be more than usually connected to communities of color (and thus possibly more conscious of racial domination); and white women about whom I had no preconceptions other than their gender and race. (Clearly, groups one and two overlapped at times. Moreover, some of the women in the third group turned out to be either gender conscious or race conscious.

Interviewees' names, year of birth, and date of first interview, in order of age:

Lisbeth Poirer (1967) 5/1/86
Lucy Fredricks (1967) 7/14/86
Cathy Thomas (1960) 2/10/85
Marty Douglass (1959) 5/12/86
Patricia Bowen (1958) 10/20/84
Tamara Green (1958) 10/18/84
Louise Glebocki (1958) 3/21/86
Beth Ellison (1955) 4/11/85
Chris Patterson (1954) 10/30/85

Sharon Ellison (1954) 10/12/85
Clare Traverso (1954) 6/15/85
Jeanine Cohen (1953) 10/4/84
Suzie Roberts (1953) 10/31/86
Helen Standish (1950) 2/22/86
Sandy Alvarez (1949) 7/25/85
Debby Rothman (1949) 9/25/85
Donna Gonzaga (1946) 5/12/86
Frieda Kazen (1945) 8/8/85
Eve Schraeger (1944) 11/13/85
Dot Humphrey (1942) 11/18/85
Margaret Phillips (1940) 10/16/85
Alison Honan (1936) 7/22/86
Joan Van Buren (1931) 6/5/86
Ginny Rodd (1930) 4/14/86
Evelyn Steinman (1930) 7/1/86
Irene Esterley (1926?)* 5/13/86
Joan Bracknell (1912) 7/10/86
Marjorie Hoffman (1905) 9/24/85
Hilda Perlman (1903) 2/14/86
Dora Hauser (1900) 2/21/86

*Declined to give age

Lisbeth Poirer (1967) 5/1/86

Lisbeth Poirer (Lisbeth told me she had changed her name after leaving home) grew up on the East Coast: Philadelphia, New York, Long Island, and Maine. She began life in upper middle class neighborhoods. After her parents' divorce, when Lisbeth was seven, she, her mother, and her brother moved frequently within working-class neighborhoods. At about fourteen, Lisbeth ran away from her mother and moved in with her father, which meant that, once again, her environment was upper middle class. Her anger and pain about her childhood were palpable: the last hour of the interview tape was barely audible, as Lisbeth's depression overwhelmed her and her voice was reduced to a murmur. After high school, Lisbeth had traveled for several months in Europe and had returned to the United States and settled in San Francisco less than four months before the interview. She was working as a telephone fund-raiser for an ecology action group and living with a group of white men and women in a rundown apartment in a poor, racially mixed section of San Francisco. I met Lisbeth in San Francisco when we both volunteered to take part in a door-to-door fund-raiser for children in Central America. As her designated canvasing partner, I was shocked by the apparent contradiction between her volunteer activity and her casually negative remarks about Latino men. As a result, I requested to interview her.

Lucy Fredricks (1967) 7/14/86

Lucy grew up in the Pacific northwest in a Seattle suburb—an island joined to the city by a causeway. Her parents, while middle-class in origin, were poor, having chosen to "drop out" of the career structure. Lucy and her siblings helped their father support the family by painting houses, and Lucy learned many art and craft skills at a young age. While she was growing up, Lucy's social environment was white except for two Asian families and one Black family. As teenagers, Lucy and a friend moved to Seattle proper and lived in a poor part of the city where many African American people lived. About a year before the interview, Lucy and her closest female friend had hitchhiked to the San Francisco Bay Area for a concert by the rock band the Grateful Dead and stayed on there. At the time of the interview, Lucy worked in a restaurant owned by an Iranian family and was spending much social time with that family and their friends, many of whom were male and recent immigrants from the Middle East. I observed Lucy at work at the restaurant and asked her to consider being interviewed.

Cathy Thomas (1960) 2/10/85

Cathy Thomas grew up in a small town outside Sacramento, California. Her parents had grown up working class. Her father was a sports coach and did well enough for the family to have bought a house by the time Cathy was about seven. However, her father's earnings were erratic because he was self-employed. After her parents' divorce, Cathy's mother supported her and her two sisters through clerical work and bookkeeping. Although primarily white, the town had a small Mexican American population and an even smaller African American one. Cathy went to school with a number of Chicano and Black students. Cathy left her home town at the end of high school to go to a prestigious state university in the San Francisco Bay Area. Cathy has a bachelor of arts degree. She works as typesetter and production manager at a small publishing house in the San Francisco Bay Area. At the time of the interviews, Cathy was lesbian, and part of the interviews involved discussion of her four-year relationship with a Chicana partner, which had ended just before the interviews took place. She lived in a rented apartment in a multiracial neighborhood in Oakland, California, and had a Chicana roommate. I met Cathy at a feminist community social gathering. I asked to interview her knowing her interest in and concern with issues about white women and racism.

Marty Douglass (1959) 5/12/86

Marty was in her mid-twenties when we met. She grew up in the 1960s and early 1970s in the working-class, mixed but predominantly white neighborhood in which she once again resided at the time of the interview. Marty's father was a blue-collar worker. Marty married before the end of high school and moved to southern California with her husband. He was both possessive and unfaithful; finally, after threatening suicide, Marty left him and returned to her mother's house. She later met and married her present husband, a welder. She worked alongside him and began an apprenticeship in welding but gave it up after the birth of her children made it financially impractical to continue. Her daughter is now in elementary school, and her son is still at home all day. Marty declared herself to be for the most part uninterested in political and social issues. Marty is Louise Glebocki's neighbor, and Louise referred me to her. Before the interview, I knew only that she was a white, working-class woman.

Patricia Bowen (1958) 10/20/84

Patricia Bowen grew up in a small Maryland town, which, as Pat described it, was culturally "semi-southern." Pat lived with her grandparents, mother, and uncles, in a space poor and crowded enough so that she shared her mother's bed until she was twelve. Her mother did clerical work; her uncles and aunts were manual and pink-collar workers. Pat described the family as "economically just one step above welfare poverty level, but with enough never to receive public assistance." Pat's father, who was absent or in jail for a lot of Pat's childhood, was from an elite East Coast family. Pat's mother paid for her to attend a private elementary school, so many of her friends were middle class, and Pat felt both uncomfortable with her middle-class schoolmates and unable to participate or hold her own with her working-class friends and neighbors. The environment in which Pat grew up was one of explicit racial hostility toward Black people. In Patricia's final year of high school, she and her parents moved to San Francisco. At the time of the interview, Pat was heterosexual, without children, and shared a rented apartment with a white male friend in a racially mixed, mainly Black-white, neighborhood in the San Francisco Bay Area. Since graduating from the University of California, Pat had been working as a waitress. I knew Pat through university networks. She volunteered to be interviewed. I began the interview knowing that she had grown up a southerner and that she had majored in women's studies.

Tamara Green (1958) 10/18/84

Tamara Green was raised, in her own words, "very solidly middle class" in Los Angeles, her father a dentist and her mother a social worker. Her parents were political liberals who had, for example, raised funds on the two occasions when Black mayoral candidate Tom Bradley ran for election in Los Angeles. The family is Jewish. Tamara grew up in an almost entirely white neighborhood. After graduating from college, Tamara worked in left-wing and feminist organizations, mainly in the cultural field. At the time of the interview, she was active politically in the movement for solidarity with Central America, was lesbian, and did not have children. She lived in a rented house shared with women friends in a racially mixed (Asian, Latino, Black, and white) neighborhood. Tamara was known to me through university women's studies networks. I interviewed her knowing of her feminist and internationally oriented activities.

Louise Glebocki (1958) 3/21/86

Louise Glebocki was 29 when we met. Louise's first five years were spent in Connecticut. The family lived on the edge of a small town, so that the house backed onto woods and fields. When Louise was six, the family moved to Los Angeles, where her mother's family lived. There Louise spent the rest of her childhood, first in a barrio with a predominantly Mexican population. Her parents worked at manual, skilled, and semi-skilled jobs. Later, her parents bought a house in a white working-class neighborhood, but Louise continued to go to school with Chicana/Chicano and white students. Louise's friendship groups and family were both Chicano and white. Louise went to the University of California, Berkeley, as an Equal Opportunity Program student. At the time of the interview, Louise made a living by cleaning houses. She was very active in a Marxist-Leninist party. Her partner of seven years at the time of the interview was a Chicano man. The couple lived together in a rented apartment, in a working-class, predominantly white neighborhood. I was referred to Louise by Cathy Thomas.

Beth Ellison (1955) 4/11/85

Beth grew up in what she described as a white, professional subdivision in a city in Virginia with her brothers, her mother, and her stepfather, who was an architect. She also spent time with her grandmother in Alabama. She studied art at college. Beth moved to the San Francisco Bay Area mainly so that she could be less closeted as a lesbian. When I met her at the time of the interview, she was a practicing artist working for a living in a record store. She was lesbian, without children, and lived alone in a rented apartment in a busy city neighborhood in the San Francisco Bay Area. I was introduced to Beth by a mutual friend and knew that she was a lesbian and a southerner before the interview.

Chris Patterson (1954) 10/30/85

Chris Patterson was in her early thirties when we met. She was born to a middle-class family in Long Island, the oldest of three children. Growing up in an all-white town, she remembered that Black people lived in the next town over. A Catholic, she was taught by her parents to feel different from and superior to other white ethnic groups, including Jews, Poles, and Germans. Chris remembered a warm relationship with a Black male biology teacher she had in school and the tension that later pervaded her high school during the first years of its desegregation program. Chris went to college in Virginia and was shocked by the more explicit anti-Black racism she encountered there. Coming out as a lesbian, Chris remained for several years in two southern cities and was active in building lesbian communities. Chris had moved to the San Francisco area and settled in Oakland less than a year before the interview. She shared a rented house with a group of white women and was self-employed as a housepainter. I contacted Chris after describing my project and my quest for interviewees at a feminist community event. She volunteered to be interviewed. When I began the interview, I knew only that she was a feminist.

Sharon Ellison (1954) 10/12/85

Sharon Ellison is Beth Ellison's sister-in-law. The interview was difficult: Sharon and her husband had recently moved and were barely unpacked, so the interview took place in the one available room in the apartment, in the presence of Sharon's husband. Possibly because of this, Sharon appeared self-conscious and embarrassed. Sharon grew up in a military family whose home base was east Tennessee. However, they had moved frequently: within the southern United States, to Alaska, to West Germany, and to Norway. Sharon felt that she had been sheltered from racist ideas by her parents, but nonetheless recalled the tension conveyed to her by white teachers and other adults when, the year she was in fourth grade, her school in Atlanta desegregated along with the rest of the city. Sharon and her husband had relocated to the San Francisco area about six months before the interview took place. They had moved for a variety of reasons, including career advancement for both of them and the desire for a more liberal environment than Memphis, their previous home. Sharon had been to law school, but when we met had a temporary lower management job in the personnel department of a business. Her husband worked in the computer industry. The couple lived in a rented apartment in a class- and race-mixed city neighborhood. I contacted Sharon Ellison via Beth Ellison.

Clare Traverso (1954) 6/15/85

Clare Traverso grew up in a small agricultural town near San Diego, California, one of six children. Clare described her family as poor, remembering, for example, wearing hand-me-down clothes and having only one pair of shoes at a time while she was growing up. Clare's father was a housepainter who worked for a large company. Her parents were active Christians, "fundamentalist, but not moral majority." The town's population was white, Mexican American, and Native American. Clare has a bachelor of arts degree in social work, but now works as a bilingual education teacher of Mexican, Chicano, Asian, and white students in an agricultural town. Clare chose teaching as a profession as a context in which it is possible to broaden consciousness of social issues. Clare is heterosexual, married, and does not have children. Her husband is a self-employed craftsman. They owned a house in a class-mixed, predominantly white neighborhood in Santa Cruz County, California. I was given Clare's name by a colleague who was conducting research with the students at Clare's school. I began the interview with Clare knowing only that she worked in a multiethnic school.

Jeanine Cohen (1953) 10/4/84

Jeanine was born in South Africa to Jewish parents active in the movement against apartheid. Her father owned a dry-cleaning business. Although surrounded by an extremely racist regime, Jeanine grew up with a great deal of close and loving contact with Black as well as white adults. Jeanine left South Africa when she was eight, when her family moved to London. Jeanine is a lesbian, does not have children, and lived in a shared, multiethnic household of women. In the interview we explored Jeanine's six-year relationship with a Black woman. Jeanine has been active politically in a range of feminist and antiracist organizations. Jeanine graduated from high school and is certified in performing arts and manual trades. She was employed at the time of the interview as a hospital clerical worker. I was referred to Jeanine by Tamara Green. I began the interview knowing that she was feminist and South African.

Suzie Roberts (1953) 10/31/86

Suzie Roberts was born and raised in a middle-class Los Angeles family. Her mother is Jewish, but she kept this information from her children until Suzie found out by accident as a teenager. Suzie married a white classmate right after high school, but left him a year later, running away to Mexico with an older Mexican man who was the couple's next door neighbor. Suzie stayed with him for six years, and they had two children. At the time of the interview, Suzie and her children lived in the San Francisco Bay Area, in a rented house in a predominantly white neighborhood. When we met, she had recently completed a bachelor of arts degree and was a child care worker. In recent years, she had actively explored and developed a relationship with Jewish culture, sending the children to Hebrew school and celebrating the Jewish holidays. At the time of the interview, she had been in a relationship with an African American man for several years. I was referred to Suzie by a colleague who happened to be Suzie's tenant. I knew before the interview that she was the mother of children of mixed heritage.

Helen Standish (1950) 2/22/86

Helen Standish grew up middle class in a company town in Massachusetts where her father was head of one of the company's research divisions. Her mother did not work outside the home. Helen's town was all white. She saw Black people when she went (rarely) to the next town over. Helen's mother taught her to make distinctions between whites and to view her own people (who, her mother said, had come to the United States on the *Mayflower*) as being on the highest rung of the status ladder. Helen was miserable at home with her physically and psychologically abusive parents, and she was relieved to move to New York to go to art school after high school. Majoring in art and education, Helen then worked as a substitute teacher, mostly in poor, working-class, and racially conflictual parts of the city. After art school, in the mid-1970s, Helen and the African American man with whom she was then in a relationship moved to the West Coast, partly, she said, to escape New York's racial tension and its hostility toward biracial couples. Helen remains on the West Coast, working as a part-time receptionist at a health spa. She had no children and lived alone in a rented apartment. I asked Helen if she would consent to an interview after I had seen her several times on my way into the health spa. I knew only that she worked there.

Sandy Alvarez (1949) 7/25/85

Sandy Alvarez was born and raised in racially mixed (Black, Latino, Asian, white) working-class neighborhoods in Los Angeles. Her father, a plumber, became permanently disabled when Sandy was twelve, and her mother began paid work as a secretary. Sandy's father died four years later. Sandy's parents were both activists in integration issues. Sandy graduated from a university in southern California. She now teaches bilingual (Spanish-English) education in a high school. Her husband is Chicano, and they have a son in elementary school and a daughter in preschool. They owned a home in a middle-class neighborhood in a small, residential, largely white community in Santa Cruz County. I was given Sandy's name by a colleague who was doing research with the students at Sandy's workplace. Before interviewing Sandy, I knew only that she taught in a multiracial school.

Debby Rothman (1949) 9/25/85

Debby Rothman was born in New York City to Jewish parents, both of whom were teachers. Because of their involvement in civil rights, Debby grew up meeting many Black men, women, and children and learning about Black music and arts. Debby lived in New York, in primarily Catholic neighborhoods where she was seen as unusual both as a Jew and as an atheist. The family moved to the San Francisco Bay Area when Debby was seven. Debby began and dropped out of college in the late 1960s, finally completing her bachelor's degree back in New York in the mid-1970s. In the interviews, we discussed both Debby's long-term relationship with an African American man and the challenges of her job at the time of the interviews as a white member of a predominantly Black labor union executive. A recurrent theme was Debby's concern to verbalize the difficulty of interracial work without feeding racism or invalidating the possibility of such work. I was able to contact Debby thanks to a colleague who was undertaking research in a different part of the labor union. I knew that she was a white activist in a multiracial union.

Donna Gonzaga (1946) 5/12/86

Donna Gonzaga grew up in Sacramento, the capital of California, in a working-class family. Her father, a skilled electrician, died when Donna was eight. Thereafter, Donna's mother supported the family through clerical work. Donna remembered being in school with white, Black, and Chicano students and being dimly aware of the class and status differences between the three groups. As a teenager, Donna was sent for several years to live with her grandparents in Utah. Donna met and married her husband in her final year of high school. The couple had two children. Her daughters, now in their twenties, spent the latter part of their childhoods living with their father. Donna moved to the San Francisco area in the late 1960s and did clerical work. She met antiracist and Black Power activists with whom she became friendly and politically involved. From then on, Donna had been active in antiracist and, later, feminist organizations. At the time of the interview, Donna was lesbian and living with two white women friends in a rented house in a racially mixed (mainly Black and white) working-class neighborhood and working at a feminist nonprofit organization. I was referred to Donna by Jeanine Cohen, and I knew at the start of the interview that she was feminist, lesbian, and involved in the movement against U.S. intervention in Central America.

Frieda Kazen (1945) 8/8/85

Frieda grew up in a small town in New Jersey, in one of the first Jewish families to move in alongside the mainly Italian and Irish American population. Frieda's father owned a laundry. The town was all white. New York City was a fifteen-minute drive away, and as a teenager, Frieda spent much time there with her school friends. After graduating from college, Frieda taught art in a Harlem elementary school and became involved in multiracial community projects on the Upper West Side of Manhattan. Frieda described the period with warmth; it felt like an ideal context where people worked together across age, sex, and race lines. Frieda met and married her husband, a Black man, in New York. After their divorce she moved to California. After a period of work developing multicultural curricula, she opened her own small retail business. She is heterosexual, does not have children, and lived in a rented city apartment with her African American partner in the San Francisco Bay Area. I was referred to Frieda through my doctor, who knew Frieda to be a member of an organization for multiracial families.

Eve Schraeger (1944) 11/13/85

Eve grew up in an upper middle class family in an all-white Chicago suburb. Her family is Jewish, but it was not until she was an adult that Eve explored and expanded the meaning of Jewish identity for herself. After graduating from an East Coast university, Eve moved to California. She worked for the welfare department in the San Francisco Bay Area for eighteen months, then left her job—in part, she said, because she found herself coming to dislike her Black clients with a passion that frightened her. In the early seventies, Eve both "came out" and "dropped out" in the lesbian feminist movement, practicing what she called downward mobility in the effort to separate from patriarchal society. In the few years preceeding the interview, however, Eve had made conscious efforts to reenter professional life and was by the time of the interview a home owner and a self-employed interior designer. She saw herself as consciously reclaiming her upper middle class identity and valuing it as much as her lesbianism and Jewishness. Eve lived alone, in an upper middle class and largely white neighborhood. I contacted Eve for the first time when I described my quest for interviewees at a feminist community event. She volunteered to be interviewed, saying that she was perturbed by her own growing racist attitudes.

Dot Humphrey (1942) 11/18/85

Dot Humphrey grew up in rural Kansas, the oldest of three children. Her father was a mechanic who repaired farm machinery, and her mother worked as postmistress in a rural post office. Living in a small, homogeneous, monoreligious community, her family was marginal because her father had been excommunicated from the church after enlisting to fight in World War II. Taken to church by friends, Dot heard white and African missionaries and decided to go to Africa as a missionary herself. With the help of her parents, Dot consciously used education as a means to escape her rural and class positioning. She went to college and earned bachelor's and master's degrees, the first on either side of her family to do so. During graduate study, she met and married her husband. The two were part of a group of radical philosophers and "nonconformers." The couple moved to New York City and soon afterward adopted a child whose heritage was Black and white. Dot left her husband and came out as a lesbian in the late 1960s in the context of the newly emergent feminist movement. Her daughter stayed with her, but her son (who is not adopted) remained with Dot's ex-husband. At the time of the interview, Dot was an editor at a San Francisco Bay Area publishing house. She and her daughter lived in a rented house in a racially mixed (Black, white) neighborhood. I was put in contact with Dot Humphrey by my neighbor. Before the interview, I was aware that she was a lesbian and that she had a daughter of biracial heritage.

Margaret Phillips (1940) 10/16/85

Margaret Phillips was born and grew up in Chicago, in a wealthy family. Her father was a businessman and landowner. Margaret moved to San Francisco with her mother when she was sixteen; she would have "come out" as a debutante had it not been for her parents' divorce. At the time of the interview, Margaret was married to a stockbroker and had just moved out of the city to an exclusive, predominantly white residential community overlooking San Francisco Bay. Margaret had three children, the youngest in college. Her oldest son had been to Jamaica several years before the interview and joined the Rastafarian movement. (Margaret described his trip to Jamaica in respectful and sympathetic terms.) We discussed at some length her struggles to adapt to her son's Rastafarianism and to welcome his Jamaican partner into the home and family. Margaret herself professed a long-standing interest in cultural diversity, and had worked for several years in a project developing multicultural curricula. She had recently qualified as a counselor but was not working at the time of the interview, having chosen to focus on settling the family into their new home. I was referred to Margaret by Frieda Kazen. Before the interview, I knew that she and Frieda had been co-workers and that Margaret had a Rastafarian son.

Alison Honan (1936) 7/22/86

Alison Honan grew up Los Angeles and Palo Alto, California.
She described her Los Angeles home as a typical two-bedroom,
one-bathroom "tract" house. Alison's father had a succession of
jobs: he owned a gas station, managed a bar, and later sold real
estate. Her mother for the most part did not work outside the
home, although—unusually for the times—she opened a pet shop
when Alison was thirteen. Through childhood Alison remembered always living in neighborhoods with people racially and
ethnically like herself. She also remembered her father expressing
disapproval of a racially mixed couple the family saw in a restaurant and his subtle discouragement of her dating a Catholic boy
(her family was Protestant). Alison graduated from college in the
late 1950s and married soon after. She and her husband were introduced by a friend to right-wing politics in the early 1960s, and
Alison had been a committed right-winger ever since, viewing
herself as part of the "moral majority" and close in spirit to the
John Birch Society, although not a member. Alison had two
daughters, the youngest still in college. She lived with her second
husband in an exclusive upper middle class area of Santa Cruz
County. Alison ran her own advertising agency with a woman
partner. I was referred to Alison by Evelyn Steinman, who informed me in general terms that Alison was politically to the
right.

Joan Van Buren (1931) 6/5/86

Joan Van Buren grew up in a Jewish family, in a working-class,
mainly Italian American and German American neighborhood in
Queens, New York. Her parents ran a hardware store, and as a
result, Joan said, they had little time for her when she was a child.
Her husband is Dutch but has lived in the United States since the
end of World War II. Joan has two daughters and a son, all living
away from home by the time of the interview. Joan graduated
from college but—because of her own experience of having
working parents—chose to stay home with her children rather
than working outside the home, although this meant they had to
work hard to make ends meet on her husband's salary. Joan and
her husband had been active in the Democratic party and, before
that, in integration activities in southern California. Although she

considered herself to be in favor of integration, she said that she would be upset if Black people moved into her neighborhood, because it would, she felt, reduce the value of her property. Joan and her husband, who is an engineer for a large corporation, lived in their own house in a middle-class, largely white neighborhood in Santa Cruz County. I met Joan through a women's club that I contacted in order to solicit interviewees. Joan volunteered to be interviewed. When I met her, I knew only that she belonged to the club and that she was willing to be interviewed.

Ginny Rodd (1930) 4/14/86

Ginny Rodd grew up on a small, rented farm in Alabama, one of eleven children. From the age of seven, she helped in the kitchen and on the farm, as well as going to school and doing homework. As she put it, "I never had much of a kid's life." Ginny married at fifteen, having met her husband in church. She did most of the field work on her own and her parents' farm, until, in 1955, her farm went bankrupt after a hailstorm destroyed the crops. At that point, Ginny, her husband, and their two sons moved to California, where her husband became a roofer and she worked in the canneries. Ginny was, at the time of the interview, head housekeeper at a residential children's home. In Alabama, Ginny said, she had had minimal contact with Black people, and was in fact taught to fear and avoid them. Since moving to California, she had met Black people and Chicanos through her children and at work. Although she strongly disapproved of marriage between Black and white people, her daughter, with whom she lived, was married to a man of Chicano, Filipino, and white descent, and the couple had an adopted son, also of tricultural heritage. Ginny was a widow by the time of the interview. She lived in her own house, sharing it with her daughter, son-in-law, and their children. I met Ginny through a friend who was a co-worker of Ginny's. My friend arranged to introduce me to all the white women workers in the children's residential home, and Ginny agreed to be interviewed.

Evelyn Steinman (1930) 7/1/86

Evelyn Steinman declined to discuss her life before the age of eighteen, saying that her memories were too unpleasant. Through stray remarks she made during the interview, I gathered that she had grown up on the South Side of Chicago, had been poor, and was half Jewish. She met and married her husband, who came from an income bracket much higher than her own, at the age of 19. The couple moved to California the following year, living in Los Angeles for fourteen years and then moving to the San Francisco area. Evelyn has a son who was 26 and in college at the time of the interview. Her husband was a very senior executive in an engineering firm. After his retirement, the couple ran their own consulting business until 1985. Evelyn had recently completed a bachelor of arts degree. She was vehement about the need to assert her Jewish identity in the face of anti-Semitism. In thinking about social issues, Evelyn argued that society was "too soft" on welfare recipients and viewed herself as having moved away from a "do-gooder" attitude that she had held in the past. At the time of the interview, Evelyn and her husband lived in their own house, in an upper middle class section of Santa Cruz County. I was referred to Evelyn through a professional women's group of which she is a member. Evelyn volunteered to be interviewed in response to a general call for participants.

Irene Esterley (1926?) 5/13/86

Irene Esterley chose not to tell me her exact age, describing herself as "mature." However, since she was retired, had been a young child during the Depression and a teenager by the time the United States entered World War II, I assumed that she was in her early sixties at the time of the interview. Irene grew up in Detroit, and the family fortunes rose and fell with the U.S. economy, poor during the Depression, but much wealthier during and after the war, since her father by that time owned a munitions factory. Irene spent her early years in her grandmother's house in a mainly Jewish neighborhood (her parents were non-Jewish German Americans). Irene finished her high school years at an exclusive girls' day school, and the family moved to a middle-class neighborhood at this time. At no time when she was growing up did Irene live in a mixed-race neighborhood, although she did encounter people of color as maids and employees, and in the downtown area. Irene has a bachelor's degree and is a certified teacher. She taught elementary school in both southern and northern California. Irene has three grown children, and grandchildren too. One son continued to live with her and her husband, owing to his ill health. Irene's husband was at the time of the interview a business executive in California's Silicon Valley. Irene continued to play a leading role in several professional women's organizations. The couple lived in their own home in a suburban, largely white neighborhood in Santa Cruz County. I was referred to Irene through a professional women's group of which she is a member. Irene volunteered to be interviewed in response to a general call for participants.

Joan Bracknell (1912) 7/10/86

Joan was born in Oakland, California, where her grandparents rented and ran a hotel and bar. Joan's parents were separated, and her mother helped with the hotel. The working-class neighborhood in which she lived and the schools she attended were, even at that time, racially mixed. After high school, Joan trained as an office worker and worked until her retirement in 1985. Joan described herself as "not religious." She described herself as having friends and acquaintances from different racial and ethnic groups and as a strong believer in tolerance and respect for differences. Joan was never married and did not have children. She lived alone in a rented apartment in a racially and class-mixed Oakland neighborhood. Joan was my neighbor. We had often greeted one another on the street. I asked whether I could interview her, and she agreed. Before the interview, I knew only that she was white and liked cats.

Marjorie Hoffman (1905) 9/24/85

Marjorie Hoffman described herself as "curious, questioning, and nonconformist." She was born in Maine on the U.S.-Canadian border, to Jewish New Yorkers, the seventh of nine children. Her father, a tailor, made a living selling clothes to workers in the Maine lumber camps. The town where she was born had a population of around three thousand and was white except for one Native American man. African American men who worked as Pullman porters came into town with the trains. The community was mainly Catholic; hers was the only Jewish family. When Marjorie was in fourth grade, the family moved to Portland, Maine, and four years later to New York City, where Marjorie first encountered people of color in large numbers. Partly influenced by her sister, Marjorie joined the Communist Party in her early twenties and was also an active unionist and electoral campaigner. After working for the federal government in Washington, D.C., and New York City, Marjorie went south in the late 1940s to work in an innovative race relations institute on a Black university campus. At the time of the interview, despite severe health problems, Marjorie remained active in the Gray Panthers, an organization for seniors' rights. I was referred to Marjorie by Frieda Kazen, who described her to me as an older radical woman.

Hilda Perlman (1903) 2/14/86

Hilda was born in Russia. As a Jew, she experienced discrimination at the hands of individuals and the state. In 1922, relatives already in the United States paid for her and her siblings' passage to Chicago. There, Hilda worked as a seamstress until around 1930, when she moved to California and studied Russian and home economics at the University of California, Berkeley, working her way through school by means of teaching and translating Russian. When World War II began, Hilda worked as a translator at the War Office. She spent the rest of her working life in a white-collar job in city government and lived for most of that time in the same rented apartment in the heart of downtown San Francisco. Hilda is married but has no children. Her husband lives in northern California. Hilda now lives in a residential home for the elderly, which is where I met her. I was referred to her by the staff at the home and knew only that she was a resident and that she was Jewish.

Dora Hauser (1900) 2/21/86

Dora Hauser lived in the same home for the elderly that Hilda Perlman lived in. Dora, although also Jewish, like many of the men and women in the community-run home, disliked the other residents and considered them "foreign" and unlike herself. Dora grew up in an affluent section of Manhattan, New York, the oldest of two daughters. The family had been wealthy: Dora's father owned a chain of retail stores and kept a stable of horses in the country. Although she knew of poor and nonwhite areas in New York City, she said that she had never had a reason to go to any of them during her childhood or adult life. Dora met and married her husband, a lawyer much older than herself, in 1922. They had two daughters and lived in another affluent section of New York City. Her husband died after fifteen years of marriage, leaving Dora with children of twelve and fourteen. Asked if her parents helped her at this time, Dora responded, "I didn't need help—I went to work." Dora did secretarial work while her children grew up. After they left home, Dora became a traveling companion and secretary to a woman academic. The two lived together for thirty-eight years, traveling in Europe, India, and New Zealand. When her friend became frail, Dora moved her into a residential home in southern California, following her into it shortly after. When her friend died, Dora moved north to the San Francisco Bay Area, to be in a home closer to her daughter. She was not happy there, and she stressed during the interview that she planned to move back to southern California as soon as possible. I met Dora through the residential home staff, whom I approached in order to solicit interviewees.

Notes

1. Introduction: Points of Origin, Points of Departure

1. Following Nancy Hartsock, "The Feminist Standpoint: Developing the Ground for a Specifically Feminist Historical Materialism," in *Discovering Reality*, ed. Sandra Harding and Merrill B. Hintikka (Dordrecht: D. Riedel, 1983), 283–310, the word "standpoint" has two linked meanings. The first is the perspective that arises out of a class's or gender's received and unanalyzed engagement with its material environment, perceived through the worldview of the dominant group. The second is the self-conscious perspective on self and society that arises out of a class (or gender) grouping's critical apprehension of itself and its location in relation to the system it inhabits. With respect to gender, Hartsock styles the former "women's standpoint" and the latter "feminist standpoint." No such distinction is currently available for my purposes. In referring here to whiteness as a standpoint, I intend, loosely, an analogy with Hartsock's "women's standpoint." The most appropriate analogy for Hartsock's "feminist standpoint" would be "white antiracist standpoint." At points in this book, I and some interviewees articulate elements of a white antiracist standpoint. Finally, it should be emphasized that the analogy is by no means perfect, since both "feminist" and "proletarian" standpoints refer to the self-conscious engagements of oppressed groups with their own positioning, whereas, of course, a "white antiracist standpoint" refers to self-conscious and self-critical engagement with a *dominant* position in the racial order.

2. "Discourses" may be understood in this book as historically constituted bodies of ideas providing conceptual frameworks for individuals, made material in the design and creation of institutions and shaping daily practices, interpersonal interactions, and social relations. "Western" is capitalized here to draw attention to its status as a discursive rather than a geographical construct. In the geographical sense, "west" is of course a relative term (tied to "east," "north, and "south," as well as to a particular point in space from which a given calculation emanates). But "west," *in* the West, tends to be understood to refer to the capitalist European countries, North America, Australia, New Zealand, and, on occasion, Japan(!). Discursively, too, "West" and "Western" are relational terms, constructed out of opposition to non-Western Others or "Orientals." Westernness implies a particular, dominative relationship to power, colonial expansion, a belonging to center rather than margin in a global capitalist system, and a privileged relationship to institutions—be they academic or oriented to mass communication—for the production of knowledge. Not all people in the (pseudogeographical) West/west are, within the terms of a discourse on West–non-West, Westerners. This is because the cultural content of Westernness draws on Christian, rationalist, north and west European customs and patterns of thought and because, discursively, Westernness is racially exclusive and tends to mean only Caucasian. Thus, for example, Ward Churchill, in describing the stages of European colonization of Native Americans, remarks that, "In the beginning, troops arrive to butcher the indigenous population. Later, the 'savages' are seen as worthy of being 'educated' and 'civilized' to white, *Western* standards, deal-

ing a devastating blow to the cultures possessed by the survivors of the slaughter."
Ward Churchill, *Fantasies of the Master Race: Literature, Cinema and the Colonization of
American Indians*, ed. Annette Jaimes (Monroe, Maine: Common Courage Press, 1992),
264 (emphasis mine).

3. I use "second wave" to refer to feminism from the late 1960s to the present.
"Third wave" has at times been used to characterize, optimistically, the emergence of
distinctively multiracial feminisms through the 1980s.

4. Examples of the published record of Black-white feminist dialogue in particular
are Tia Cross, Frieda Klein, Barbara Smith, and Beverley Smith, "Face-to-Face, Day-
to-Day: Racism CR [Consciousness Raising]," *Heresies* 3: 3, 66–67; Elly Bulkin, Minnie
Bruce Pratt, and Barbara Smith, *Yours in Struggle: Three Feminist Perspectives on Anti-
Semitism and Racism* (Brooklyn, N.Y.: Long Haul Press, 1984; Ithaca, N.Y.: Firebrand,
1988); Gloria I. Joseph and Jill Lewis, *Common Differences: Conflicts in Black and White
Feminist Perspectives* (Garden City, N.Y.: Anchor, 1981). See also Chandra Talpade
Mohanty, Ann Russo, and Lourdes Torres, eds., *Third World Women and the Politics of
Feminism* (Bloomington: Indiana University Press, 1991), ix, for reference to the con-
ference Common Differences: Third World Women and Feminist Perspectives, University of Illinois, Urbana-Champaign, April 1983.

5. Combahee River Collective, "A Black Feminist Statement," in *Capitalist Patriarchy and the Case for Socialist Feminism*, ed. Zillah R. Eisenstein (New York: Monthly
Review Press, 1979), 362–72. The statement argues for the need to analyze U.S. society
in terms of four interlocking axes of oppression based on race, class, gender, and sexuality. It also articulates an identity politics that linked the positioning of Black women
who are targets of all four systems of domination with a unique purview and political
agency.

6. In fact, bell hooks and Chela Sandoval, two women I met at that time at the
University of California, Santa Cruz, have written precisely about the political and
strategic implications for women of color of their positioning within webs of power
and systems of domination. Both of these women have been critical to my thinking
about racism, and Sandoval's work has been crucial to my thinking about power and
political strategy. bell hooks, *Ain't I a Woman? Black Women and Feminism* (Boston:
South End Press, 1981); *Feminist Theory: From Margin to Center* (Boston: South End
Press, 1984); *Talking Back: Thinking Feminist, Thinking Black* (Boston: South End Press,
1989). Chela Sandoval, "The Struggle Within: Women Respond to Racism—Report on
the National Women's Studies Conference, Storrs Connecticut" (Oakland, California:
Occasional Paper, Center for Third World Organizing, 1982) (revised version of this
paper is published in *Making Face, Making Soul, Haciendo Caras: Creative and Critical
Perspectives by Women of Color*, ed. Gloria Anzaldúa, [San Francisco: Aunt Lute, 1990],
55–71); "U.S. Third World Feminism: The Theory and Method of Oppositional Consciousness in the Postmodern World," *Genders* 10 (Spring 1991): 1–24.

7. I owe this term to Stuart Hall, "Race, Articulation, and Societies Structured in
Dominance," in *UNESCO: Sociological Theories, Race and Colonialism* (Paris: UNESCO
Press, 1980), 305–45.

8. For accounts of the uses and effectiveness of consciousness raising in the second
wave of feminism, see Anna Coote and Beatrix Campbell, *Sweet Freedom: The Struggle
for Women's Liberation* (London: Picador, 1982); Alice Echols, *Daring to Be Bad: Radical
Feminism in America, 1967–75* (Minneapolis: University of Minnesota Press, 1989);
Katie King, "The Situation of Lesbianism as Magical Sign: Contests for Meaning in the
U.S. Women's Movement, 1968–72," *Communications* 9 (1986): 65–91.

9. From a white feminist perspective, the clearest articulation of this position is
Hartsock, "The Feminist Standpoint." Articulations of a similar epistemological stance
by U.S. women of color include Combahee River Collective, "A Black Feminist Statement"; Aida Hurtado, "Relating to Privilege: Seduction and Rejection in the Subordi-

nation of White Women and Women of Color," *Signs* 14, no. 4 (1989): 833–55; and Patricia Hill Collins, "The Social Construction of Black Feminist Thought," *Signs* 14, no. 4 (1989,): 745–73.

10. A key text here is Cherríe Moraga and Gloria Anzaldúa, eds., *This Bridge Called My Back: Writings by Radical Women of Color* (Watertown, Mass.: Persephone, 1981; New York: Kitchen Table Women of Color Press, 1983).

11. Among others, see Hazel Carby, "White Woman Listen! Black Feminism and the Boundaries of Sisterhood," Center for Contemporary Cultural Studies, *The Empire Strikes Back: Race and Racism in '70s Britain* (London: Hutchinson, 1981), 212–35; Kum Kum Bhavnani and Margaret Coulson, "Transforming Socialist Feminism: The Challenge of Racism," *Feminist Review* 23 (Summer 1986): 81–92.

12. See, for example, Angela Y. Davis, *Women, Race and Class* (New York: Random House, 1981), 202–21.

13. The founding text here is, I believe, the Combahee River Collective's "A Black Feminist Statement." I will discuss more recent contributions later.

14. For example, Bernice Johnson Reagon, "Coalition Politics: Turning the Century," in *Home Girls: A Black Feminist Anthology*, ed. Barbara Smith (New York: Kitchen Table Women of Color Press, 1983), 356–69; Cherríe Moraga and Gloria Anzaldúa's concept of "El Mundo Zurdo/The Left Handed World," *This Bridge Called My Back*, 195–96.

15. Ruth Frankenberg, "Different Perspectives: Interweaving Theory and Practice in Women's Work," qualifying essay, Board of Studies in the History of Consciousness, University of California, Santa Cruz, 1983.

16. Among such developments, Chicana scholars have examined how the figure of La Malinche constructs Chicana femininity (for example, Norma Alarcon, "Chicana's Feminist Literature: A Revision Through Malintzin/or Malintzin: Putting Flesh Back on the Object," Moraga and Anzaldúa, *This Bridge Called My Back*, 182–90. Similarly, Hortense Spillers builds on the work of African American historians to show how, given the material conditions of Black women's lives, they were "excluded" from racially dominant notions of femininity, "Mama's Baby, Papa's Maybe: An American Grammar Book," *Diacritics*, Summer 1987: 65–81. Rayna Green, in "The Pocahontas Perplex: The Image of Indian Women in American Culture," in *Unequal Sisters*, ed. Ellen Carol DuBois and Vicki L. Ruiz (New York: Routledge, 1990), 15–21, analyzes the ideological construction of the figure of Native American women within a colonial matrix.

17. Such work has been undertaken by, for example, Gloria I. Joseph and Jill Lewis, *Common Differences*, who examine the differences in perspective, experience, and sense of self between white and Black women; Vron Ware, *Beyond the Pale: White Women, Racism and History* (London: Verso, 1992), who articulates in particular the place of white womanhood in the discursive economies of racism and imperialism; and Teresa L. Amott and Julie A. Matthaei, *Race, Gender, and Work: A Multicultural History of Women in the United States* (Boston: South End Press, 1991), who by juxtaposing and contrasting the histories of U.S. women across racial and ethnic lines enable greater attention to the specification of gender by race and class.

18. Patricia Zavella, "The Problematic Relationship of Feminism and Chicana Studies," *Women's Studies* 17 (1988): 123–34.

19. Norma Alarcon, "The Theoretical Subjects of *This Bridge Called My Back* and Anglo-American Feminism," in *Haciendo Caras*, ed. Anzaldúa, 356–69.

20. Chandra Talpade Mohanty, "Feminist Encounters: Locating the Politics of Experience," *Copyright* 1, no. 1 (1984); Donna J. Haraway, "Situated Knowledges: The Science Question and the Privilege of Partial Perspective," in Donna J. Haraway, *Simians, Cyborgs and Women: The Reinvention of Nature* (New York: Routledge, 1991), 183–202.

21. Foremost in this regard were Elly Bulkin ("Hard Ground: Jewish Identity, Racism and Anti-Semitism") and Minnie Bruce Pratt ("Identity: Skin, Blood, Heart") in Bulkin, Pratt, and Smith, *Yours in Struggle*, 89–228 and 9–64; Mab Segrest, *My Mama's Dead Squirrel: Lesbian Essays on Southern Culture* (Ithaca, N.Y.: Firebrand, 1985); Adrienne Rich, "Disloyal to Civilization: Feminism, Racism, Gynephobia," in Adrienne Rich, *On Lies, Secrets and Silence: Selected Prose, 1966–1978* (New York: Norton, 1979), 275–310; and Adrienne Rich, "Notes Toward a Politics of Location," in Adrienne Rich, *Blood, Bread and Poetry: Selected Prose, 1979–1985* (New York: Norton, 1986), 210–31.

22. Among the works I have found extremely helpful in this regard, see Stuart Hall, "Race, Articulation"; Centre for Contemporary Cultural Studies, *The Empire Strikes Back*; Michael Omi and Howard Winant, *Racial Formation in the United States: From the 1960s to the 1980s* (New York: Routledge and Kegan Paul, 1986); Cornel West, "Race and Social Theory: Towards a Genealogical Materialist Analysis," in *The Year Left, 2, Toward a Rainbow Socialism—Essays on Race, Ethnicity, Class and Gender*, ed. Mike Davis et al. (London: Verso, 1987), 74–90; Paul Gilroy, *There Ain't No Black in the Union Jack* (London: Hutchinson, 1987); David Theo Goldberg, ed., *Anatomy of Racism* (Minneapolis: University of Minnesota Press, 1990).

23. Omi and Winant, *Racial Formation*, 3.

24. See, for example, Virginia R. Dominguez, *White by Definition: Social Classification in Creole Louisiana* (New Brunswick, N.J.: Rutgers University Press, 1986); Peggy Pascoe, "Race, Gender and Intercultural Relations: The Case of Interracial Marriage," *Frontiers* 12, no. 1 (Summer 1991).

25. I am very much indebted to the work of Michael Omi and Howard Winant (in *Racial Formation*) for their periodization of U.S. race discourse. However, my analysis diverges from theirs in a range of ways, including the names I have given to specific periods or tendencies, my emphasis on the continued salience of "essentialist racism," and my focus on daily life rather than on intellectual movements, political processes, and social movements.

26. Omi and Winant, *Racial Formation*, 14–15.

27. Ibid., 14–24.

28. Ibid., 25–51.

29. Ibid., 4.

30. Toni Cade, *The Black Woman: An Anthology* (New York: Mentor, 1970); Sara Evans, *Personal Politics: The Origins of the Women's Liberation Movement in the Civil Rights Movement and the New Left* (New York: Vintage, 1980); Paula Giddings, *When and Where I Enter: The Impact of Black Women on Race and Sex in America* (New York: Bantam, 1984); Alma Garcia, "The Development of Chicana Feminist Discourse, 1970–1980," in *Unequal Sisters*, ed. DuBois and Ruiz, 418–31.

31. The term "color-blindness" is in some ways convenient because it is commonly used. I find it troubling, however, partly because it places a value judgment on a physical disability, and partly because it offers a quasi-physiological description of what is in fact a complex of social and political processes. Moreover, as I will argue in later chapters of this book, differences of racial identity and their connections to positions of domination and subordination are, for the most part, evaded within this discursive repertoire rather than literally not seen.

32. See, for example, Cornel West, "Race and Social Theory."

33. I am indebted to Chetan Bhatt for suggesting to me the term "repertoire."

34. Scholarship on the cultural and discursive legacies of colonialism is, by now, extensive. A helpful introduction to the field is Robert Young, *White Mythologies: Writing History and the West* (London: Routledge, 1990). Although by no means the first moment of engagement with the topic, a founding moment of widespread interest in the critical study of colonial discourses in the U.S. academy is the publication of Edward Said's *Orientalism* (New York: Random House, 1978).

35. For documentation and analysis of the fabrication of the "cannibal" within co-lonial discourse, see, for example, Peter Hulme, *Colonial Encounters: Europe and the Native Caribbean, 1492–1797* (New York: Methuen, 1986). For analysis of a complex colonial "bricolage" see Harryette Mullen, *The Psychoanalysis of Little Black Sambo*, Oc-casional Papers, Group for the Critical Study of Colonial Discourse, University of Cal-ifornia, Santa Cruz, 1987.

36. The term "epistemic violence," coined by Gayatri Chakravorty Spivak, was used by her in a keynote address to the Europe and Its Others Conference: Essex Con-ference on the Sociology of Literature, University of Essex, England, July 1984.

37. Said, *Orientalism*.

38. Gayatri Chakravorty Spivak, "The Rani of Sirmur," in *Europe and Its Others*, ed. Francis Barker et al. (Colchester: University of Essex, 1985), 128–51; Chandra Talpade Mohanty, "Under Western Eyes: Feminist Scholarship and Colonial Dis-courses," *Feminist Review*, Autumn 1988: 60–88; Trinh T. Minh-ha, "Difference: A Special Third World Women Issue" (special issue, "She, the Inappropriate/d Other") *Discourse* 8 (Fall–Winter, 1986–87); outside the arena of the critical study of colonial discourse, see also Toni Morrison, *Playing in the Dark: Whiteness and the Literary Imag-ination* (Cambridge, Mass.: Harvard University Press, 1992).

39. Spivak, "The Rani of Sirmur," 128.

40. There are exceptions to this generalization. In U.S. sociology, one may note among them David Wellman, *Portraits of White Racism* (Cambridge: Cambridge Uni-versity Press, 1977; revised edition forthcoming 1993); and Bob Blauner, *Black Lives, White Lives: Three Decades of Race Relations in America* (Berkeley: University of Cali-fornia Press, 1989). Both studies, however, are less about identity per se or the expe-rience of living as white and racially privileged in the United States than about attitudes to racial others and their social contexts.

41. There are again important exceptions here. These include Sallie Westwood, *All Day, Every Day* (London: Pluto, 1984), a study of a multiracial British factory work force that does indeed examine how race, culture, and gender shape the experiences of white and black workers; Kum Kum Bhavnani, *Talking Politics: A Psychological Framing for Views from Youth in Britain* (Cambridge: Cambridge University Press, 1991), a mul-tiracial study of British school-leavers' political attitudes and expectations of paid work; and David R. Roediger, *The Wages of Whiteness: Race and the Making of the American Working Class* (London: Verso, 1991).

42. Again, one may note exceptions here, among them the feminist autobiograph-ical work of Rich, "Disloyal to Civilization" and "Politics of Location"; Segrest, *My Mama's Dead Squirrel*; Bulkin, "Hard Ground"; and Pratt, "Identity."

43. There is a supreme irony involved in rereading this paragraph after the Los Angeles rebellion of April 1992 in the aftermath of the acquittal of four Los Angeles police officers in the brutal beating of African American Los Angelan Rodney King. Even before April 1992, however, for each of these statements about regional differ-ences in racism, it would be possible to claim the opposite, and with some merit, too. With regard to "blatant" racism, even before the 1991 videotaping of the attack on King, charges of excessive use of force and of attack dogs by police were frequent, although less well publicized before the King incident than after it. In terms of far-right and white supremacist activism, Tom Metzger, leader since the mid-1980s of the major neo-Nazi organization White Aryan Resistance, is based on the West Coast, and his radio show, "Race and Reason," was broadcast on San Francisco radio during the period in which the interviews took place. Further, the youth wing of White Aryan Resistance is active in the greater San Francisco Bay Area. Public discourse on the West Coast also includes more "mainstream" racial tension: in 1991, for example, five white male teachers in the San Francisco Unified School District brought a "reverse discrim-ination" suit against the school board (Burt Buzan and Kenneth D. Gallegos, "Politics

of Resentment Divide San Francisco Teachers," *San Francisco Weekly*, September 4, 1991).

2. White on White: The Interviewees and the Method

1. All interviewees are referred to by pseudonyms.

2. Seven women were in their twenties; eight were in their thirties; five were in their forties; four were in their fifties; one was in her sixties; one was in her seventies; and two were in their eighties. One woman was 93.

3. This list totals more than thirty because of the double counting of retirees.

4. In characterizing the "neutral" research persona, I am drawing both on Ann Oakley's critical characterization in "Interviewing Women: A Contradiction in Terms," in *Doing Feminist Research*, ed. Helen Roberts (London: Routledge and Kegan Paul, 1981), 30–61, and on my own experiences of fieldwork training at the University of California, San Francisco, September 1983–March 1984.

5. Oakley, "Interviewing Women."

6. Sherna Gluck, "What's So Special about Women? Women's Oral History," *Frontiers* 11, no. 2 (Summer 1977; special issue on women's oral history): 3–14.

7. Luisa Passerini, "Work Ideology and Consensus under Italian Fascism," *History Workshop Journal* 8 (Autumn 1979): 82–108.

8. James Clifford, Introduction, *Writing Culture: The Poetics and Politics of Ethnography*, ed. James Clifford and George Marcus (Berkeley: University of California Press, 1986), 7.

9. Luisa Passerini, "Memory: Résumé of the Final Session of the International Conference on Oral History, Aix-en-Provence, 26 September, 1982," *History Workshop Journal* 5 (Spring 1983): 195.

10. Roland Barthes, *S/Z: An Essay*, trans. Richard Miller (New York: Hill and Wang, 1974), 5.

3. Growing Up White: The Social Geography of Race

1. As I stated earlier, all names are pseudonyms.

2. See, for example, many of the contributions to Cherríe Moraga and Gloria Anzaldúa, eds., *This Bridge Called My Back: Writings by Radical Women of Color* (Watertown, Mass.: Persephone, 1981; New York: Kitchen Table Women of Color Press, 1983).

3. Discussion of the decisions Beth's mother made are beyond the scope of this paper since I did not interview her, but only her daughter. However, it is possible to speculate that, in relation to the Black doctor and his family, a sense of class similarity overrode or mitigated race difference in making Beth's mother feel it acceptable for the family to move in. In contrast, she did not accept Beth's move to a racially mixed neighborhood that was also a low-income area. It is also possible that, for Beth's mother, the presence of one or two Black people did not disrupt her sense of the "whiteness" of the environment, whereas a greater number of Black people, in school or in a neighborhood, was more disturbing.

4. As always, there is an embedded history here, since up until the 1960s as many as half of all Black women in paid employment worked as domestic workers. See, for example, Julianne Malveaux, "Ain't I a Woman: Differences in the Labor Market Status of Black and White Women," in *Racism and Sexism: An Integrated Study*, ed. Paula S. Rothenberg (New York: St. Martin's, 1988), 76.

5. Judith Rollins's study, *Between Women: Domestics and Their Employers* (Philadelphia: Temple University Press, 1985), also points to the "invisibility" of Black domestic workers in the contemporary United States (see especially pp. 207ff.).

6. I have chosen to stay with Clare's term, "Mexican American," here, for it is hard to guess what name or names the Mexican-descended community in that town might have given themselves.

7. Angela Y. Davis, *Women, Race and Class* (New York: Random House, 1981), 172–201.

8. Megumi Dick Osumi, "Asians and California's Anti-Miscegenation Laws," in *Asian/Pacific American Experiences: Women's Perspectives*, ed. Nobuya Tsuchida (Minneapolis: Asian/Pacific American Learning Resource Center and General College, University of Minnesota, 1982), 1–37.

9. Vron Ware, in *Beyond the Pale: White Women, Racism and History* (London: Verso, 1992), analyzes in detail the ways white women are discursively conceived as potential targets of sexual assault by men of color in the ideological economies of colonialism and racism (see especially Part 1, "The White Woman's Burden? Race and Gender in Popular Memory," 1–46).

4. Race, Sex, and Intimacy I: Mapping a Discourse

1. *Loving v. Virginia* 338, U.S.1, 87, S.Ct., 1817, 18L.Ed.2d 1010.

2. For example, Reginald Horsman, in "Scientific Racism and the American Indian in the Mid-Nineteenth Century," *American Quarterly* 27 (May 1975): 152–68, argues that from a seventeenth-century Christian standpoint, whiteness and white people connoted purity, while blackness and African people were associated with dirt, corruption, and evil. Indigenous Americans, in contrast with both of these images, were in fact viewed as part of nature rather than as part of the human world—an ideology that from the white viewpoint justified, in addition to a ban on interracial relationships, the elimination of Indians from the environment as "pests." The notion of Manifest Destiny, of white people as rightful possessors of the continent, was, in short, premised on a cosmological argument that conveniently benefited those who believed in it.

3. My use of the term "scientific racism" indicates only form, not greater accuracy or truth value.

4. Horsman, "Scientific Racism," 166–67.

5. Ibid., 155 and elsewhere.

6. In Herbert Gutman, *The Black Family in Slavery and Freedom, 1750–1925* (New York: Pantheon, 1976), and elsewhere.

7. Megumi Dick Osumi, "Asians and California's Anti-Miscegenation Laws," in *Asian/Pacific American Experiences: Women's Perspectives*, ed. Nobuya Tsuchida (Minneapolis: Asian/Pacific American Learning Resource Center and General College, University of Minnesota, 1982), 2. I am especially indebted to Osumi for this discussion of the history of antimiscegenation with respect to Asian/Pacific Americans.

8. Ibid., 8.

9. Patricia Hill Collins, *Black Feminist Thought: Knowledge, Consciousness, and the Politics of Empowerment* (Boston: Unwin Hyman, 1990), 67–90.

10. See, for example, Angela Y. Davis, *Women, Race and Class* (New York: Random House, 1981), 172–201; see also the video "Ethnic Notions," Marlon Riggs, director, Marlon T. Riggs Productions, 1987.

11. Elaine Kim, *Asian American Literature* (Philadelphia: Temple University Press, 1982), 173–213.

12. Peggy Pascoe, "Race, Gender and Intercultural Relations: The Case of Interracial Marriage," *Frontiers* 12, no. 1 (Summer 1991): 7.

13. Ibid.

14. For example, in 1970 there were 65,000 Black-white married couples out of a total of 44,597,000 married couples in the United States; in 1980 the equivalent figures were 167,000 out of 49,714,000; in 1989, the figures were 219,000 Black-white married

couples out of a total of 52,924,000 married couples in the United States. These figures do not, of course, include heterosexual, gay, or lesbian domestic partners, nor interracial couples other than Black-white. It should also be noted that interracial partnerships are still few in comparison with same-race ones, for, expressed as percentages, Black-white couples increased from 0.1 percent of married couples in 1970 to 0.3 percent in 1980, and to 0.4 percent in 1989 (U.S. Bureau of the Census, *Statistical Abstract of the United States: 1991* 111th Edition [Washington, D.C.: U.S. Government Printing Office, 1991], 44).

15. For example, Kenneth Ballhatchet, in *Race, Sex and Class under the Raj: Imperial Attitudes and Policies and their Critics, 1793–1905* (London: Wiedenfeld and Nicholson, 1980), suggests that this is the case in India.

16. As Virginia Dominguez points out, as recently as 1982, a Louisiana court decided that a woman who had filed suit to be considered white, was Black on the grounds that she was one thirty-second Black. Dominguez, *White by Definition: Social Classification in Creole Louisiana* (New Brunswick, N.J.: Rutgers University Press, 1986), 1–5.

17. More than from a concern for purity or the maintenance of racial hierarchy, the hostility of communities of color toward interracial relationships may stem at times from a view of whites as oppressors with whom one should not mix, or from a refusal to accept the terms of racism by being accepted as a "token" or by "assimilating." Anger may also emerge as a response to an aspect of what may be termed "racist sexism," which shapes standards of physical attractiveness in the culture and constructs white women as more attractive than women of color, both to white and nonwhite men. (Besides these arguments "against" relationships with whites, there are of course arguments "for" relationships within communities of color—a concern to build, strengthen, and value the Chicano, African American, Asian, and Native communities; an emphasis on self-valuing and valuing others within the racial-cultural group, in opposition to negative stereotyping by the dominant culture. There are of course other aspects to cultural nationalist or separatist politics not related to the question of interracial relationships.)

18. See, for example, Mary Douglas, *Purity and Danger: An Analysis of the Concepts of Pollution and Taboo* (London: Routledge and Kegan Paul, 1966).

5. Race, Sex, and Intimacy II: Interracial Couples and Interracial Parenting

1. I am excluding Margaret, who did not choose her daughter-in-law, but including Dot Humphrey, who did choose her child.

2. This discussion is also limited by the fact that it draws on a very small number of mothers and children.

6. Thinking Through Race

1. *Repertoire* is defined by *Webster's Unabridged Dictionary* (New York: Simon & Schuster, 1983) as "the stock of operas, dramas, etc., which can be readily performed by a company, from their familiarity with them; those parts, songs, etc. which are usually performed by an actor or vocalist; hence, generally, a number of things which can be readily and efficiently done by a person by virtue of his familiarity with them." I am indebted to Chetan Bhatt for his suggestion that I use the word *repertoire* in this context.

2. As I noted in chapter 1, I am intentionally avoiding the term "color-blind," in part because it deploys and judges negatively a physical disability, and in part because it is misleading in that this discursive repertoire is organized around evading difference

or acknowledging it selectively rather than literally not "seeing" differences of race, culture, and color.

3. This sentiment echoes that of some of the women quoted in chapter 4, including Ginny herself, who suggested that children of "mixed" heritage were apt to be blamed for their parents' sins.

4. Thanks to David Wellman, University of California, Santa Cruz, for informing me that the imagined memory of "push day" is shared by many whites in Detroit and elsewhere, and is not a part of Irene Esterley's conceptual landscape alone.

5. In the titles of this section and the next, I am drawing on the title of Audre Lorde's "The Transformation of Silence into Language and Action," *Sister Outsider* (Freedom, Calif.: Crossing, 1984), 40–44. Lorde's title emphasizes a vital goal of feminism. Yet, as Mab Segrest has stated on more than one occasion—including a lecture at the University of California at Santa Cruz in April 1988—feminists are at times more successful at completing the first part of the transformation than the second.

6. These women's descriptions are similar in form and direction to those of white feminists who have in the past decade published their reevaluations of the structuring of their lives by race—for example, Elly Bulkin, "Hard Ground: Jewish Identity, Racism, and Anti-Semitism," in Elly Bulkin, Minnie Bruce Pratt, and Barbara Smith, *Yours in Struggle: Three Feminist Perspectives on Anti-Semitism and Racism* (Brooklyn, N.Y.: Long Haul Press, 1984; Ithaca, N.Y.: Firebrand, 1988), 89–228; Minnie Bruce Pratt, "Identity: Skin, Blood, Heart," in Bulkin, Pratt, and Smith, *Yours in Struggle*, 9–64; Mab Segrest, *My Mama's Dead Squirrel: Lesbian Essays on Southern Culture* (Ithaca, N.Y.: Firebrand, 1985); and Adrienne Rich, "Notes Toward a Politics of Location," in Adrienne Rich, *Blood, Bread, and Poetry: Selected Prose, 1979–1985* (New York: Norton, 1986), 210–31. They also mirror in certain ways the writing of women of color about the ways in which racism has structured their daily lives. But while women of color for the most part describe racialization and the experience of being targeted by racism as an unavoidable reality, consciousness of racism emerges in white women's stories as something that has to be striven for.

7. On November 3, 1979, Klansmen opened fire on a civil rights march organized by the Communist Workers' Party in Greensboro. Five party members were killed, and nine others were injured. James Ridgeway, *Blood in the Face: The KKK, Aryan Nations, Nazi Skinheads and the Rise of a New White Culture* (New York: Thunder's Mouth, 1990), 79, 100.

8. This strategy is so prevalent as to be difficult to document in any meaningful way. See, for example, Linda Alcoff, "Cultural Feminism versus Poststructuralism: The Identity Crisis in Feminist Theory," *Signs* 13, no. 3 (1988): 405–36; Norma Alarcon, "The Theoretical Subjects of *This Bridge Called My Back* and Anglo-American Feminism," in *Making Face, Making Soul, Haciendo Caras: Creative and Critical Perspectives by Women of Color*, ed. Gloria Anzaldúa (San Francisco: Aunt Lute, 1990); Teresa de Lauretis, "Eccentric Subjects: Feminist Theory and Historical Consciousness," *Feminist Studies* 16, no.2, 1990: 115–50; and Chela Sandoval, "U.S. Third World Feminism: The Theory and Method of Oppositional Consciousness in the Postmodern World," *Genders* 10 (Spring 1991): 1–24. These essays both survey the field of recent feminist theory and make theoretical contributions in their own right about the social construction of feminist subjects.

7. Questions of Culture and Belonging

1. See, for example, Reginald Horsman, "Scientific Racism and the American Indian in the Mid-Nineteenth Century," *American Quarterly* 27 (May 1975); and Sander Gilman, "Black Bodies, White Bodies: Toward an Iconography of Female Sexuality in Late Nineteenth Century Art, Medicine and Literature," *Critical Inquiry* 12, no. 1

(Autumn 1985): 204–42. In addition, Peter Hulme, in *Colonial Encounters: Europe and the Native Caribbean 1492–1797* (New York: Methuen, 1986), examines colonial deployment of essentialist racism, together with colonial invention and projection of constructions of indigenous Caribbean peoples as, among other things, "cannibal."

2. In this regard, for example, Edward Said argues in *Orientalism* (New York: Random House, 1978) that West European discourses on the "non-West" proposed above all else the fundamental difference or "Otherness" of the so-called Orient.

3. Trinh T. Minh-ha, "Difference: A Special Third World Women Issue" (special issue, "She, the Inappropriate/d Other"), *Discourse* 8 (Fall–Winter 1986–87).

4. Chandra Talpade Mohanty, "Under Western Eyes: Feminist Scholarship and Colonial Discourses," *Feminist Review*, Autumn 1988: 60–88.

5. On colonial constructions of tradition, for example, Lata Mani's study of British colonial and missionary discourses on India shows how, within those discourses, Indian culture (or in the terms of the era, "tradition") was invarably viewed as a sphere of consciousness that, although potentially controlling the actions of indigenous people, was not itself formed or reformulated in relation to material or political considerations. Lata Mani, "Contentious Traditions: The Debate on *Sati* in Colonial India," *Cultural Critique* 7 (Fall 1987): 119–56; and *Contentious Traditions: The Debate on* Sati *in Colonial India, 1780–1830*, forthcoming, University of California Press.

6. Key works here are Johannes Fabian, *Time and the Other: How Anthropology Makes Its Object* (New York: Columbia University Press, 1983); James Clifford and George Marcus, *Writing Culture: The Poetics and Politics of Ethnography* (Berkeley: University of California Press, 1986); and James Clifford, *The Predicament of Culture: Twentieth-Century Ethnography, Literature and Art* (Cambridge, Mass.: Harvard University Press, 1988). See also Arjun Appadurai, "Putting Culture in Its Place," *Cultural Anthropology* 3, no. 1 (February 1988).

7. See, for example, Renato Rosaldo, *Culture and Truth: The Remaking of Social Analysis* (Boston: Beacon, 1989); James Clifford and Vivek Dhareshwar, eds., *Traveling Theory, Traveling Theorists, Inscriptions* 5 (1989; special issue), Center for Cultural Studies, University of California, Santa Cruz. In addition, the *Public Culture* bulletin, University of Pennsylvania, analyzes cultural transformation in a transnational context.

8. Stuart Hall, "Gramsci's Relevance for the Study of Race and Ethnicity," *Journal of Communication Inquiry* 10, no. 2: 26.

9. Paul Gilroy, *There Ain't No Black in the Union Jack* (London: Hutchinson, 1987), 17.

10. Raymond Williams, *The Country and the City* (New York: Oxford University Press, 1978).

11. The classic statement of this position is W. E. B. Du Bois's concept of the "double consciousness" of Americans of African descent. Two recent feminist statements of similar positions are Patricia Hill Collins, *Black Feminist Thought: Knowledge, Consciousness, and the Politics of Empowerment* (Boston: Unwin Hyman, 1990); and Aida Hurtado, "Relating to Privilege: Seduction and Rejection in the Subordination of White Women and Women of Color," *Signs* 14, no. 4: 833–55.

12. Gilroy, *There Ain't No Black*, 17.

13. See, for example, Winthrop Talbot, ed., *Americanization* (New York: H. W. Wilson, 1917), esp. Sophonisba P. Breckinridge, "The Immigrant Family," 251–52; Olivia Howard Dunbar, "Teaching the Immigrant Woman," 252–56, and North American Civic League for Immigrants, "Domestic Education among Immigrants," 256–58; and Kathie Friedman Kasaba, " 'To Become a Person': The Experience of Gender, Ethnicity and Work in the Lives of Immigrant Women, New York City, 1870–1940," doctoral dissertation, Department of Sociology, State University of New York, Binghamton, 1991. I am indebted to Kathie Friedman Kasaba for these references and for her discus-

sions with me about working-class European immigrants to the United States at the turn of this century.

14. Gilroy, *There Ain't No Black*.

15. For example, Irish feminists in the United Kingdom have spoken and written about the extent to which anti-Irish discrimination is still rife in Britain, articulated on the cultural level in terms of distrust or hostility from the dominant British culture, and on the political and economic level in terms of the colonial and neocolonial relationships that obtain between mainland Britain on the one hand and Ulster and Eire on the other. Being Irish in the United Kindom, in short, does have political saliency, and in this context relationships of political allegiance have developed between Irish and Black women in Britain. See debates in the pages of the British feminist journals *Spare Rib* and *Outwrite* through the 1980s.

16. Ashkenazi Jews are not the only white group with a history of having been deemed racial Others in the United States. Irish Americans, southern Italians, and Celts are among the groups who share this history. On this point, see, for example, Mr. Dillingham, *Dictionary of Races or Peoples*, Reports of the Immigration Commission, Committee on Immigration (Washington, D.C.: Government Printing Office, 1911). I am indebted to Kathie Friedman Kasaba for this reference.

17. For a detailed study of "ethnicities by choice," see Mary Waters, *Ethnic Options* (Berkeley: University of California Press, 1990).

18. Elly Bulkin, in "Hard Ground: Jewish Identity, Racism and Anti-Semitism," in Elly Bulkin, Minnie Bruce Pratt, and Barbara Smith, *Yours in Struggle: Three Feminist Perspectives on Anti-Semitism and Racism* (Brooklyn, N.Y.: Long Haul Press, 1984; Ithaca, N.Y.: Firebrand, 1988), 89–288, addresses the need to disentangle and distinguish between forms of oppression at specific historical moments (see esp. 110–11).

19. Toni Morrison, in *Playing in the Dark: Whiteness and the Literary Imagination* (Cambridge, Mass.: Harvard University Press, 1992), incisively clarifies, through analysis of the U.S. literary canon, the ways both whiteness and (white) Americanness are constructed by means of the production and deployment of fictive "Africanist" Others.

20. See, for example, Teresa Amott and Julie Matthaei, *Race, Gender, and Work: A Multicultural Economic History of Women in the United States* (Boston: South End Press, 1991). Amott and Matthaei use "white" and "European American" interchangeably.

21. As, for example, by organizations like the National Association for the Advancement of White People and the White Aryan Resistance.

22. Both of these points take me well beyond the scope of this book. On the former point, see, for example, Paul Gilroy, *There Ain't No Black*. On the question of whiteness and femininity and the construction of both in the context of racist and colonial discourses, see Vron Ware, *Beyond the Pale: White Women, Racism and History* (London: Verso, 1992).

Epilogue: Racism, Antiracism, and the Meaning of Whiteness

1. As I have repeatedly emphasized, this does not mean that all white individuals have absolute privilege, any more than all male individuals have absolute privilege. Rather, it means that individuals whose ascribed characteristics include whiteness (or maleness) will find the benefits of that ascription accruing to them.

2. Antonio Gramsci, *Selections from the Prison Notebooks*, ed. and trans. Quintin Hoare and Geoffrey Nowell Smith (New York: International Publishers, 1971), 324.

Bibliography

Alarcon, Norma. "Chicana's Feminist Literature: A Re-vision Through Malintzin/or Malintzin: Putting Flesh Back on the Object." In *This Bridge Called My Back: Writings by Radical Women of Color*, edited by Cherríe Moraga and Gloria Anzaldúa, 182–90. Watertown, Mass.: Persephone, 1981; New York: Kitchen Table Women of Color Press, 1983.

———. "The Theoretical Subject(s) of *This Bridge Called My Back* and Anglo American Feminism." In *Making Face, Making Soul, Haciendo Caras: Creative and Critical Perspectives by Women of Color*, edited by Gloria Anzaldúa, 356–69. San Francisco: Aunt Lute, 1990.

Alcoff, Linda. "Cultural Feminism versus Poststructuralism: The Identity Crisis in Feminist Theory." *Signs* 13, no. 3 (1988): 405–36.

Amott, Teresa, and Julie Matthaei. *Race, Gender, and Work: A Multicultural Economic History of Women in the United States*. Boston: South End Press, 1991.

Anzaldúa, Gloria, ed. *Making Face, Making Soul, Haciendo Caras: Creative and Critical Perspectives by Women of Color*. San Francisco: Aunt Lute, 1990.

Appadurai, Arjun. "Putting Culture in Its Place." *Cultural Anthropology* 3, no. 1 (February 1988).

Ballhatchet, Kenneth. *Race, Sex and Class under the Raj: Imperial Attitudes and Policies and their Critics, 1793–1905*. London: Wiedenfeld and Nicholson, 1980.

Barthes, Roland. *S/Z: An Essay*. Translated by Richard Miller. New York: Hill and Wang, 1974.

Bhavnani, Kum Kum. *Talking Politics: A Psychological Framing for Views from Youth in Britain*. Cambridge: Cambridge University Press, 1991.

———, Margaret Coulson. "Transforming Socialist Feminism: The Challenge of Racism." *Feminist Review* 23 (Summer 1986): 81–92.

Blauner, Bob. *Black Lives, White Lives: Three Decades of Race Relations in America*. Berkeley: University of California Press, 1989.

Bulkin, Elly, Minnie Bruce Pratt, and Barbara Smith. *Yours in Struggle: Three Feminist Perspectives on Anti-Semitism and Racism*. Brooklyn, N.Y.: Long Haul Press, 1984; Ithaca, N.Y.: Firebrand, 1988.

Cade, Toni. *The Black Woman: An Anthology*. New York: Mentor, 1970.

Centre for Contemporary Cultural Studies. *The Empire Strikes Back: Race and Racism in '70s Britain*. London: Hutchinson, 1981.

Churchill, Ward. *Fantasies of the Master Race: Literature, Cinema and the Colonization of American Indians*. Edited by Annette Jaimes. Monroe, Maine: Common Courage Press, 1992.

Clifford, James. *The Predicament of Culture: Twentieth-Century Ethnography, Literature and Art*. Cambridge, Mass.: Harvard University Press, 1988.

———, and Vivek Dhareshwar, eds. *Traveling Theory, Traveling Theorists*. Inscriptions 5 (1989; special issue). Center for Cultural Studies, University of California, Santa Cruz.

———, and George Marcus, eds. *Writing Culture: The Poetics and Politics of Ethnography.* Berkeley: University of California Press, 1986.

Collins, Patricia Hill. "The Social Construction of Black Feminist Thought." *Signs* 14, no. 4 (1989): 745–73.

———. *Black Feminist Thought: Knowledge, Consciousness, and the Politics of Empowerment.* Boston: Unwin Hyman, 1990.

Combahee River Collective. "A Black Feminist Statement." In *Capitalist Patriarchy and the Case for Socialist Feminism,* edited by Zillah R. Eisenstein, 362–72. New York: Monthly Review Press, 1979.

Coote, Anna, and Beatrix Campbell. *Sweet Freedom: The Struggle for Women's Liberation.* London: Picador, 1982.

Cross, Tia, Frieda Klein, Barbara Smith, and Beverley Smith. "Face-to-Face, Day-to-Day: Racism CR." *Heresies* 3, no. 3: 66–67.

Davis, Angela Y. *Women, Race and Class.* New York: Random House, 1981.

De Lauretis, Teresa. "Eccentric Subjects: Feminist Theory and Historical Consciousness." *Feminist Studies* 16, no. 2 (1990): 115–50.

Dillingham, Mr. *Dictionary of Races or Peoples.* Reports of the Immigration Commission, Committeee on Immigration, Washington, D.C.: Government Printing Office, 1911.

Dominguez, Virginia R. *White by Definition: Social Classification in Creole Louisiana.* New Brunswick, N.J.: Rutgers University Press, 1986.

Douglas, Mary. *Purity and Danger: An Analysis of the Concepts of Pollution and Taboo.* London: Routledge and Kegan Paul, 1966.

Dubois, Ellen Carol, and Vicki L. Ruiz, eds. *Unequal Sisters: A Multicultural Reader in U.S. Women's History.* New York: Routledge, 1990.

Echols, Alice. *Daring to Be Bad: Radical Feminism in America, 1967–75.* Minneapolis: University of Minnesota Press, 1989.

Evans, Sara. *Personal Politics: The Origins of the Women's Liberation Movement in the Civil Rights Movement and the New Left.* New York: Vintage, 1980.

Fabian, Johannes. *Time and the Other: How Anthropology Makes its Object.* New York: Columbia University Press, 1983.

Frankenberg, Ruth. "Different Perspectives: Interweaving Theory and Practice in Women's Work," qualifying essay, Board of Studies in the History of Consciousness, University of California, Santa Cruz, 1983.

Giddings, Paula. *When and Where I Enter: The Impact of Black Women on Race and Sex in America.* New York: Bantam, 1984.

Gilman, Sander. "Black Bodies, White Bodies: Toward an Iconography of Female Sexuality in Late Nineteenth Century Art, Medicine and Literature." *Critical Inquiry* 12, no. 1 (Autumn 1985): 204–42.

Gilroy, Paul. *There Ain't No Black in the Union Jack.* London: Hutchinson, 1987.

Gluck, Sherna. (1977). "What's So Special about Women? Women's Oral History." *Frontiers* 11, no. 2 (Summer 1977; special issue on women's oral history): 3–14.

Goldberg, David Theo, ed. *Anatomy of Racism.* Minneapolis: University of Minnesota Press, 1990.

Gramsci, Antonio. *Selections from the Prison Notebooks.* Edited and translated by Quintin Hoare and Geoffrey Nowell Smith. New York: International Publishers, 1971.

Gutman, Herbert. *The Black Family in Slavery and Freedom, 1750–1925.* New York: Pantheon, 1976.

Hall, Stuart. "Race, Articulation, and Societies Structured in Dominance." *UNESCO: Sociological Theories, Race and Colonialism,* 305–45. Paris: UNESCO Press, 1980.

———. "Gramsci's Relevance for the Study of Race and Ethnicity." *Journal of Communication Inquiry* 10, no. 2 (1986): 5–27.

Haraway, Donna J. "Situated Knowledges: The Science Question and the Privilege of Partial Perspective." In Donna J. Haraway, *Simians, Cyborgs, and Women: The Reinvention of Nature*, 183–202. New York: Routledge, 1991.

Hartsock, Nancy. "The Feminist Standpoint: Developing the Ground for a Specifically Feminist Historical Materialism." In *Discovering Reality*, edited by Sandra Harding and Merrill B. Hintikka, 283–310. Dordrecht: D. Riedel, 1983.

hooks, bell. *Ain't I a Woman? Black Women and Feminism*. Boston: South End Press, 1981.

———. *Feminist Theory: From Margin to Center*. Boston: South End Press, 1984.

———. *Talking Back: Thinking Feminist, Thinking Black*. Boston: South End Press, 1989.

Horsman, Reginald. "Scientific Racism and the American Indian in the Mid-Nineteenth Century." *American Quarterly* 27 (May 1975): 52–168.

Hulme, Peter. *Colonial Encounters: Europe and the Native Caribbean 1492–1797*. New York: Methuen, 1986.

Hurtado, Aida. "Relating to Privilege: Seduction and Rejection in the Subordination of White Women and Women of Color." *Signs* 14, no. 4 (1989): 833–55.

Joseph, Gloria I., and Jill Lewis. *Common Differences: Conflicts in Black and White Feminist Perspectives*. Garden City, N.Y.: Anchor, 1981.

Kasaba, Kathie Friedman. " 'To Become a Person': The Experience of Gender, Ethnicity and Work in the Lives of Immigrant Women, New York City, 1870–1940." Doctoral dissertation, Department of Sociology, State University of New York, Binghamton, 1991.

Kim, Elaine. *Asian American Literature*. Philadelphia: Temple University Press, 1982.

King, Katie. "The Situation of Lesbianism as Magical Sign: Contests for Meaning in the U.S. Women's Movement, 1968–72." *Communications* 9 (1986): 65–91.

Lorde, Audre. "The Transformation of Silence into Language and Action." In *Sister Outsider*, 40–44. Freedom, Calif.: Crossing Press, 1984.

Malveaux, Julianne. "Ain't I a Woman: Differences in the Labor Market Status of Black and White Women." In *Racism and Sexism: An Integrated Study*, edited by Paula S. Rothenberg, 76–79. New York: St. Martin's, 1988.

Mani, Lata. "Contentious Traditions: The Debate on *Sati* in Colonial India." *Cultural Critique* 7 (Fall 1987): 119–56.

———. *Contentious Traditions: The Debate on* Sati *in Colonial India, 1780–1830*. University of California Press, forthcoming.

Mohanty, Chandra Talpade. "Feminist Encounters: Locating the Politics of Experience." *Copyright* 1, no. 1 (1984).

———. "Under Western Eyes: Feminist Scholarship and Colonial Discourses." *Feminist Review*, Autumn 1988: 60–88.

———, Ann Russo, and Lourdes Torres, eds. *Third World Women and the Politics of Feminism*. Bloomington: Indiana University Press, 1991.

Moraga, Cherríe, and Gloria Anzaldúa, eds. *This Bridge Called My Back: Writings by Radical Women of Color*. Watertown, Mass.: Persephone, 1981; New York: Kitchen Table Women of Color Press, 1983.

Morrison, Toni. *Playing in the Dark: Whiteness and the Literary Imagination*. Cambridge, Mass.: Harvard University Press, 1992.

Mullen, Harryette. *The Psychoanalysis of Little Black Sambo*. Occasional papers, Group for the Critical Study of Colonial Discourse, University of California, Santa Cruz, 1987.

Oakley, Ann. "Interviewing Women: A Contradiction in Terms." In *Doing Feminist Research*, edited by Helen Roberts, 30–61. London: Routledge and Kegan Paul, 1981.

Omi, Michael, and Howard Winant. *Racial Formation in the United States: From the 1960's to the 1980's*. New York: Routledge and Kegan Paul, 1986.

Osumi, Megumi Dick. "Asians and California's Anti-Miscegenation Laws." Asian/
    Pacific American Experiences: Women's Perspectives, edited by Nobuya Tsuchida,
    1–37. Minneapolis: Asian/Pacific American Learning Resource Center and General
    College, University of Minnesota, 1982.
Pascoe, Peggy. "Race, Gender and Intercultural Relations: The Case of Interracial Mar-
    riage." Frontiers 12, no. 1 (Summer 1991).
Passerini, Luisa. "Work Ideology and Consensus under Italian Fascism." History Work-
    shop Journal 8 (Autumn 1979): 82–108.
———. "Memory: Résumé of the Final Session of the International Conference on Oral
    History, Aix-en-Provence, 26 September, 1982." History Workshop Journal 5 (Spring
    1982).
Reagon, Bernice Johnson. "Coalition Politics: Turning the Century." In Home Girls: A
    Black Feminist Anthology, edited by Barbara Smith, 356–69. New York: Kitchen
    Table Women of Color Press, 1983.
Rich, Adrienne, "Disloyal to Civilization: Feminism, Racism, Gynephobia." In
    Adrienne Rich, On Lies, Secrets and Silence: Selected Prose, 1966–1978. New York:
    Norton, 1979.
———. "Notes Toward a Politics of Location." In Adrienne Rich, Blood, Bread and
    Poetry: Selected Prose, 1979–1985. New York: Norton, 1986.
Ridgeway, James. Blood in the Face: The KKK, Aryan Nations, Nazi Skinheads and the
    Rise of a New White Culture. New York: Thunder's Mouth Press, 1990.
Roediger, David. The Wages of Whiteness: Race and the Making of the American Working
    Class. London: Verso, 1991.
Rollins, Judith. Between Women: Domestics and Their Employers. Philadelphia: Temple
    University Press, 1985.
Rosaldo, Renato. Culture and Truth: The Remaking of Social Analysis. Boston: Beacon,
    1989.
Said, Edward. Orientalism. New York: Random House, 1978.
Sandoval, Chela. "The Struggle Within: Women Respond to Racism—Report on the
    National Women's Studies Conference, Storrs, Connecticut." Occasional paper,
    Center for Third World Organizing, Oakland, California, 1982. Revised for Making
    Face, Making Soul, Haciendo Caras: Creative and Critical Perspectives by Women of
    Color, edited by Gloria Anzaldúa, 55–71. San Francisco: Aunt Lute, 1990.
———. "U.S. Third World Feminism: The Theory and Method of Oppositional Con-
    sciousness in the Postmodern World." Genders 10 (Spring 1991): 1–24.
Segrest, Mab. My Mama's Dead Squirrel: Lesbian Essays on Southern Culture. Ithaca,
    N.Y.: Firebrand, 1985.
Spillers, Hortense. "Mama's Baby, Papa's Maybe: An American Grammar Book." Dia-
    critics, Summer 1987: 65–81.
Spivak, Gayatri Chakravorty. "The Rani of Sirmur." In Europe and Its Others, edited by
    Frances Barker et al., 128–51. Colchester: University of Essex, 1985.
Talbot, Winthrop, ed. Americanization. New York: H. W. Wilson, 1917.
Trinh T. Minh-ha, ed. "Difference: A Special Third World Women Issue." Discourse 8
    (Fall–Winter 1986–87; special issue, "She, the Inappropriate/d Other").
Ware, Vron. Beyond the Pale: White Women, Racism and History. London: Verso, 1992.
Waters, Mary. Ethnic Options. Berkeley: University of California Press, 1990.
Wellman, David. Portraits of White Racism. Cambridge: Cambridge University Press,
    1977; revised edition forthcoming, 1993.
West, Cornel. "Race and Social Theory: Towards a Genealogical Materialist Analysis."
    In The Year Left, 2, Toward a Rainbow Socialism—Essays on Race, Ethnicity, Class and
    Gender, edited by Mike Davis et al., 74–90. London: Verso, 1987.
Westwood, Sallie. All Day, Every Day. London: Pluto, 1984.

Williams, Raymond. *The Country and the City*. New York: Oxford University Press, 1978.

Young, Robert. *White Mythologies: Writing History and the West*. London: Routledge, 1990.

Zavella, Patricia. "The Problematic Relationship of Feminism and Chicana Studies." *Women's Studies* 17 (1988): 123–34.

Index

Compiled by Eileen Quam and Theresa Wolner

Ruth Frankenberg is an assistant professor of American studies at the University of California at Davis. She received a Ph.D. degree in 1988 from the University of California at Santa Cruz. She holds an undergraduate degree in social and political sciences from the University of Cambridge, U.K. Her work is situated at the intersection of feminist, race, and cultural studies and focuses on the critical analysis of racial domination and multicultural curriculum development. She has written on building multiracial women's studies curricula, academics' responses to Edward Said's *Orientalism*, and the meaning and utility of the concept of the "postcolonial." In addition to teaching and research, Frankenberg has been involved in feminist, antiracist, and antifascist activism. Ruth Frankenberg was born in Cardiff, Wales, grew up in Manchester, England, and came to the United States in 1979.